The Self-Publi...

MW01030600

"An essential reference to the best publishing resources for every self published author. Highly recommended!"
　—**Mark Coker,** <u>Smashwords</u> founder

"Independent authors need a team to help create a fantastic finished product, and finding the right people can be a challenge when you first start out. This book will help authors to locate professionals to edit, publish and market their work—helping them to stand out in the crowded marketplace."
　—**Joanna Penn,** <u>The Creative Penn</u>

"Time is money. You'll save a lot of both by referring to this easy-to-use resource. I'll be promoting this valuable guide and urging my own author clients to use it."
　—**Joan Stewart,** <u>The Publicity Hound</u>

"Wish this guide existed when I started self-publishing. It outlines the process beautifully, directs you where to go and saves months of research. A treasure chest I plan to open often."
　—**Jason Matthews,** <u>How to Make, Market and Sell Ebooks</u>

"This reference is for every author because, whether you sell out to a large publisher or publish yourself, the author must do the promoting. Publishers do not promote books.
　—**Dan Poynter,** <u>The Book Futurist</u>

"As a marketing person and publishing instructor, a guide like this is long overdue. It's a much needed resource and guide for authors and publishers to help them find high quality industry professionals. Thoroughly researched and curated by two people I greatly respect and admire, this book will take the guesswork out of self-publishing. This short-cut to the top pros—editors, designers, marketers, bloggers, distributors—is just exactly what we've all been waiting for. This book is a must-have for any author or publisher!"
　—**Penny Sansevieri,** <u>Author Marketing Experts</u>

"There are countless self-publishing guides telling you how you should self-publish. With *The Self-Publisher's Ultimate Resource Guide*, there's finally a definitive source getting to the nuts and bolts of the process. In one book, authors have all they need to self-publish professionally and successfully."

—**Henry Baum,** Self-Publishing Review

"Awesome is not profound enough a word for this resource. In my consults with struggling authors, one of the most common questions I receive is "who can I get to help me." Why anyone hasn't created this resource before now befuddles me. Now we have *The Self-Publishers Ultimate Resource Guide* from the masterminds of self-publishing, and I endorse it wholeheartedly times ten. I'll be recommending this to all my readers."

—**C. Hope Clark,** Founder Funds for Writers and Author *The Carolina Slade Mysteries* and *The Edisto Island Mysteries*

"Wow—what an amazing resource! Finally there's one place where anyone who wants to self-publish can find top editors, designers, printers and more. This is a real life-saver, a must-have guide for every indie author."

—**Alexis Grant,** founder of The Write Life

"Wow... what an amazing wealth of resources for authors. This is a great reference book for any author to add to their library. I highly recommend this book!"

—**Shelley Hitz,** owner of Training Authors

"Finally, hundreds of the resources you need compiled conveniently under one cover. This rich resource should be at every author's elbow."

—**Patricia Fry,** author of 47 books, speaker, book editor and former executive director of SPAWN (Small Publishers, Artists and Writers Network)

"This is a comprehensive, "must-have" reference for anyone writing a book or thinking about it. Joel provides a thorough and thoughtful approach to the hundreds of vendors offering services to writers at all stages of their projects."

—**Patricia Benesh,** Author Assist

This book is a living document

Although we have tried to gather the most valuable resources for indie authors, it's inevitable that some have been missed, and new products and services are constantly being introduced. We want your help to make it even better. If you know of a person, company, product, or service of value to independent authors that's not included in this guide, please let us know. You can send submissions to be included in the next edition of The Self-Publisher's Ultimate Resource Guide to: editor@spresourceguide.com.

Thank you

REVISED AND EXPANDED

2016
EDITION

New: Guidance from industry experts on 35 resource topics

The
Self-
Publisher's
Ultimate
Resource
Guide

Every Indie Author's Essential Directory
to Help You Prepare, Publish, and
Promote Professional Looking Books

JOEL FRIEDLANDER
BETTY KELLY SARGENT

Marin Bookworks
369-B Third Street, #572
San Rafael, CA 94901

Quantity sales: Special discounts are available on quantity purchases by corporations, associations, and others. For details, contact the "Special Sales Department" at the publisher's address above.

Printed in the United States of America

ISBN 978-0-936385-38-9 - Trade paper
ISBN 978-0-936385-39-6 - ePub

2nd Edition

Credits:

Research: Josslyn Shapiro
Fact checking and production: Christi Love, Kate Tilton
Copyediting: Wyn Hilty
Design: Marin Bookworks, http://www.thebookdesigner.com

For our friends, and families,
and self-publishers everywhere.

Author a great book, Publish it quickly and Entrepreneur your way to success. Self-publishing isn't easy, but it's fun and sometimes even lucrative. Plus, your book could change the world.

—Guy Kawasaki, *APE: Author, Publisher, Entrepreneur: How to Publish a Book*

TABLE OF CONTENTS

Introduction

What's the hardest part of becoming a self-publisher? Figuring out who's who, what's what, and where and how to find the right resources to make your book the best it can be. Traditional publishers know all this. They work with some of the best editors, designers, copy editors, proofreaders, publicists, marketers, ad agencies, and salespeople in the country. That's their job, and they do it well. But for indie authors who don't have access to these people, and often don't even know who they are, trying to find top freelance professionals to help them write, produce, and sell their book can be a nightmare.

We had no idea how urgent the need for a curated, comprehensive resource guide for indie authors was until, much to our surprise, the 2015 edition of *The Self-Publisher's Ultimate Resource Guide* launched at number one in its category on Amazon. Once we started getting positive feedback from hundreds of readers and began to realize just how essential this Resource Guide was, we decided to expand it significantly in the new, 2016 edition. Here's what we've done:

- Invited a select group of self-publishing industry leaders to share their expertise by writing a cutting-edge, thought-provoking introduction to the section of the guide that pertains to their expertise. For example, Penny Sansevieri tells us what really matters when it comes to Marketing and Publicity, Carla King explains shortcuts to E-book Conversion, and Ingram's Robin Cutler demystifies the confusing world of Book Distribution.

- Added two new categories: Book Shepherds and Author Assistants, bringing the total number of categories up to thirty-five.

- Increased the number of listings significantly and deleted any out-of-date or questionable listings. As many of you know, we already update the e-book version of *The Self-Publisher's Ultimate Resource Guide* every four months to keep it the most comprehensive and up-to-date resource guide on the market. For this 2016 edition we are providing our readers with a major revision.

Our goal in this edition of *The Self-Publisher's Ultimate Resource Guide* is the same: to make the process of finding everything you need to self-publish successfully much easier for you. Instead of scrolling through hundreds of websites looking for an editor with a solid background in trade publishing or an experienced designer to create a smashing cover for your book, we've done that work for you. Not only will this guide save you hours of hit-and-miss research, but you can also be assured that when you contact a person or group on our list, that resource will be professional and current. No more discovering a blogger who seems to be speaking directly to you, only to realize that she hasn't posted a new entry since 2012.

Here's how the Ultimate Resource Guide works. We have divided our recommended resources into three sections: Prepare, Publish, and Promote. In the Prepare section, we list the people you need to help you get your manuscript ready to publish, such as developmental editors, copyeditors and proofreaders, indexers, illustrators, cartoonists, cover and interior book designers, and translators. We have also included helpful writing software in this section, as well as image sources, grants and funding for writers, professional and trade associations, and our take on the best books for writers.

The Publish section lists resources to help you with e-book conversion and print-on-demand (POD) for the print version of your book, as well as our curated list of subsidy publishers and short-run printers. We also include top book production software; helpful links to sites covering services to help you create your book by providing information on bar codes, copyright, and ISBNs; and the best, most up-to-date books on self-publishing.

In the Promote section, you'll find the best resources to help you get your book out into the marketplace; attract targeted readers; and sell, sell, sell. Here we include website designers for authors, social media consultants, book review services, and press release services and sources. We also list fifty-five of the best current blogs for self-publishers, as well as sources for book blog tours, marketing and publicity professionals, news and views sources, distributors, retailers, sites that list e-books, writing contests, fellowships and prizes for indie authors, and book awards for self-published authors.

One word of caution: before hiring anyone to work on your book, be sure to chat with them on the phone and find out exactly what they charge, what their timeline is, and what results you can reasonably expect from their services. If they offer you a contract, be sure to read it carefully, especially the fine print. If they don't have a contract, you might suggest sending them a simple letter of agreement. Better safe than sorry, as the saying goes.

And who are we to offer this sage advice?

Betty Kelly Sargent is the founder of BookWorks, the Self-Publishers Association (www.bookworks.com). She writes a regular column on self-publishing for *Publishers Weekly* and is a member of the Independent Editors Group (www.bookdocs.com). Betty has spent more than thirty years as an editor in the traditional publishing business in New York, most recently as editor-in-chief of William Morrow, where at one point she had three books on the New York Times best-seller list at once. She has also been executive editor at HarperCollins, executive editor at Delacorte Press, Fiction and Books editor at Cosmopolitan magazine, and book reviewer for CNN's live Sunday morning show. She is the author of seven traditionally published books and two self-published books. In addition to moderating indie publishing panels and workshops in New York City and Los Angeles, she is a member of PEN and the Authors Guild and is on the board of the New York Society Library and the authors committee of the Pasadena Festival of Women Authors. She is passionate about helping indie authors learn to navigate the ever-changing landscape of self-publishing.

Joel Friedlander is an award-winning book designer and blogger who has been launching the careers of self-publishers since 1994 from his book design and consulting practice at Marin Bookworks in San Rafael, California. Joel is a self-published author and the blogger behind TheBookDesigner.com (www.thebookdesigner.com), a popular and award-winning blog on book design, book marketing, and the future of the book. Joel is also the founder of The Self-Publishing Roadmap (www.selfpublishingroadmap.com), a training course for authors, and TheBookMakers.com (http://thebookmakers.com) and BookDesignTemplates.com (www.bookdesigntemplates.com), where he provides tools and services for authors who publish their own books. He is also a columnist for *Publishers Weekly*, speaks often at publishing industry events, and is a past president of the Bay Area Independent Publishers Association.

We hope you'll have as much fun using this guide as we have had putting it together. And please let us know if you feel there are any glaring omissions in the guide, if you yourself would like to be listed, or if you know some person or organization you feel should be included. We welcome all input and will check out your recommendations; if they meet our standards of professionalism, we will be happy to include them.

PREPARE

Making your book the best it can be is the surest route to self-publishing success. And how do you do that? You seek help from the most highly qualified professionals you can find. Just as you probably wouldn't try to build your own house or fix the brakes on your car, it is almost never a good idea to try to be your own editor, proofreader, cover designer, or indexer. Professionalism shows, and the most important thing you can do for your book once it's completed is to seek the advice of top-notch professionals. With their help, you can produce a book that looks as if it just rolled off the presses of one of the big, traditional publishing houses—and you can be certain your readers will notice.

Content & Developmental Editors

What good editors do and where indie authors can find them

The one absolutely essential service you will need, whether you are writing a novel or a guide to the best restaurants in Paris, is an editor. Traditional publishing houses provide an editor for you, but indie authors need to find an appropriate editor for their book on their own. Content and developmental editors can help you refine your concept, organize your material, be consistent, and (if you are writing fiction) keep your plot moving and create depth in your characters—just for starters. We suggest you get in touch with several editors, find one with experience who really connects with you and your book idea, and then make sure she is absolutely clear about her fees, services, and deadlines. A short letter of agreement is always a good idea.

If you are new to self-publishing, you might want to learn a little more about editors in general—what they do and why they can make such a difference for you and your manuscript. Here's a quick overview to help you get a feel for what editorial help is all about.

F. Scott Fitzgerald's editor, the famous Maxwell Perkins, said, "Just get it down on paper, and then we will see what to do with it." Perkins is the editor who convinced those in charge at the time at Scribner that *The Great Gatsby* was a masterpiece. Then he worked closely with Fitzgerald to help make it just that. In fact, if you're curious about what great editing looks like, you might want to take a look at the correspondence between these two gentlemen at Letters of Note (www.lettersofnote.com/2012/07/the-novel-is-wonder.html).

Encouraging writers to complete their manuscript is just the first step in the editorial process. In my thirty years as an editor in the traditional book-publishing world, I've seen talented editors transform hundreds of manuscripts from ordinary to extraordinary. Perhaps it is a question of reorganizing the manuscript, or maybe there's no sizzle between the lovers, or maybe the book's title is flat or misleading. Interesting that two of the titles Fitzgerald considered for his masterpiece were *The High-Bouncing Lover* and *Trimalchio in West Egg*. Thank you, Mr. Perkins.

There are four kinds of editors:

- **Developmental editors** work with you from the very beginning, often before you have even put a word on paper. They help refine your concept, figure out who you are writing for, organize your material and arrange your chapters, and work out how you are going to get Ted and Tiffany off the dark planet before the cyborgs arrive. They are right there, offering advice and counsel every step of the way. I like to think that good developmental editors are like good shrinks. They don't tell you what to do; they get you to tell yourself.

- **Content editors** start their work once you have completed yours. They help you find, become comfortable with, and nurture your voice. They may ask you to rewrite sections of your book, delete chapters because they are slowing everything down, or introduce a new character who can help the reader see things from a fresh point of view. They will ask all kinds of questions and check your facts for accuracy, your prose for readability, and your plot for plausibility. They suggest where to cut, where to expand, and where to go deeper. They make sure you keep up the momentum and point out where a character's behavior doesn't fit her personality or her dialogue doesn't ring true. At the end of this process, you should have a tight, professional, compelling manuscript that is almost ready to go to press—or, for self-publishers, to be converted to the file formats you need.

- **Copyeditors** are the technical experts. They read your completed manuscript carefully for grammar, style, spelling, and punctuation. They will point out inconsistencies and inaccuracies, and they may even rewrite a confusing sentence or two. You can always restore whatever you want, but in my experience, good copyeditors are almost always right.

- **Proofreaders** are the last to see the manuscript. They go over it after the design is completed and make sure the front and back matter, photos, and captions are all in place. They also check headings, page numbers, typefaces, subheads, and running heads and make sure all the copyeditor's corrections have been inserted properly.

How do you find a good editor?

By good, I mean good for you and your book. In my view, a top, well-qualified editor is likely to be a professional editor with lots of experience in the traditional book- publishing world. A high school English teacher probably won't cut it—not because they're not smart and literate, but because books are special, and editors who have worked on successful, traditionally published books usually have a feel for what makes a book strong, and what does and doesn't work in the marketplace. Once you have found the person you think may be right for your book, ask her where she has worked and what books she has edited. Make sure she has had experience editing the kind of book you're working on. Remember you are hiring her, not vice versa.

Where can you find this person?

- **Right here.** Just turn the page to find a curated list of top freelance book editors.

- **Get a referral.** Ask your friends, other writers, or agents you meet at writers' conferences. You can also go online. Type "freelance book editors" into Google and see what you get—but remember to do your homework and thoroughly check out any editors who appeal to you.

- **Chat with the editor.** Be clear about your goals. Ask him about his credentials and for the titles of some published books he has worked on. Do you like him? Does he seem enthusiastic about your project? It's important that you feel a positive connection with him, because you will be working together closely.

- **Has she had experience with self-publishing?** If you are considering becoming an indie author—as you probably are if you are reading this book—it can be helpful to work with an editor who has had experience with indie publishing. This is not essential, but it's a nice plus in case you have questions about the self-publishing process and need some guidance.

- **Ask about the timeline.** When can you expect to see something from him, and about how long does he think this process will take?

- **Ask what she charges.** If her fees don't fit your budget, ask if she could recommend someone else.

- **Ask for a contract.** At the very least, get a simple letter of agreement. Make sure you both agree on the schedule of payments and what will happen if either of you decides to terminate the agreement.

- **Has she had experience with self-publishing?**—If you are considering becoming an indie author—as you probably are if you are reading this book—it can be helpful to work with an editor who has had experience with indie publishing. This is not essential, but a nice plus in case you have questions with the self-publishing process and need some guidance.

Most important: trust your instincts. If you think you can work well with this person—that she respects you and you respect her—then go for it. If not, keep looking. You are the author of this original piece of work. Your name will be on the cover and the title page. It's your book, your creation, and you need to work with someone who appreciates that. Go with what feels right to you, and chances are, it will be right—for you and your book, and the editor, too.

Betty Kelly Sargent
BookWorks (www.BookWorks.com)

Adams, Catherine – New York, NY 319-321-1253
inkslingerediting@yahoo.com,
http://www.inkslingerediting.com "developmental editor +
creative mentor for books, essays, short fiction & nonfiction
pieces including transmedia publishing"

Adelstein, Marlene – Hudson Valley, NY
marlene@fixyourbook.com, http://www.fixyourbook.com
"developmental/line editing for commercial, women's, literary +
historical fiction, thrillers, mysteries, memoir, YA & screenplays"

Adian Editing – jen@adianediting.com, http://www.adianediting.
com "Jen Blood offers beta reading + copy/content/line editing
& proofreading"

Arnie Kotler Editing Services – Kihei, Maui, Hawaii 808-
875-7995 arnie@arniekotlereditingservices.com,
http://arniekotlereditingservices.com/ "Arnie Kotler offers
developmental editing, line editing, copy editing, proofreading,
ghostwriting, book packaging & more"

Arteseros, Sally – New York, NY 212-982-3246
sarteseros@bookdocs.com,
http://www.bookdocs.com/editors/sarteseros "developmental/
line editing for commercial + literary fiction including short
stories, YA, biography, history, business, science, anthropology,
religion, inspiration, essays & academic books"

Barthel, Anne J. – New York, NY 917-710-6408
info@annejbarthel.com, http://www.annejbarthel.com "line
editing to restructuring across a wide range of nonfiction, from
memoir to spirituality to personal development"

Bell, Harriet – New York, NY 212-249-5625 harrietbell@verizon.net,
http://www.bellbookandhandle.com OR hbell@bookdocs.com,
http://www.bookdocs.com/editors/hbell "editorial services
specializing in nonfiction: cookbooks, fashion, memoirs, health/diet/
fitness, psychology, business, mind/body/spirit & illustrated books"

Benesh, Patricia – San Diego, CA info@authorassist.com,
http://www.authorassist.com "writing coach specializing in

nonfiction and fiction: developmental editing, structure/plot/
character development, manuscript reviews, proposal writing"

Bernstein, Elizabeth – San Francisco, CA eb@ebc-books.com,
http://www.ebc-books.com "writing coach for short stories, novels,
narrative nonfiction, academic/technical texts & screenplays"

Black, Hillel – New York, NY 212-734-8407 hillwen@aol.com,
http://www.hillelblack.com "developmental/line editor for
literary + commercial fiction, biography/memoir, business,
history, politics, science & sports"

Bokat, Nicole – Montclair, NJ 973-509-8957
nicolebokat@gmail.com, http://www.nicolebokat.com "editing
+ ghost-writing for fiction/nonfiction including first novels &
memoirs; also guidance on self-publishing process"

✓ **Buchanan, Averill** – Belfast, UK averill@averillbuchanan.com,
http://www.averillbuchanan.com "development editing, copyediting, proofreading, indexing"

Burbank, Toni – Brooklyn, NY toniburbank@bookdocs.com,
http://www.bookdocs.com/editors/tburbank "developmental/
line editing, manuscript evaluation + proposal writing with
particular interest/expertise in psychology, health, women's
issues, spirituality & self-help"

Carbone, Linda – Ardsley, NY 914-374-8790
lindacarbone@optonline.net, http://www.
publishersmarketplace.com/members/LindaCarbone/
"nonfiction developmental/line editing, book doctor & writing
coach; welcomes first-time authors"

Carr, David Colin – Point Richmond, CA 510-232-3098
david@davidcolincarr.com, http://www.davidcolincarr.com
"fiction and nonfiction developmental editing, specializing in
transformative, spiritual, self-help, human growth, psychology"

Chrysalis Editorial – Washington, DC 301-704-1455
herta@chrysaliseditorial.com, http://chrysaliseditorial.com/
"Herta Feely & Emily Williamson offer manuscript critiques,

developmental edits, coaching, ghostwriting, & agent/
publishing advice for fiction & non-fiction"

Cole Norman, Anne – Brooklyn, NY acole157@gmail.com, http://
www.publishersmarketplace.com/members/acolenorman
"nonfiction developmental/line editing, book doctor +
ghostwriter for reference, mind/body/spirit, health, travel,
lifestyle, self-help, how-to & pop culture"

Dalsimer, Susan – New York, NY 212-496-9164
sdalsimer@bookdocs.com,
http://www.bookdocs.com/editors/sdalsimer "editor +
ghostwriter for literary/commercial fiction including YA, as well
as nonfiction, specializing in memoir, spirituality, psychology,
theater, film & television"

Dave King Editorial Services – Shelburne Falls, MA 413-522-7582
dave@davekingedits.com, http://www.davekingedits.com/
"reading reports, line editing, & coaching line editing"

De Angelis, Paul – West Cornwall, CT 860-672-6882
pdeangelis@bookdocs.com,
http://www.pauldeangelisbooks.com "conceptual/
collaborative editing + ghostwriting for history, current affairs,
music, biography, psychology, religion, literature, Eastern
tradition, translations & humor"

Dearman, Jill – New York, NY 212-841-0177 jill@jilldearman.com,
http://www.bangthekeys.com "developmental editing,
ghostwriting + coaching for fiction & nonfiction, plays &
screenplays"

Denneny, Michael – New York, NY 212-362-3241
mldenneny@bookdocs.com,
http://www.bookdocs.com/editors/mdenneny "structural/
line editing for literary/commercial fiction including mysteries/
thrillers + most narrative nonfiction including memoir, history,
biography, current affairs & psychology"

Dinas, Paul – New York, NY 646-932-4916
dinas.paul@gmail.com,http://www.bookdocs.com/editors/pdinas

OR http://www.pauldinasbookeditor.com "conceptual/ collaborative editing + ghostwriting for history, current affairs, music, biography, psychology, religion, literature, Eastern tradition, translations & humor"

Dolin, Arnold – New York, NY 212-874-3419 abdolin@sprynet.com, consulting-editors.com/Consulting_Editors_Alliance/ Meet_the_Editors.html "editing + consulting for fiction/ nonfiction specializing in contemporary issues/politics, popular psychology, business, memoir/biography, literary fiction, gay fiction, theater, films & music"

Ehrenfeld, Temma – New York, NY 212-316-1840 expertediting@rocketmail.com, http://expertediting.org "editing + ghostwriting for fiction & nonfiction writers including novels, memoirs, journalistic or personal essay & academic/ scientific manuscript especially in the humanities/psychology"

Faulkner Editorial Services – Los Angeles, CA 310-391-3705 monica.faulkner@gmail.com, http://www.laeditorsandwritersgroup. com/about-our-members/monica-faulkner "manuscript evaluation, developmental/line editing, copyediting, proofreading, also writing coach & publishing consultant"

Fetterman, Bonny – New York, NY 718-739-1057 bonnyfetterman@theeditorscircle.com, http://theeditorscircle.com/bonny_v__fetterman.html "consulting, developmental/line editing specializing in Jewish history, religion, biblical studies, biography, memoir, Holocaust studies & historical fiction"

Flynn, Sarah – Annapolis, MD 410-626-9952 sarahflynn@comcast.net, http://www.publishersmarketplace. com/members/SarahFlynn/ "developmental/line editing + book doctor for general fiction, mystery, biography, history, cookbooks, African-American, memoirs, current affairs/politics & narrative nonfiction"

Gaskin, Carol – Sarasota, FL 941-377-7640 carol@editorialalchemy.com, http://www.editorialalchemy.com

"editing for literary/commercial fiction + general nonfiction including mystery/thriller, historical fiction, sci-fi, psychology, self-help, mysticism/spirituality, religion/mythology, archaeology/arts/history & juvenile/YA"

Gatewood Satter, Nan – New Paltz, NY 845-256-0504 nangatewoodsatter@gmail.com, consulting-editors. com/Consulting_Editors_Alliance/Meet_the_Editors.html "specializing in literary/commercial fiction + narrative nonfiction; memoir, first novels, personal growth & social justice, including the development of emerging writers"

Gelles-Cole, Sandi – Woodstock, NY 914-679-7630 sandigc@aol.com, http://www.literaryenterprises.com "developmental editing + writing coach for fiction, including plot/character/pacing & nonfiction organization/structuring"

Greenstein, Ruth – New York, NY 212-741-1393 rg@greenlinepublishing.com, http://www.greenlinepublishing.com/greenstein.htm "substantive editing, co-writing, ghostwriting, coaching + platform development for fiction and nonfiction including memoirs & poetry"

Groff, David – New York, NY 212-645-8910 davidagroff@gmail.com, http://www.davidgroff.com "editing + consulting focusing on narrative nonfiction, memoir, literary & popular fiction"

Hammett, William – New Orleans, LA (metro area) wmhammett@aol.com, http://www.freelanceghost.com "editing, ghostwriting + mentoring for ghostwriters, covering most fiction & nonfiction topics/genres"

Hanna, Annetta – Maplewood, NJ 973-763-5140 annettahanna@hotmail.com, http://www. publishersmarketplace.com/members/AnnettaHanna/ "developmental/line editing, ghostwriting book doctor + publishing consultant for biography, business/investing/finance, history, health, travel, mind/body/spirit, lifestyle memoirs/ autobiographies, narrative nonfiction, self-help & design"

✓ **Heckman, Emily** – Santa Barbara, CA 917-837-3817
emilyheckman@aol.com,
http://www.bookdocs.com/editors/eheckman "developmental/
line editing + publishing consultant specializing in narrative
nonfiction, women's health, spirituality/religion, psychology,
current events & commercial literary fiction including mysteries/
thrillers (no sci-fi/fantasy)"

Hinzmann, Hilary – New York, NY 212-942-0771
hinzmann@earthlink.net, http://consulting-editors.com/
Consulting_Editors_Alliance/Meet_the_Editors.html "editor,
book doctor, collaborator + ghostwriter specializing in history,
science, technology, business, sports, music, political/social
issues, biography/memoir & fiction"

Holtje, Bert – Jersey City, NJ 201-320-2337
bert@the-consulting-editor.org, http://www.
publishersmarketplace.com/members/consultingeditor
"manuscript development, ghostwriting + book doctor
specializing in general fiction, business/investing/finance,
health, mind/body/spirit & science"

Jablonski, Carla – Brooklyn, NY editorial@carlajablonski.com,
http://www.carlajablonski.com/home.html "developmental/
line editing specializing in children's books, YA, adult fantasy, sci-
fi & historical fiction"

Jackson Fallon, Kathryn – editorseditor@gmail.com, https://
www.publishersmarketplace.com/members/editorseditor
"developmental/line/substantive editing + ghostwriting
specializing in financial, business & economic text including
proficiency working with non-native speakers of English"

Josephy, Jennifer – New York, NY 212-744-0874
jenjosedit@gmail.com, http://consulting-editors.com/
Consulting_Editors_Alliance/Meet_the_Editors.html "editorial
services specializing in diet/health, biography/memoirs, history,
lifestyle, cookbooks, food-related & travel narratives, the art
world, women's issues & dogs"

Kaplan, Rob – Cortlandt Manor, NY 914-736-7182 robkaplan@theeditorscircle.com, http://www.theeditorscircle.com/rob_kaplan.html "editing, ghostwriting + collaborating for nonfiction including business, self-help, popular psychology, parenting, history & other subjects"

Kern, Judith – New York, NY 212-249-5871 kernjt@aol.com, http://consulting-editors.com/Consulting_Editors_Alliance/Meet_the_Editors.html "editorial services specializing in self-help, spirituality, lifestyle, food, health/diet, mysteries & women's fiction"

kn literary arts – http://knliterary.com/ "editorial services ranging from outlines to developmental editing"

LaFarge, Ann – Millbrook, NY 845-677-3361 alafarge@aol.com, http://www.publishersmarketplace.com/members/annlafarge/ "developmental/line editing, ghostwriting + book doctor specializing in general fiction, memoir, biography & narrative nonfiction"

Lakin, C.S. – San Francisco, CA http://www.livewritethrive.com "Susanne offers manuscript evaluations, developmental/copyediting, proofreading + coaching for new writers of fiction & nonfiction"

Lalli, Carole – New York, NY 212-744-6097 clalli3@gmail.com, http://consulting-editors.com/Consulting_Editors_Alliance/Meet_the_Editors.html "editor + ghostwriter for nonfiction, specializing in food, wine, lifestyle & cookbooks"

Leon, Susan – Larchmont, NY 914-833-1422 sleon@bookdocs.com, http://www.bookdocs.com/editors/sleon "developmental editing, rewrites, ghostwriting + book doctor specializing in memoir/autobiography, historical fiction & story-driven nonfiction"

Levine, Robert – New York, NY 212-535-3346 operafella@gmail.com "developmental editing, ghostwriting + book doctor specializing in nonfiction travel, art & music"

Lieberman, Beth – Los Angeles, CA 310-403-1602 bethlieberman@theeditorscircle.com, http://theeditorscircle.com/beth_lieberman.html

"developmental/content editing specializing in psychology/
motivational, Judaica, women's issues, Los Angeles-interest,
parenting, memoir + technique coaching for fiction & guidance
on indie publishing"

Los Angeles Editors & Writers Group – Los Angeles, CA
http://www.laeditorsandwritersgroup.com "LA-based editors/
writers covering all genres of literary/mainstream fiction +
nonfiction including medicine/science, health, psychology,
parenting, self-help, popular culture, the arts, business/finance,
spirituality, memoir & natural history"

Mancini Bothwell, Ali – Brooklyn, NY 917-301-3062
ali.bothwell@gmail.com,
http://www.publishersmarketplace.com/members/AliMancini/
"developmental editing to final polish for general fiction,
mystery/suspense/thriller, biography, history, travel, lifestyle,
juvenile, fantasy/sci-fi, pregnancy/parenting & sports"

Marek, Richard – Westport, CT 203-341-8607 rwmarek@earthlink.net,
http://www.bookdocs.com/editors/rmarek "manuscript
evaluation, editing + ghostwriting for fiction & nonfiction"

McCafferty, Danelle – New York, NY 212-877-9416
writerseditor@gmail.com, http://consulting-editors.com/
Consulting_Editors_Alliance/Meet_the_Editors.html
"developmental/line editing + rewrites for thrillers/mysteries/
true crime, women's contemporary & historical fiction, romance,
inspirational/self-help, religion/spirituality & theater"

McClellan, Anita – Belmont, MA 617-575-9203
adm@anitamcclellan.com, http://www.anitamcclellan.com
"developmental editor, book doctor & writer's coach specializing
in nonfiction"

Miner, Sydny – Pelham, NY
sminer@bookdocs.com OR sydny.miner@gmail.com,
http://www.bookdocs.com/editors/sminer "manuscript
evaluation, editing, rewriting, ghosting/collaborating for fiction
+ nonfiction, with expertise in cookbooks, food and nutrition,

diet/health/exercise, parenting, psychology, relationships, self-help, history, popular culture, & memoir"

Moore Sproul, Lindsey – Brooklyn, NY lindsey.moore@gmail.com, https://www.publishersmarketplace.com/members/lindseymoore "developmental/line editing, ghostwriter + book doctor for general fiction, mystery, biography, lifestyle, pop culture & humor"

Morgan, James – Little Rock, AR 501-690-2503 jamesmorgan144@gmail.com, http://www.publishersmarketplace.com/members/jamesmorgan "developmental/line editing, ghostwriting + book doctor for general fiction, biography, business/investing/finance, history, health, travel, mind/body/spirit, lifestyle & sports"

Nash, Jennie – Santa Monica, CA 310-400-6382 matt@noblankpages.com, www.noblankpages.com "book/author coach offering editorial guidance + motivation for writers at all stages through structured class format"

Nicholas, Nancy – New York, NY nacnich@cs.com, http://consulting-editors.com/Consulting_Editors_Alliance/Meet_the_Editors.html "editorial services for fiction including first novels, historical fiction, mysteries, biographies/autobiographies, history, theater, hobbies & gay issues"

NY Book Editors – New York, NY 888-959-3082 M-F 9a-5p EST info@nybookeditors.com, http://nybookeditors.com "25 editors with extensive experience in publishing offering manuscript evaluation, content + copyediting, proofreading, ghostwriting & coaching"

Obadia, Elianne – Tempe, AZ wmidwife@aol.com "manuscript midwife handling all aspects of editing + coaching from development to completion"

O'Connell, Diane – New York, NY 866-821-4164/570-359-4669 diane@writetosellyourbook.com, http://www.writetosellyourbook.com "editorial + consulting services for first-time & indie authors of fiction/nonfiction"

Osborn, Alice – Raleigh, NC 919-971-9414 alice@aliceosborn.com, http://aliceosborn.com "editor specializing in spirituality, sci-fi/ fantasy & military fiction"

Paine, John – Montclair, NJ 973-783-5082 jpaine@johnpaine.com, http://www.johnpaine.com "developmental/line editing & ghostwriting for fiction & nonfiction"

Peck, Alice – Brooklyn, NY 917-494-7259 alicepeck@alicepeck.com, http://alicepeckeditorial.com "editorial services from concept to final manuscript for fiction & nonfiction including first-time novelists"

Peske, Nancy – Shorewood, WI 414-763-7094 nancy@nancypeske.com, http://www.nancypeske.com "developmental/line editor, ghostwriter & publishing consultant for nonfiction writers"

Rashbaum, Beth – New York, NY 212-228-9573 bethrashbaum@gmail.com, http://www.bookdocs.com/editors/brashbaum "line editing, rewrites, ghostwriting + collaborating for nonfiction including memoir/ biography/autobiography, investigative journalism, Judaica, health/wellness, yoga, psychology & popular science"

Rigney, Melanie –Arlington, VA info@editorforyou.com, http://www.editorforyou.com "manuscript evaluation, content/ developmental editing for primarily nonfiction (no poetry, screenplays, proofreading or copyediting)"

Rinzler, Alan – San Francisco, CA alan@alanrinzler.com, http://www.alanrinzler.com OR Publishers Marketplace: Alan Rinzler, "manuscript consulting, developmental editing (character, story, narrative voice) & self-publishing advice, specializing in general fiction, mystery/ suspense/thriller, fantasy/sci-fi, juvenile/YA, biography/memoir, history, religion, African-American, science & paranormal"

Robertson, Ed – South Pasadena, CA 707-373-6458 ed@edrobertson.com, http://www.edrobertson.com "collaborative editor/writer + ghostwriter specializing in memoirs, biographies, film/television & books about celebrities"

✓ **Rojany Buccieri, Lisa** – Los Angeles, CA 818-707-1042
editorialservicesofla@gmail.com,
http://www.editorialservicesofla.com "line editing,
ghostwriting, self-publishing edit, page layout/packaging +
creative/literary consulting for fiction, nonfiction, YA, children's
& picture books"

Rosengard, Alice – New York, NY 212-662-4323
arosengard1@gmail.com, http://www.publishersmarketplace.
com/members/secretweapon/ "manuscript evaluation +
developmental/line editing for literary/mainstream fiction
including history, biography, memoir, current affairs & science"

Ross, Hilary – New York, NY 212-724-6756 hilary@hilaryross.net,
http://www.publishersmarketplace.com/members/hross
"structural + line editing for general fiction & nonfiction
including mystery/thrillers/suspense & romance (romance is a
specialty)"

Sanger, Joan – New York, NY 212-501-9352 joansanger@aol.com,
http://consulting-editors.com/Consulting_Editors_Alliance/
Meet_the_Editors.html "developmental/content editing for
mainstream/commercial fiction, primarily legal + medical
thrillers, mysteries, contemporary women's fiction & biography/
autobiography"

Sargent, Betty Kelly – New York, NY 917-287-1966
bettysargent@me.com,
http://www.bookdocs.com/editors/bsargent "manuscript
evaluation, line editing + collaborative writing for fiction/
general interest nonfiction including biography/memoir, health,
self-help & women's issues/interests"

Schwartz, Susan A. – New York, NY 212-877-3211
susan.sas22@gmail.com,
http://www.susanschwartzeditor.com
OR susanschwartz@theeditorscircle.com,
http://www.theeditorscircle.com/susan_a__schwartz.html
"editing, consulting + ghostwriting for fiction (all general
categories including thrillers & women's interest) plus popular

nonfiction (health, parenting, business, relationships, memoirs & reference books on all subjects)"

Sciarra Poynter, Toni – New York, NY tonionemail@yahoo.com, http://consulting-editors.com/Consulting_Editors_Alliance/Meet_the_Editors.html "specializing in nonfiction including wellness/health/medicine, psychology, science, lifestyle, important social/cultural trends, women's issues, family issues, career/workplace issues, personal improvement & narrative nonfiction"

Siegfried, Carin – Charlotte, NC 704-608-6559 carin@cseditorial.com, http://www.cseditorial.com OR http://twoeditorsandacomma.com "development/content editing for all genres except fantasy/sci-fi & religion (no copyediting)"

Spencer King, Janet – New York, NY 212-371-1479 janet@bookdevelopmentgroup.com, http://www.bookdevelopmentgroup.com/about-us/janet-spencer-king "manuscript evaluation, content/line editing, consulting + project management for self-publishing authors including fiction & nonfiction"

Taylor-Fox, Barry & Nadine – Burbank, CA 818-917-5362 info@taylor-fox.com, http://taylor-fox.com "editing + ghostwriting for business, memoirs, health, inspirational & philosophy"

Touchstone Editing – contact@touchstone-editing.com, http://www.touchstone-editing.com "Touchstone Editing provides editing & proofreading services for authors across genres, in YA, NA, & Adult categories"

Turok, Katharine – New York, NY 207-460-7477 kturok@gmail.com, http://wordsintoprint.org/editors/ "developmental/substantive/line editing + ghostwriting for literary/mainstream fiction & general nonfiction including memoir, contemporary issues/politics, natural history, travel, psychology, film/theater/arts, poetry, reference & translations"

Vezeris, Olga – New York, NY 212-744-8842 olga@bookdevelopmentgroup.com, http://www.

bookdevelopmentgroup.com/about-us/olga-vezeris "concept development, in-depth manuscript editing + self-publishing project management/consulting for fiction, nonfiction & audiobooks"

Victory Editing – Monroe, Louisiana anne@victoryediting.com, http://victoryediting.com "Anne Victory offers developmental editing, proofreading & oops detection"

Wade, James O'Shea – Yorktown Heights, NY 914-962-4619 jwade@bookdocs.com, http://www.bookdocs.com/editors/jwade "line editing, rewriting, ghostwriting + collaboration for most nonfiction, specializing in military history/memoirs, general history, autobiography, intelligence and foreign policy, science, & business, plus thrillers & male-oriented fiction (no how-to books, cookbooks or illustrated books)"

Weber, Karl – Irvington, NY 914-478-1983 karlweberliterary@yahoo.com, http://www.karlweberliterary.com "developmental editing + consulting for nonfiction including business, politics, current affairs, self-help, personal development, memoir & popular reference"

Wilde, Michael – Hudson, NY 518-672-7172 michaelwildeeditorial@earthlink.net, http://www.publishersmarketplace.com/members/mewilde/ "developmental/line editor + book doctor for nonfiction, including history, biography/memoir, behavioral sciences, political science, economics, education, social sciences & mainstream/literary fiction including children/YA"

Zack, Elizabeth – Convent Station, NJ 973-984-7880 ezack@bookcraftersllc.com, www.bookcraftersllc.com "editorial critique, content edit, consulting + coaching for self-improvement, memoir, inspiration, parenting, health/fitness, spirituality, popular culture, career, romance, fantasy, YA/children, women's interest & thriller/mystery"

Copyeditors & Proofreaders

What's the difference, and why are they essential?

Once your manuscript is finished, the keen eyes of copyeditors and proofreaders (for print books) will ensure that your book has none of the embarrassing typographical errors, factual inaccuracies, or continuity mistakes that so often plague self-published books. If you want your book to look and feel professionally published, it is essential that you work with a copyeditor for your e-book and a copyeditor and proofreader for the print edition. Often copyeditors are proofreaders as well, so you get two for the price of one.

Copyediting and proofreading are two different editorial skills, but there is a lot of confusion about how they differ. Copyeditors work on a manuscript before it is typeset. Proofreaders compare the typeset page proofs that have come back from the printer with the original copyedited manuscript to make sure all the changes suggested by the copyeditor have been inserted properly into the printed pages.

Copyeditors used to mark their corrections, edits, and style suggestions on the original manuscript (usually in blue pencil) before it was sent to the printer. These days, they often input their changes to the document in a word processing program such as Microsoft Word.

Here's a list of some of the things they do to improve your manuscript:

- Make sure the manuscript makes sense and reads smoothly
- Check spelling, grammar, punctuation, abbreviations, capitalization, and syntax
- Standardize notes, reference lists, and bibliographies
- Make style decisions based on *The Chicago Manual of Style*
- Standardize the use of quotations, numbers, italics, and foreign words
- Format the manuscript (chapter titles, subheads, and running heads)
- Check the accuracy of facts
- Eliminate the overuse of passive voice
- Point out clichés
- Make sure the tone and voice are consistent throughout

Proofreaders take the page proofs that have come back from the printer and check to make sure all the changes suggested by the copyeditor have been made properly. They make sure the photos are in the right place, the captions are correct and fit the photo, the page numbers are correct, there are no widows (dangling words or phrases at the top of a page)—essentially, that all the pages are error-free and the book is ready for the first printing, or for print on demand if that's what you have chosen.

Betty Kelly Sargent
BookWorks (www.BookWorks.com)

Adian Editing – jen@adianediting.com, http://www.adianediting.
com "Jen Blood offers beta reading + copy/content/line editing
& proofreading"

AIA Editing – AIAadmin@awesomeindies.net,
http://awesomeindies.net/for-authors/full-editing-services
"small team offering copy/line editing & proofreading"

Ascend Editing & Critique Services – Chicago, IL
maryvitas@ascendediting.com, http://www.ascendediting.com
"Mary Vitas offers manuscript critiques + copy/content/line
editing & proofreading"

Audet, Carole – Orillia, ON Canada 705-325-9439
carole@allwritesource.com, http://www.allwritesource.com
"Carole Audet offers editorial services + self-publishing support/
consulting for authors of spiritual, inspiration & self-help works"

Baum, Cate – London, UK editor@indiebookediting.com,
http://www.indiebookediting.com "line/copyediting +
proofreading specializing in self-published/indie books; also UK
to US English as well as proficiency in Spanish & French"

bigwords101 – San Francsico, CA 707-529-0092
info@bigwords101.com, http://www.bigwords101.com
"Copyediting + proofreading for all genres, fiction & nonfiction"

BubbleCow – Liverpool, UK garysmailes@bubblecow.co.uk,
http://bubblecow.com "line editing + detailed editor's report,
also proofreading & eBook cover design for indie authors
(partner of Humble Nations premade covers)"

CambridgeEditors – 617-876-2855
harte@cambridgeeditors.com OR
editors@cambridgeeditors.com, http://cambridgeeditors.com/
"Non-fiction editors focusing on scholarly & academic
books including research proposals, journal articles, creative
manuscripts by writers & poets, & corporate & institutional
publications"

Carter, Kathy – Peoria, IL 309-685-6389 M-F 9a-5p CST
kathy@carteredit.com, http://carteredit.com "substantive

+ copyediting for nonfiction trade books, including liberal religion/spirituality, philosophy, history, science, reference, health/wellness/nutrition, self-improvement, financial, communication, computer skills & how-to"

Chrysalis Editorial – Washington, DC 301-704-1455 herta@chrysaliseditorial.com, http://chrysaliseditorial.com/ "Herta Feely & Emily Williamson offer manuscript critiques, developmental edits, coaching, ghostwriting, & agent/ publishing advice for fiction & non-fiction"

Clio Editing Services – clioediting@gmail.com, http://clioediting.com "Eliza Dee offers substantive, copy + line editing & proofreading for indie authors"

DocuMania – dcma@vermontel.net, http://www.documania.us "Copyediting and substantive editing for most fiction genres, memoir & commercial nonfiction."

Ducharme, Sue – Boston, MA 603-522-0134 sducharme@roadrunner.com, http://www. authorsresourceguide.net/12095/sue-ducharme-textworks OR http://www.publishersmarketplace.com/members/ SueDucharme/ "developmental/line editing, copyediting + proofreading for most fiction & nonfiction genres"

Ebook Editing Pro – North Kingstown, RI ebookeditingpro@gmail.com, http://www.ebookeditingpro.com "small team of professional eBook copyeditors for fiction + nonfiction who can also write the book blurb"

Editcetera – Berkeley, CA 510-849-1110 http://www.editcetera.com "association of approx. 100 (prescreened) freelance publishing professionals offering full range of editorial services including developmental/copyeditors, proofreaders & indexers"

EditFor.me – Dallas, TX 661-524-5573 blake@editfor.me, http://www.editfor.me "Blake Atwood provides copyediting, ghostwriting, & book consultation services."

Editorial Freelancers Association – New York, NY 866-929-5425/212-929-5400 M-F 9a-5p EST office@the-efa.org, http://www.the-efa.org "EFA directory lists members by specialty + skill set, including editing, proofreading, indexing, translators & researchers"

Elliott, Lee – Wendell, NC 919-752-6158/919-332-2629 managingeditor@elliotteditorial.com, http://www.elliotteditorial.com "copyediting, line editing, proofreading, developmental editing + indexing"

Faulkner Editorial Services – Los Angeles, CA 310-391-3705 monica.faulkner@gmail.com, http://www.laeditorsandwritersgroup.com/about-our-members/monica-faulkner "manuscript evaluation, developmental/line editing, copyediting + proofreading, also writing coach & publishing consultant"

Finishing Touches Editing – Santa Rosa, CA 707-528-2265 esther@FinishingTouchesEditing.com, http://www.FinishingTouchesEditing.com "Copyediting, proofreading, ghostwriting, blogs, press releases + content creation"

Garrett, Michael – Clay, AL mike@manuscriptcritique.com, http://www.manuscriptcritique.com "copyediting, line editing, proofreading + book doctor for commercial fiction"

Hilty, Wyn – Redmond, WA whilty@comcast.net "copyediting + proofreading for fiction/nonfiction of all types, including sci-fi/fantasy, K-12 education, how-to & popular reference"

Honeycutt, Sharon – Winamac, IN freelancer1968@gmail.com, https://www.elance.com/s/skh0711 "content/copyediting, proofreading + ghostwriting for fiction & nonfiction"

Indie Books Gone Wild – Atlanta, GA yassabook2012@gmail.com, http://indiebooksgonewild.blogspot.com "team of line editors dedicated to the indie author, also offering print book formatting, beta-reading & proofreading"

Linda Jay Editorial Services – Petaluma, CA 415-320-0083 LindaJay@aol.com, http://wordsbylj.com/ "Linda Jay is a book manuscript copyeditor with decades of experience. She edits about 25 book manuscripts a year for indie authors. Genres include business, novels, memoirs, spirituality, women's issues, academic topics, fantasy (zombies, vampires). She is comfortable working with authors whose second language is English"

Lindgren, Mike – New York, NY 212-481-6488 mike_lindgren@yahoo.com, http://www.mikelindgren.net OR http://www.publishersmarketplace.com/members/ mikelindgren "copyediting, proofreading + copywriting for general fiction, biography, history, travel, lifestyle, sports, pop culture, music, art & critical theory"

Markman, Marla – Corona, CA 951-471-2526 marla@ marlamarkman.com, http://marlamarkman.com "creating, editing, managing content for a range of media, from magazines + books to websites & marketing collateral"

Marsh, Adam – San Francisco, CA 415-564-3100 marshadam@msn.com, http://www.publishersmarketplace. com/members/marshadam "developmental/line editing, copyediting, proofreading, copywriting, ghostwriter + book doctor for most fiction & nonfiction"

McCullough, Carrie – Augusta, GA 706-564-7998 carrie@carriemccullough.com, http://carriemccullough.com "content + line editing, also author profiles for social media networking including Facebook, Twitter & blogs"

PenUltimate Editorial Services – Kelowna, BC Canada 778-478-0877 info@penultimateword.com, http://penultimateword.com "Arlene Prunkl works primarily with self-publishing authors as freelance editor, manuscript evaluator + proofreader for both fiction & nonfiction"

PeopleSpeak – Laguna Hills, CA 949-581-6190 pplspeak@att.net, http://www.detailsplease.com/peoplespeak "Sharon Goldinger offers content/copyediting, proofreading, manuscript evaluation, research + fact checking & publishing consulting"

Proofable – Cambridge, UK enquiries@proofable.com, http://www.proofable.com "online job board; prescreened freelance copyeditors, proofreaders, copywriters + translators submit bids to match client project posts"

Quinlin, Jenny – jennyq@historicaleditorial.com, http://historicaleditorial.blogspot.com "developmental/copyediting + proofreading specializing in historical fiction, romance & fantasy; also custom/premade covers for those genres"

Quirk, Kevin – Crozet, VA 434-823-7629 kevin@yourbookghostwriter.com, http://www.yourbookghostwriter.com "content/line editing, proofreading, ghostwriter + coach specializing in autobiography/memoir & purpose-driven nonfiction"

Ridley, Elizabeth – Brookfield, WI 414-476-9925 liz@elizabethridley.com, http://www.elizabethridley.com OR http://www.publishersmarketplace.com/members/sparkscoop/ "developmental/line editing, copyediting, proofreading + book doctor for most fiction & nonfiction"

Robertson, Ed – South Pasadena, CA 707-373-6458 ed@edrobertson.com, http://www.edrobertson.com "copyediting, line editing, copywriting + ghostwriter, specializing in history, memoirs & biography"

Rubenthaler, Kira – Coos Bay, OR 541-944-6479 editing@bookflydesign.com, http://www.bookflydesign.com "Bookfly Design; copyediting + proofreading for indie authors, self-publishers & small presses"

Sigrid MacDonald Copyediting & Critiques – Ottawa, ON Canada sigridmac13@hotmail.com OR sigridmacdonald@rogers.com, http://sigridmacdonald.blogspot.com "copyediting, proofreading, manuscript evaluation & self-publishing coach, also blog with helpful writing tips: http://beyourowneditor.blogspot.com"

Smith, Robin – Candler, NC 828-633-0525
robinsmithink@charter.net, http://www.robinsmithink.com
"manuscript evaluation, content editing, line editing &
copyediting"

StyleInSites – 415-699-9371 info@styleinsites.com,
http://www.styleinsites.com "Elissa Rabellino offers a full range
of editorial services from line editing to proofreading"

Sue Klefstad Indexing & Proofreading Services –
Monticello, IL 217-762-7453 sue@suetheindexer.com,
http://www.suetheindexer.com "indexing + APA- & AMA-style
proficient proofreading specializing in psychology, science/
medical, business/financial, the arts, education & children's
literature"

TK Proofreading – Spring Hill, QLD Australia (08) 98381225
tonykeen25@gmail.com, http://www.tkproofreading.com.au
"Tony Keen (qualified journalist) offers structural editing, line
editing & proofreading"

The Write Companion – Roswell, NM 575-910-4836
alignor.lignor@gmail.com, http://www.thewritecompanion.com
"Amy Lignor & Mary Carrier will edit, ghostwrite, review and/or
provide content for your literary project"

Writer's Helper – Gibsons, BC Canada http://www.writershelper.com
"Audrey Owen offers substantive, line + copyediting for self-
publishing authors specializing in nonfiction & children's books;
website full of helpful info for indie authors"

Indexers

Most people never think about how an index is created; they just look for it, use it, and find it helpful—or not. Usually the first thing most people ask the indexer is, "Do you read the whole book?" The short answer is "Yes." But it's a lot more complicated than that. Here are some of the most common questions I hear as a professional indexer, and the answers I usually give.

What is an index, anyway?

Well, it's that thing at the back of a book where you look up stuff you want to find in the book. (Not a very elegant response, admittedly, but it seems to do the trick.)

How do you get to be an indexer?

There are online correspondence courses, some colleges teach indexing, there are books on the art of indexing, some people find a mentor, and there are several online discussion groups for beginning and experienced indexers to share information, techniques, and so on. It's one of the rare professions you can legitimately learn on your own, but it's faster, and you'll learn the profession's standards, if you take a course.

Do you have to read the whole book?

Yes; how else would I know what's in it to be indexed?

Don't they have computer apps for that?

There are apps that do the background work for you, such as alphabetizing, helping you gather similar entries, and making sure cross-references are correct. (Uh-oh . . .)

What's a cross-reference, and what could be incorrect about it?

Cross-references tell the reader where to find similar or related information that they might not have thought of, such as

parrots. See also canaries

or that the information they want is located elsewhere, such as

cats. See felines.

An incorrect cross-reference might be, for example,

cats. See felines
felines. See cats.

Why is this incorrect? Because it's a loop. Cats tells you to go to felines, and felines tells you to go to cats. There's no useful information at either one, which is a very serious error.

But aren't there apps that find all the words you want and give you the page number?

Sure, if you want every single instance of every single word in the manuscript. That's actually called a concordance, not an index. It will come up with some indexable words, but it won't know what the context of "fields" is. "We saw some lovely fields" (not indexable) versus "Crop rotation includes letting certain fields lie fallow . . ." (indexable). Apps also can't tell if a phrase is indexable and won't show indexable phrases, such as "cows in a field," "field-management basics," and so on. Only a human can do that.

OK, I get it. But who needs an index anyway? I can't think of the last time I used one.

There are two kinds of people who use an index: the bookstore browser who wants to get a feel for the scope of the book, and the reader who wants to find something they already read. And, of course, librarians who are deciding whether to purchase a book. Most librarians won't buy a nonfiction book that doesn't have an index. Oh, and anyone who thinks they might actually be in the index. If they are, they'll almost certainly buy the book. So an index is a strong marketing tool for most books, increasing usability and strongly increasing sales.

My publisher says I'm responsible for indexing my book. Why can't I do it myself? You just said I could teach myself how to do it.

Most authors don't make good indexers of their own work. They get too close to the topic and don't look at it from a reader's point of view. They think every point is important and therefore should be indexed. A professional indexer looks at the text as the reader would. They will avoid those passing mentions I talked about; they will know what related topics should be cross-referenced and how to structure the index with many access points so that a reader has the easiest route to the information they want. If you, as the author, have written a book with references to felines and never once use the word "cat," then you probably wouldn't put the word in the index as a main entry, and a lot of readers will never find your information on cats. A professional indexer knows that a reader would look for "cat" rather than "feline" in an index, even if the word never appears in the text.

Professional indexers are also able to gather information that you might not realize goes with other information. Or you, the author, might put unrelated information in the entry. Or have a ton of page numbers in an index entry without telling the reader what specific information is on those pages. Or analyze the text so that certain subentries should also be main entries with their own subentries and cross-references, and so on. These are things that authors might not know to do, or how to do.

There are a few authors who have indexed their own books and done a wonderful job—for example, Julia Child, but she was a member of the American Society for Indexing, and took the time to learn how to index well.

Which, by the way, is another obstacle for an author. It's like any other craft. You can learn it, even teach yourself, but it can take a lot of time and practice to get good at it. Wouldn't you rather spend that time working on your writing?

You've convinced me. How do I find a professional indexer, and how do I know whether the person I plan to hire is good at it?

You can usually get some referrals from your publisher or printer. If you're self-publishing and no one has any suggestions, try an Internet search for "book indexers" ("indexes" and "indexing" might get you Standard & Poors, rather than book indexers). Or try one of the professional organizations such as the American Society for Indexing. Ask colleagues. Try LinkedIn and Facebook. If you aren't certain of an indexer's ability, ask for references and samples. Do it as soon as you know you're going to publish a book, because indexing is the very last thing on the list of what needs to be done, and good indexers are busy and might not be able to fit your project in at the last minute.

Oh. How long does it take to index a book?

There are many variables, including how big the book is, the scope and density of the information, the actual physical size of the pages, how much is text versus graphics, and so on. The way indexers work also varies widely. It will generally take an experienced indexer about two weeks to do a good job on a 300-page book—less if the book has a lot of graphics, nonindexable content, and low-density content, and more, maybe much more if the book is densely packed with information, is poorly designed and organized, is about a very complex topic, is oversized, has multiple columns, and so on.

And cost?

Well, that also varies depending on the book and the indexer. You could find rates from as low as $1.50 per page to as much as $10 per page. Remember that your indexer does this for a living and has put a lot of time and effort into learning this craft. You'll have to balance the cost against the return. If your book is on the easy end and doesn't have a lot of detail, you might be able to hire a less experienced indexer whose rates might be a little lower. If you have a complex book with specialized content, you're going to be far better off paying a higher rate for someone with experience.

Most indexers charge by the indexable page (any page that has to be read for indexable content, whether there is any on that page or not). Some will agree to an hourly rate or project rate. Always remember that you get what you pay for, and that in almost every case you will have three considerations: The indexer can do it fast, cheap, or well. You can only pick two.

Rachel Rice
Rae the Indexer (www.rachelrice.com)

Rachel Rice has been a freelance indexer since 1993. Many of her clients are authors, and she enjoys working with them to create the best book possible. She likes to index a wide range of topics, including self-help, medical/veterinary, business, psychology, animal care, textbooks, and much more.

Access Points Indexing – Hood River, OR 503-312-1294
mary@accesspointsindexing.com,
http://www.accesspointsindexing.com "Mary Harper facilitates
audience-focused text analysis, multiple access points &
navigational interrelationships"

Amethyst Harbor, Inc. – amy.hall@amethystharbor.com,
http://www.amethystharbor.com "Amy Hall provides nonfiction
indexing for trade books, cookbooks + textbooks, also
copyediting & proofreading services"

Brookfield Indexing – London, ON Canada 519-432-9421
info@brookfieldindexing.com,
http://www.brookfieldindexing.com "Sergey Lobachev offers
back-of-the-book + embedded indexing specializing in a wide
range of topics in sciences/humanities for academic & trade
books"

Colleen Dunham Indexing – Buffalo, NY 505-934-5571
colleendunham1819@hotmail.com,
http://www.colleendunhamindexing.com "back-of-the-book
indexing, consulting, software feature mapping, collection
indexing, scholarly research & 'quick' indexes"

Deborah E. Patton Professional Indexing – Staunton, VA 540-
324-2721 dp@pattonindexing.com, http://pattonindexing.com
"indexes for books, journals & author websites in print or
electronic formats"

INDEX-S – Ottawa, ON Canada 613-860-5280
bcuerden@gmail.com, http://www.index-s.com "back-of-the-
book indexes, specializing in scholarly/academic texts, as well as
works that rely on knowledge of art, art history & spirituality"

Mertes Editorial Services – Alexandria, VA 703-549-4574
kmertes@hotmail.com, http://katemertes.com "Kate Mertes;
back-of-the-book, website indexing + developmental editing,
specializing in law & humanities"

Nancy C. Gerth, Ph.D. – Sagle, ID 208-304-9066
docnangee@nancygerth.com, http://nancygerth.com "30 years'

experience organizing, presenting and mapping information; covering natural sciences, humanities & trade"

Rachel Rice – Plainfield, MA 802-380-3944 rae.the.indexer@gmail.com, http://www.rachelrice.com/ "back-of-the book indexing along with indexing of journals, catalogues, & monographs. Also offers embedded indexes using Word and XML coding"

Sue Klefstad Indexing & Proofreading Services – Monticello, IL 217-762-7453 sue@suetheindexer.com, http://www.suetheindexer.com "indexing + APA- & AMA-style proficient proofreading specializing in psychology, science/medical, business/financial, the arts, education & children's literature"

Tabby Cat Communications – Camas, WA 206-432-1973 info@tabbycatco.com, http://www.tabbycatco.com "Cheryl Landes offers editing, indexing + proofreading, specializing in technical communications publishing for both print & online environments"

WordCo Indexing Services, Inc. – Norwich, CT 860-886-2532 office@wordco.com, http://www.wordco.com "WordCo facilitates discovery by providing publishers with print & embedded/digital indexes"

Cover & Interior Book Designers

What indie authors need to know about cover designers, interior designers, and formatters

---

Almost every publishing professional advising self-publishers says the same thing: focus on editing and cover design. Those are the two most important elements of your book, the ones that will make the biggest difference in how your book is received and how it will sell.

We've already discussed how working with a good editor can help make or break your book, so now let's take a look at the importance of good design, both inside and out.

Why are covers so important in book publishing?

The most important reason is that the cover will establish the brand of your book. The design will capture the essence of the book and highlight its appeal to potential readers.

In addition, you may end up using your cover design, graphics, and colors on your website, in social media, and on collateral material like posters, bookmarks, postcards, and fliers.

But a book cover has more work to do. Here are five goals every good book cover should aim to achieve:

- **Announce the genre.** Clearly, many book buyers search for books by category, niche, or genre, so this instant identification of where your book belongs is critical. If it looks like historical fiction, but it's actually a vampire romance, many potential readers may miss your book completely.

- **Telegraph the tone.** Although subtler, it's also important that the cover suggest the tone of a work, especially with fiction. Is it a brash, over-the-top page-turner, or an understated character study?

- **Explain the scope.** Especially with nonfiction, readers need to know what's included in your book and what's not—what's the subject matter, time period, setting, and skill level of the author or contributors?

- **Generate excitement.** Effective book covers have a "hook," something that intrigues, grabs you by the throat, makes a promise—something that will attract and hold a reader's attention and make them want to know more.

- **Establish a market position.** Your book cover can help browsers by letting them know where your book fits in with other, similar books they are already familiar with. Is it encyclopedic, filled with vampires, based on new groundbreaking research, loaded with resources?

Professional cover designers

For almost all authors, getting a cover for your book that touches all these bases; is attractive to the readers in your niche, category, or genre; and really helps sell your book is going to mean hiring a professional designer.

And you want a professional *book cover designer*, not just a good graphic artist, your nephew who just took an art class in college, or your friend who loves to paint and draw. Book cover design is a specialty, and even skilled graphic designers who haven't worked in book publishing aren't a good choice for this crucial task.

There are some important points to consider when you start looking for a cover designer for your book. Here are some tips on finding and working with a professional book cover designer.

Many designers have a submission form for you to fill out. It will collect the information the designer feels is most important. Whether or not they have such a form, you should be prepared with:

- Your manuscript, even if it isn't finished
- The final title and subtitle for your book
- Your name as you'd like it to appear on the cover
- Your publishing company logo, if you have one
- Some idea of who the audience is for your book
- Samples or links to examples of book covers in your category that you like, as well as ones you don't like

Also keep in mind that designers vary in the work they perform. Some only do book covers, some only do interiors, some do both, and some, particularly designers with a studio and a staff, may also be able to create an author website, handle your printing, and supply you with other graphics for your publishing company or book promotion.

If you find a designer who can "do it all" for you, you'll save yourself a lot of time and trouble coordinating the work of several people.

Tips on working with your cover designer

- Check the designer's portfolio to make sure she understands and has worked in your genre, category, or niche.

- Make sure the designer's fee is within your budget.
- If you need to have the work completed by a specific date, make sure this is communicated to the designer at the outset, and that he agrees to your schedule.
- Review the designer's contract or agreement under which the work will be done.
- Let your designer know exactly what you'll need besides the basic front cover. *& Back cover*
- Review the formats you'd like to receive your cover in when it's done: PDF for uploading to print on demand, a JPG of the front cover for your e-book, a high-resolution file, etc.
- Supply the designer with necessary background material (see the list above).
- Give the designer photos or drawings that you think will be useful as background or visual inspirations.
- Don't dictate that the designer *must* use those elements, but leave it up to her—that's why you hired a pro!
- Talk over the various approaches to your cover in the sample designs she will provide you with.
- Remember that you and your designer are *collaborators* trying to reach the best approach to packaging your book for sale.

About contracts and agreements

Although many indie authors skip this step, it's wise to have a written agreement with your designer that addresses the exact work to be done, what it will cost, how payments will be made, how either person can cancel the contract if they wish, and the ownership of the artwork used to create the cover as well as the files the designer creates to produce your reproduction-quality PDF for printing or your JPG for your e-book.

This may seem embarrassing at first, but it can save a lot of heartache and expense later if your project doesn't turn out the way you expect. This also applies to interior designers, formatters, photographers, models, and illustrators—in other words, you need a contract or a letter of agreement with anyone who is creating something to be used in the publication of your book.

Beyond the book

Keep in mind that you may want to extend the branding established on your cover beyond the book itself. For instance, some designers will be happy to also provide:

- Graphics for your website
- Bookmarks
- Posters
- Social media graphics like Facebook headers and Twitter cards
- E-mail newsletter templates

Each of these is an opportunity to extend your brand and reach more potential readers.

Interior designers and formatters

The interior of a book is the complete opposite of its cover, from a design perspective. While you want your cover to stop people, compel them to have a closer look, and generate excitement for the story within, you want the opposite from your interior. And while cover design changes with the seasons, reflecting current tastes in design "fashion," in some ways book interiors have remained largely unchanged for hundreds of years.

Many books do not need a "custom" interior because our requirements for books can be reduced to three essentials:

- The book needs to be easily *readable*
- The design should not get between the *author and reader*
- The interior needs to conform to *industry standards*

Readability

Book interiors are long-form documents that need to be easy to read, and that's what should inform most of your decisions. When your designer chooses fonts, establishes page margins, and creates navigational aids like contents and running heads, she will at all times be keeping the reading experience in mind.

Staying out of the way

While design flourishes such as illustrated chapter openings, ornamental text breaks, and other devices can help establish an appropriate tone for your book, none of these elements should intrude on the reader to the point that the reading experience is compromised.

Industry standards

Sure signs of a book that's been produced by an amateur author can usually be traced to an ignorance of or disregard for standards. For instance, a book whose pages are numbered with the odd pages on the left will be a "red flag" to any book professional who examines the book, and that may not be the effect you're trying to create.

What book professionals? People like bookstore buyers, book reviewers, authors you have asked for a testimonial, media bookers, and others. We rely on these people to help us bring our books to market and spread our message. Don't create a book that looks "off" or amateurish to them.

Creating the cover and interior for your book should be an enjoyable part of your book publishing process, so take a deep breath and realize you'll only go through this once—for each book!

Joel Friedlander
The Book Designer (www.thebookdesigner.com)

1106 Design – Phoenix, AZ 602-866-3226 office@1106design.com, http://1106design.com "cover + interior book design, proofreading & editorial services"

99 Designs – 800-513-1678 http://99designs.com "crowd-sourced design; post your project/budget and designers worldwide submit proposals to choose from"

Aartpack Inc. – Carlisle, MA 617-566-3080 info@aartpack.com, http://www.aartpack.com "cover + interior book design, specializing in education, health & corporate publications"

Abacus Graphics – Oceanside, CA 760-724-7750 jrw@abacusgraphics.com, http://www.abacusgraphics.com "book covers, graphics, website design + collateral marketing materials for authors"

Abrams, Mark – Brooklyn, NY 917-450-6833 lookmark@earthlink.net, http://www.markabramsdesign.com "book cover design for all fiction + nonfiction genres"

ACD Book Cover Design – New York, NY 917-455-2184 "designs for print, print-on-demand, & e-book publishing"

Alchemy Book Covers & Design – jacypods@gmail.com, http://www.alchemybookcovers.com "Keri Knutson offers custom + premade covers, interior design elements, logos, banners & other marketing/promotional materials"

Alphabet Soup Group – Mountain Lakes, NJ 973-335-4849 lili@alphabetsoupgroup.com, http://www.alphabetsoupgroup.com "typographic + interior book design for print & digital formats including art direction, book jackets, promotional materials"

ALSO – Chicago, IL 773-527-6587 jenny@also-online.com, http://www.also-online.com "small design studio for book covers/interiors, illustration, animation, branding & web design"

Andrew Newman Design – Marstons Mills, MA 508-420-1161 newmandesign@gmail.com, http://andrewnewmandesign.com "book covers, illustrations, branding, logos & website design"

Arisman Design Studio – Essex, MA 978-768-7063
    judith.arisman@verizon.net, www.arismandesign.com "cover/
    interior book design + illustration including layout, typesetting,
    photo research & retouching"

Atomic Covers – Tampa, FL http://www.atomiccovers.com "Johnny
    Atomic, illustrator + cover artist specializing in sci-fi/fantasy,
    works with top studios in entertainment industry as well as
    indie authors looking for custom-painted cover design"

Author's Voice Publishing – jan@authorsvoicepublishing.com,
    http://www.AuthorsVoicePublishing.com "Full service
    studio offers cover and interior book design & production,
    editorial services, photo research & alterations, ISBN, LCCN, &
    promotional materials, for authors of fiction & non-fiction"

BeauteBook – New York, NY 646-736-7444 info@beautebook.com,
    http://www.beautebook.com "cover/interior book design, dust
    jackets for hard/paperback POD, eBook formatting, website
    design & book marketing materials"

Berg Design – Albany, NY 518-495-9409 edatkeson@gmail.com,
    http://www.edatkeson.com/bpages/berg.htm "cover + interior
    book design for mainly nonfiction, especially the sciences"

David Bergsland – David@bergsland.org,
    http://www.bergsland.org "interior & font designer"

BH Communications – New York, NY 212-982-6502
    brice@bhcommunications.com,
    http://www.bhcommunications.com "cover/interior book
    design for primarily nonfiction, + branding & website design"

Blair, Kelly – Brooklyn, NY kelly@kellyblair.com, http://kellyblair.com
    "art direction, design + illustration for fiction & nonfiction book
    covers"

Book Cover Cafe – Brisbane, Australia anthony@bookcovercafe.com,
    http://www.bookcovercafe.com "artist/graphic designer
    Anthony Puttee offers custom book cover design + editorial,
    publishing advice/consulting, marketing & author-platform
    building services for the indie author"

Book Cover Express – Nova Scotia, Canada cstevenson@accesswave.ca, http://cathistevenson.com/word/book-cover-design "Cathi Stevenson designs custom covers for print + eBooks in most fiction & nonfiction genres"

The Book Designers – Fairfax, CA 415-491-5426 info@bookdesigners.com, http://www.bookdesigners.com "full-service studio including cover/interior design, editing, production, printing & eBook conversion"

Bookfly Design – Coos Bay, OR 541-944-6479 covers@bookflydesign.com, http://www.bookflydesign.com "small studio offering customized cover design + editing services for indie authors"

Books and Branding – Jersey City, NJ 201-420-8205 sndi@verizon.net, http://booksandbranding.com "Susan Newman offers cover + interior book design, web design & brand development"

Brand, Christopher – New York, NY 646-257-0945 mail@christopher-brand.com, http://www.christopher-brand.com "graphic designer + illustrator for book covers & interiors"

Branderburg, Jeff – San Francsico, CA 415-298-3099 imagecomp@icloud.com, http://JeffBrandenburg.com "designs books & assist self-publishing authors in getting their books published in a variety of formats, from hard cover books to ebooks"

Budd Publishing – Ottawa, Ontario Canada 613-824-9707 ev@buddpublishing.com, http://buddgraphics.com/consulting/ "Evelyn Budd is a registered graphic designer who specializes in book cover & interior design"

Cox-King Multimedia – Geneva, NY 315-719-0141 9a-5p EST info@ckmm.com, http://www.ckmm.com "full-service studio offering book covers/jacket design, including interior layout, typesetting, editing + collateral/promotional materials; will only work with experienced self-publishers"

CreativINDIECovers – Portland, OR 971-270-2017
derekmurphy@creativindie.com,
http://bookcovers.creativindie.com "Derek Murphy offers
custom + DIY cover design, interior print/eBook formatting and
DIY templates, WordPress author website design & ISBN's"

Damonza – Cape Town, S. Africa damonza@damonza.com,
http://damonza.com "predesigned/custom covers + layout/
formatting for print & eBooks as well as book trailers"

David Gee Book Design – davidgeebookdesign@gmail.com,
http://davidgeebookdesign.tumblr.com "designer with
advertising background specializing in book covers"

DeVicq Design – New York, NY 646-957-4839 roberto@devicq.com,
http://www.devicq.com "book cover designer + illustrator
specializes in designing with typography"

Desktop Miracles Inc. – Stowe, VT 802-253-7900
barry@desktopmiracles.com, http://www.desktopmiracles.com
"full-service studio specializing in cover/interior book design,
formatting & print production management"

Digital Vista Inc. – Massapequa, NY 516-799-5277
info@digitalvista.net, http://www.digitalvista.net "book cover
design packages at multiple price points + book trailers &
collateral materials"

DLC Designs – Kalamazoo, MI http://dcoll1.wix.com/dlcdesigns
"Donna Collier offers custom/premade covers for print +
eBooks, 3D ads, website/blog banners, buttons & logos for indie
authors"

Dorian, Mars – Berlin, Germany md@marsdorian.com,
http://www.marsdorian.com "artist with bold graphic style for
book covers + illustration; also offers coaching on building your
brand & online presence"

DreamUp – Hollywood, CA 323-645-8220 support@dreamup.com,
https://dreamup.com "DeviantArt spinoff; crowdsourcing
platform to find creative professionals for cover design, websites
+ illustration by posting your project/budget & screening bids"

Dunn+Associates Design – Hayward, WI 715-634-4857 info@dunn-design.com, http://www.dunn-design.com "design studio specializing in book covers + book marketing tools & logos"

Ebook Indie Covers – ebook.indie.covers@gmail.com, http://ebookindiecovers.com "Melody Simmons offers premade + custom covers for eBooks/paperbacks, Facebook/ website banners, promo materials & book trailers"

Ebook Launch – admin@ebooklaunch.com, http://ebooklaunch.com "premade + custom cover designs, eBook formatting for Smashwords premium catalog, Amazon KDP, Google Books & POD formatting for CreateSpace"

Erelis Design – Belgrade, Serbia http://nadaorlic.wix.com/book "Nada Orlic, book cover designer, illustrator + website designer"

Extended Imagery – Chicago, IL carl@extendedimagery.com, http://extendedimagery.com "Carl Graves offers custom book covers, illustration + motion graphics/animation for clients including best-selling indie author JA Konrath"

Fiona Jayde Media – fiona@fionajayde.com, http://fionajaydemedia.com "custom + premade covers, web design, editorial services & promotional materials"

Fiona Raven Book Design – Vancouver, BC Canada 604-568-4158 info@fionaraven.com, http://www.fionaraven.com "cover + interior book page design & production"

Foster Covers – Fairfield, IA 641-472-3953/800-472-3953 info@fostercovers.com, http://www.fostercovers.com "leading book cover designer for fiction + nonfiction"

Gates Sisters Studio, Inc. – New York, NY 212-614-1439 kathleen@gatessisters.com, http://www.gatessisters.com "book interior + cover design, advertising & web design services"

A Good Thing, Inc. – New York, NY 212-687-8155 arichman@agoodthingink.com, http://www.agoodthingink.com "cover + interior book design for mainly nonfiction, academic, directories & journals"

Gray318/Jonathan Gray – London, UK +44 (0) 7956 173218
jon@gray318.com, http://gray318.com "London-based book
cover designer"

Haggar, Darren – New York, NY darrenhaggar@gmail.com,
http://darrenhaggar.com "book cover designer + art director"

Humble Nations – Prague, CZ humblenations@gmail.com,
http://humblenations.com "premade covers + customized
designs using stock images, with fast turnaround"

IndieBookLauncher – Brampton, ON Canada 905-791-2349
info@indiebooklauncher.com,
http://www.indiebooklauncher.com/aboutus.php "cover
design, developmental/copyediting, eBook production/digital
distribution + ISBN's"

Indie Designz – contact@indiedesignz.com,
http://www.indiedesignz.com "specializing in premade/custom
cover design + interior formatting for print & eBooks"

Itzhack Shelomi Design – Scarsdale, NY 212-689-7469
studio@ishelomi.com, http://www.ishelomi.com "cover/interior
design/formatting for trade books (mainly kids) + textbooks
(mainly medical); also offers production & editorial services"

JD Smith Design – Carlisle, Cumbria UK info@jdsmith-design.co.uk,
http://www.jdsmith-design.com "graphic designer Jane Dixon-
Smith offers eBook, paperback + hardcover dust jacket design,
typesetting & promotional/marketing materials for authors"

Kabak, Carie – Missouri carriekabak@icloud.com,
http://carriekabak.wix.com/graphics "print & eBook cover
design, photo & image editing, + promotional graphic design"

Keenan Design – London, UK +44 (0) 7957 102466
keenan@keenandesign.com, http://www.keenandesign.com
"Jamie Keenan, book cover designer for American + British
fiction & nonfiction"

Kit Foster Design – Edinburgh, UK kitfosterdesign@gmail.com,
http://www.kitfosterdesign.com "graphic designer specializing

in custom book covers for print/eBooks, also offering ready-made eBook covers & banners"

Lai, Chin-Yee – New York, NY 917-209-2888 design@chinyeelai.com, http://www.chinyeelai.com "book cover + jacket designer for fiction & nonfiction"

Laura Duffy Design – New York, NY 347-834-1027 laura@lauraduffydesign.com, http://lauraduffydesign.com "specializing in cover design for fiction + nonfiction as well as marketing & publicity materials"

Lightbourne Inc. – Wilsonville, OR 800-697-9833/503-542-3551 shannon@lightbourne.com, http://lightbourne.com "book covers + interior layouts, eBooks, website design, branding & marketing services"

LLPix Designs – Linton, IN 812-798-9117 laura@llpix.com, http://www.llpix.com "Laura Wright LaRoche, photographer & graphic designer of custom + premade covers, book trailers, logos & author swag"

Memory Works Publishing – Sedona, AZ 928-284-0222 http://www.memoryworkspublishing.com "cover/interior design, layout, editorial services + ISBNs, specializing in biographies, memoirs, family history & photo books"

Minor, Wendell – Washington, CT 860-868-9101 wendell@minorart.com, http://www.minorart.com "artist and illustrator specializing in children's books"

Monkey C Media – San Diego, CA 619-955-8286 info@monkeycmedia.com, http://monkeycmedia.com "book cover &interior designs"

OctagonLab – Switzerland support@octagonlab.com, http://octagonlab.com "custom book cover design packages, banners & logos"

Pearson, David – London, UK +44 (0) 20 7837 6654 david@typeasimage.com, http://typeasimage.com "London-based designer specializing in book covers/jackets + branding"

Precision Graphics – Champaign, IL 217-359-6655 info@precisiongraphics.com, http://www.precisiongraphics.com "print + eBook design plus illustration primarily for science, math, medical & educational textbooks"

Rivershore Books – 763-670-8677 info@rivershorebooks.com, http://rivershorebooks.com/ "Cover design and book formatting for fiction, nonfiction, & poetry"

Robert Pizzo Illustration/Design – Redding, CT 203-938-0663 rp@robertpizzo.com, http://www.robertpizzo.com "illustrator/designer specializing in graphic illustrations + infographics for book covers/interiors & promotional materials"

Robin Ludwig Design – Palm Coast, FL 386-338-3388 robin@gobookcoverdesign.com, http://www.gobookcoverdesign.com "custom book covers + graphic design for print/online marketing & author swag"

Rock and Hill Studio – m3woods@gmail.com, http://rockandhillstudio.com "complete services for print + digital books, from cover art & design to editing & formatting"

Romance Novel Covers – support@romancenovelcovers.com, http://www.romancenovelcovers.com "stock image website specifically for romance novelists with large selection of non-exclusive images, premade + customized covers"

Rothman, Julia – Brooklyn, NY 917-885-7963 julia@also-online.com, http://www.juliarothman.com "partners with ALSO (Chicago) on designs for book interiors/covers, also illustration, advertising & branding"

Salamander Hill Design – Elgin, QC Canada 450-264-6787 david@salamanderhill.com, http://www.salamanderhill.com "David Drummond, founder/principal specializes in book cover design, illustration & promotional materials"

Shadow Canyon Graphics – Golden, CO 303-278-0949 dnshadow@earthlink.net, http://www.shadowcanyongraphics.com "full-service graphics studio offering cover/interior design, page composition, indexing, illustration, editing & project management"

Shaw, Heather – Traverse City, MI shaw.heather00@gmail.com, http://www.thumbtack.com/mi/traverse-city/editors/book-design-editing "book design + layout, eBook conversion, editorial services & web design for authors"

Stillpoint Digital Press – Mill Valley, CA 415-381-1408 editor@stillpointdigital.com, http://stillpointdigital.com "David Kudler and team offer cover/interior design, editing, fact checking, web design, indexing, & more"

Syd Gill Design – Vancouver, BC Canada sydgill99@gmail.com, http://www.sydgill.com "custom + premade book covers, wallpaper, banner art & other promotional graphics"

Ten Berge, Jeroen – Wellington, NZ +64-212-936381 jeroenslimited@gmail.com, http://jeroentenberge.com "custom book covers, illustration & branding for best-selling as well as first-time authors"

Tobin, Isaac – Chicago, IL isaac@isaactobin.com, http://www.isaactobin.com "book covers/interiors, illustration & type design"

Vedic Design – Bridgewater, NJ book-cover@vedicdesign.com, http://www.vedicdesign.com "small design firm specializing in affordable custom royalty-free book covers & logos"

Velvet Wings Design – Sydney, AU k.rose2727@gmail.com, http://velvetwingsdesign.com "Rose Newland makes book covers for ebooks and POD"

Vila Design – El Salvador villatat@gmail.com, http://www.viladesign.net "Tatiana Vila offers cover design for eBooks + POD paperbacks & eBook formatting"

Words Plus Design – Tecumseh, MI 888-883-8347/517-423-9092 wordsplusdesign@comcast.net, http://www.wordsplusdesign.com "book covers, interior page design/layout, promotional materials & light editing/proofreading services"

Image Sources

Finding an image for your book cover

Image desperation is a sad, sad thing. If you're a graphic designer, you've undoubtedly run into this problem during your career. If you're attempting to design your own book cover, it's something you need to watch out for.

Image desperation is when the project manager can't find or can't afford a good image for a project, so she decides to "make do." Making do can include using the wrong image, such as a dog instead of a wolf; a dental syringe instead of an insulin syringe; or a waning gibbous moon instead of a full moon. Sometimes this has more to do with lack of research than true desperation, but even when you've done your research you can make blunders that leave others shaking their heads. We've all seen those low-resolution images combined with clip art that are supposed to fool the reader. They don't.

Microstock agencies

Since your book cover is the "handshake that greets the world" for your project, you should make it work—and keep in mind that it has to look good even when it is only one inch high in a thumbnail ad. It takes just as much effort to create a bad book cover as it does a good book cover in today's image-rich world. That wasn't the case even ten years ago, when images were difficult to find. Back then, digital cameras were quite expensive, at least ones that shot in high resolution, and there were only a few low-priced stock art agencies around. CD collections that offered thousands of images for only a few dollars usually weren't even worth the few dollars. Behind closed doors in publishing houses, art directors would budget thousands of dollars to license the right photograph, hire a photographer to take one, or find an illustrator to create the perfect image for the cover. Then microstock agencies started popping up online almost overnight.

These companies work almost exclusively online and accept images from photographers and artists all over the world, both amateur and professional. Once this method of doing business caught on, images became available for as little as $10. Some companies even offered them for as low as $1 each. Package deals and memberships were also introduced at far more reasonable costs than ever before. Sometimes $500 a year would allow you unlimited downloads and reproductions of an image.

These days, things seem to be shifting back to higher costs for memberships and single images, and most companies now have a reproduction limit (although a very high one, usually 100,000 or more) on using images. The rising prices are due mainly to the fact that the smaller agencies are being bought by much larger corporations that can charge more because there's less competition. In spite of this, it's still fairly easy to find affordable images, and there are even some sites that offer high-resolution images for free. If you can't find the perfect picture to license, you can take one yourself with a good digital camera or hire a professional photographer. If those solutions are not possible, you can always consider going with a text-only cover. Well-laid-out text can be wonderful, and the best-sellers' lists are full of books with text-only covers.

Finding the right image

First, you need to decide what message you want your cover to send. Avoid too many small scenes on a cover. Not only will they not be seen in a thumbnail, they'll confuse the reader and make things look cluttered. It's more important to set the mood for the book. You're not going to want a cheerful cartoon on a murder mystery, but neither are you going to want a picture of a severed arm, a getaway car, four or five characters, and a tropical island all on one cover. Study the bestseller lists carefully. If you are designing a cover for a murder mystery, with a primarily American target market, you might want to start by studying books written by John Grisham, David Baldacci, Michael Connelly, and James Patterson. They all sell well in America. In general, they have big text that's easy to see at thumbnail size. They limit the number of colors they use. The imagery is in the background, often a blurry figure or a significant landmark from the city the book is set in. You're not going to see identifiable people on many. Most of their books have several covers that are used for different formats, or have changed for a variety of reasons throughout the years. Sometimes you will see identifiable characters printed after a movie based on the book comes out. That's used to tie the book in with the movie promotions.

When you're ready to start your own online image search, you'll find thousands of pictures with a click of your mouse. In fact, you'll probably have a difficult time choosing which microstock site to visit first, but when you do, head straight to the licensing agreement—often called the End-User License Agreement, or EULA for short. You'll need to read image licenses carefully. Make sure you'll be able to use the image commercially for your book cover and for marketing campaigns.

Once you've done that, you will want to create an account. In fact, you'll probably want to create an account at every microstock site you like. It will make things much easier later on. You can sign up for free with most sites, and they'll make a "lightbox" available for you where you can save potential images, or you can download "comps" (low-resolution, watermarked versions of an image) and keep them in a folder with the agency information and image number. Once you've found a few pictures you think will work, send the links or comps to your designer, if you're using one, to make sure she can work with them. If you're doing the work yourself, then you'll need to check a few things. First, keep in mind that for a print book you need to be working at 300 dpi. (Dpi means dots per inch. Please note that I'm using dpi and ppi—which stands for pixels per inch—interchangeably for the purposes of this article.) So for a 6 x 9 print book, the image will need to be 1800 x 2700 pixels if it's going to cover the full cover, plus you'll need .125 inches for bleed (defined below). I got the pixel size by multiplying the book width of 6 inches by the dpi of 300 and then multiplying the book height of 9 inches by the dpi of 300.

If your book is only going to be available electronically, you'll still need the 300 dpi size because Amazon currently wants covers submitted at 1000 pixels on the longest side, but for best quality, they recommend 2500 pixels. You won't have to worry about bleed for an e-book cover, though.

What to check when you're choosing an image

1. **Artifacting.** This is a compression problem that will reduce reproduction quality. Blow the image up to 200 or 300 percent and see if fuzzy dots and/or jagged lines and/or a boxy, broken pattern start to appear all over

the image. If these are visible, the picture won't reproduce well.

2. **Pixilation.** These jagged edges can happen on any image, but particularly with illustrations. Scale the image to the size you plan to use and zoom in to make sure all the curved lines are smooth. If you're using line art, work with the vector (EPS) graphic if possible. Vector images can be increased to any size and still retain their quality. Many stock art sites offer you the option to download the vector or EPS format. You will need a program like Adobe Illustrator or the free Inkscape program to work with vector images, but you can open and look at them in Photoshop, InDesign, and many other software graphics programs. Just make sure your software program supports the file type before paying for a vector image.

3. **CMYK conversion.** Because RGB (Red, Green, Blue) images are what TVs, monitors, and other electronic devices display, and they are typically smaller in size than CMYK (Cyan, Magenta, Yellow, Black) images, stock agencies almost always only offer the RGB version of images. Printers, on the other hand, will in most cases be using CMYK to print the book cover. Some printers will accept an RGB file (many won't), but they'll "flip it on the fly" when they get it, meaning there's no color control, so your pretty pink might end up printing magenta, your rich black will be gray, and your oranges will look rusty. You can usually take the RGB image into a program like Photoshop or the free online editor Pixlr and make some adjustments to the color to make it look just as good in CMYK as it does in RGB.

4. **Bleed**. Make sure your image will work when it's laid out with bleed. Bleed is a small amount of paper (usually .125 inches) that is trimmed off the book during binding. That means you'll need to make sure your full spread cover file (with back, front, and spine) has an additional .125 inches at the top, bottom, left, and right. If you have a background image, it will have to extend out that far so it can be trimmed off.

5. **Test print**. You're always going to see some distortion on a computer screen, particularly with line art. If you're unsure about whether it's being caused by the monitor or if it's a real issue, have a test print done. Some print bureaus will do this for you, but you can take it to any place that has a commercial quality laser printer, like Staples or FedEx. It only costs a few dollars to have a full-sized color print made.

Originality

So you've found the perfect image. It looks wonderful on the test print, the license works, you can afford it . . . and then you see it on another book. What do you do? Well, if the book is not in your genre, I say use it anyway. Even the big publishing companies are sourcing images from the same places self-publishers are these days, so it's going to happen. Do you really think someone is going to say, "Gee, I'd buy that book if I hadn't seen the same image on another book last week"? Not likely. If the book is in your genre, or you might be accused of copying, then you should consider looking for a different image or find a unique way to incorporate the image on your cover so it doesn't look the same as the other book. Keep in mind that the models on romance covers are used in multiple images. There's a fairly limited number of images and models available compared to the number of romance books being produced (particularly in the supernatural genres). So even if it's a different image, chances are your sexy vampire will be a sexy pirate on another book at some point. What I would avoid doing is following the herd. I've seen dozens and dozens of self-published book covers with not only the same images but also the same fonts, the same layouts, and the same colors. Be original. Create your own brand. Look at what they're doing in your genre overseas in the UK, Australia, or even Canada for inspiration. Quite often books are released with different covers for specific markets (the original Harry Potter not only had different covers, but the title was different in the United States from elsewhere).

If you're creating your own cover, it should be a labor of love. If you're not enjoying every minute of it, hire a professional.

Cathi Stevenson
Book Cover Express (www.BookCoverExpress.com)

Cathi has been designing book covers for more than fifteen years and has worked on more than two thousand projects for traditional publishing houses and self-publishing authors. She worked in a printing bindery where she did everything from typesetting to burning plates to binding books. After getting a degree in behavioral psychology, she worked as a writer, editor, and page layout designer with a major newspaper for eight years before leaving to become a freelance writer. Soon after that, the Internet opened up a whole new world of clients, and she was able to start Book Cover Express.

Associated Press Images – New York, NY 212-621-1930 http://www.apimages.com "contemporary + historical images from the Associated Press including rights-managed/ microstock/royalty-free stock photography & music tracks"

BigStock Photos – New York, NY 855-272-5125 support@bigstockphoto.com, http://www.bigstockphoto.com "subscription-based or prepaid packages provide access to a vast collection of royalty-free stock photos & illustrations"

Bridgeman Images – New York, NY (also London, Paris, Berlin) 212-828-1238 edward.whitley@bridgemaimages.com, http://www.bridgemanimages.com/en-US "specializing in hi-res, rights-managed, fine art, cultural & historical images for reproduction"

CanStockPhoto – Halifax, NS Canada support@canstockphoto.com, http://www.canstockphoto.com "microstock agency offering royalty-free stock photography, graphics + clip art available by subscription, prepaid credit or 1-time purchase"

Corbis Images – New York, NY 800-260-0444 sales@corbis.com, http://www.corbisimages.com "set up account to purchase royalty-free/rights-managed stock photos + illustrations including editorial & fine art images"

DreamsTime – Brentwood, TN 615-771-5611/800-243-1791 M-F 9a-7p EST http://www.dreamstime.com "royalty-free stock photography + video footage available for purchase with free sign-up including some free images"

First Light – Toronto, ON Canada 416-597-8625 info@firstlight.com, http://www.firstlight.com "division of Design Pics with access to all Design Pics galleries of royalty-free + rights-managed stock photography & video" (other divisions: http://www.pacificstock. com & http://www.axiomphotographic.com)

FotoSearch – Waukesha, WI 800-827-3920/262-717-0740 fotosearch@fotosearch.com, http://www.fotosearch.com "search engine/aggregator for worldwide royalty-free, rights-managed stock photography, footage, illustration + clip art for licensing & purchase"

FreeDigitalPhotos – London, UK +44 (0) 203 086 8635 (post-sales service only) http://www.freedigitalphotos.net "royalty-free images available for free (small size/low-res) + published creator credit or paid (larger/high-res) with both standard & extended licensing options"

Getty Images – 800-462-4379 sales@gettyimages.com, http://www.gettyimages.com "multiple option subscriptions allow access to royalty-free/rights-managed editorial + archival stock photos, videos & music"

Image Zoo – Vancouver, BC Canada 877-274-6243/604-687-8477 info@imagezoo.com, http://www.imagezoo.com "royalty-free, rights-managed + custom illustrations from more than 400 artists offering a wide range of styles"

iStockPhoto – Calgary, AB Canada 866-478-6251 http://www.istockphoto.com "monthly/annual subscription or prepaid credits allow access to royalty-free photos, illustrations, vector images, video clips & audio tracks"

MasterFile – Toronto, ON Canada 800-387-9010/416-929-3000 M-F 8:30a-7p EST info@masterfile.com, http://www.masterfile.com "royalty-free, rights-managed images, vectors + illustrations available for licensing/purchase individually or by subscription"

RGB Stock – http://www.rgbstock.com "free stock images for blogs, websites + other non-commercial use including books if not primary content, extended use/licensing only with permission artist"

Shutterstock – New York, NY 866-663-3954/646-419-4452 support@shutterstock.com, http://www.shutterstock.com "multiple subscription options or prepaid credits for access to huge library of standard + enhanced license, royalty-free stock photos, vectors, illustrations, clip art, video footage & music"

Stock Exchange – Calgary, AB Canada http://www.sxc.hu "subsidiary of Getty Images offering free stock images through

member sharing; does not clear model releases & permission
must be obtained from image creator for any use not stated in
standard license agreement"

Stock Free Images – Brentwood, TN 800-243-1791 M-F 9a-7p EST
http://www.stockfreeimages.com "royalty-free stock images
(small/low-res) provided by DreamsTime contributors for free
download with link back to site + larger/high-res images &
extended licensing available for fee"

Book Shepherds & Publishing Consultants

Adding power to your book's success

As an author, unless you are a "pro" in publishing, you'll need to get some help. Who do you call? Is it a book coach, publishing consultant, or book shepherd?

Book coaches, book consultants, and book shepherds

There's a new breed of publishing consultants out there. Is there a difference between a book coach, a book consultant, and a book shepherd? Many think they are all the same, but they aren't.

With each, being a guide for the author is critical. Some plug ahead, leading the way; others offer you choices while giving you input about the pros and cons of each; and still others encourage you to find your own options and make your choice. Some are proactive; others reactive. What you don't want is someone who is nonactive.

Book coaches are quite good at encouraging you—after all, who couldn't use a cheerleader during a challenging process? One of the unwritten rules in most "coaching rule books" is that the coaching client (that's you) is not given specific directions on how to do something or solve a problem. You get to determine the final solution. Often coaches respond to your statements and questions with other questions.

You: I need a cover designer for my book . . .
What resources do you need to find one?

You: I hear it's important to begin a blog for my book . . .
Good idea. What would you call it? How do you think you would go about creating one?

What coaches are really good at is keeping their authors focused on developing strategies to accomplish whatever they need to do. They do it with discovery and dialogue, moving the author through the process by listening, helping her set goals, and holding her accountable for taking the steps necessary to achieve those goals.

If you say you need to connect with a cover designer within the next two weeks, the book coach will hold your feet to the fire at the two-week mark. The book coach's goal is to help you achieve your goal—whatever that is. Coaches don't set the agenda. You do.

Book consultants are not as interested in working with you on the nitty-gritty details of book authoring—guiding you in writing, publishing, or developing your book. Nor are they as into dealing with whatever hiccups you encounter along the way. What they do is tell you step by step how to get where you want to go.

You need a printer—*here are three to contact.*

You need a cover designer—*here are three that work well for your type of book.*

You need an interior designer—*there's only one I think will be a fit for your book; I will refer you to her.*

Book consultants often create a program for you—a process they have crafted telling you how to succeed.

If you are a self-starter and don't need any monitoring or ongoing appointments, you can save money using a book/publishing consultant. That is, as long as you are someone who can take on the to-do list yourself and don't require much hand-holding or brainstorming during the process.

Caution: It's not unusual for successful authors to call themselves book coaches or consultants as they share their experiences in publishing with a novice author. While they often have valuable information to share, frequently the novice is required to adopt the system the veteran has developed based on his personal experience. Publishing is rarely a one-size-fits-all enterprise, however, so make sure what they suggest is appropriate for the book you are writing.

Book shepherds should have a depth of experience within the publishing and writing fields (both as an author and working within the publishing business with authors). You need someone who has connections with vendors and associates who will bring your book concept and vision to life; can assist you in creating the actual book; has marketing moxie; and understands book selling, niche markets, and how book publishing works. Not only will they show you what book publishing and authoring is all about, but they will work with you throughout the creation and launch of your book as well.

Book shepherds work with authors to build a strong foundation—teaching them about publishing, creating a blueprint with timelines to meet goals, and then implementing a plan of action to meet those goals. They can keep you from making mistakes that could lead to thousands of dollars in losses, not to mention time down the drain. Book shepherds want to create a book that looks good, feels good, and that the author takes great pride in.

Book shepherding is an author-centric approach focusing on the author's agenda: discovering the story behind the story and revealing resources most authors don't realize they have. They do all that along with bringing a team together that designs and produces your book. Their essential goal is to ensure your voice and vision are honored. The result should be a book you are proud of.

What your book publishing advisors should be looking for

1. **Does the idea or manuscript have legs?** Does it make sense and is it media worthy? What makes it unique so that it can shine within its genre or category?

2. **Is there is a niche for the book?** The more you find a niche for yourself, the bigger your market becomes. It's much better to be the whale in the pond than the sardine in the ocean. When you develop a niche market, you become the go-to person—for media, for consulting, for speaking, for books.

3. **Have you done any research to support the concept?** Writers should be doing research ... even the best storytellers have to dig down, learning the craft as they weave their magic—background, arcing, and story lines all have components that are rarely pulled from the air. Surveys and studies often become the basis of best-selling nonfiction. Some research is incredibly in-depth; other background is more casual. Research brings in other voices that the author can question, compliment, or shred.

4. **If writing nonfiction, are you an expert?** This doesn't necessarily mean that you have academic degrees—it means you have invested a lot of time in the topic area and your knowledge of the subject is deeply engrained in experience.

5. **Are you prepared to invest time, energy, and money into developing and supporting your book?** To create a successful book, all three are needed. Your time—the project is not going to be completed overnight. Your energy—the creation, development and birthing of a book is equivalent to a full time job—do you have the commitment? And your money—while self-publishing has made publishing a book much more affordable than ever before, it's still not free.

6. **Do you understand what a return on investment (ROI) is?** Will you be stymied by the overall costs of a book—from preproduction through postproduction?

7. **Do you embrace publishing as a business?** Or is it an encounter of the casual kind?

8. **Do you have a platform or a following that will support the book—creating book sales and begin building a buzz?** Too many authors fail by simply believing that if they write it and print it, readers will come. Wrong. You have to reach out to your readers . . . you need to do the work to connect with others and start the buzz machine.

9. **Have you thought about, or written, a plan for how your book will be marketed?** This question should probably be number one—without having a plan for how you are going to create, launch, and roll out your book, it will be invisible.

10. **Does your family support the project?** Without support, authoring is a lonely road. There are times when you need to focus so much attention on the book that little else gets done. Family and colleagues need to be on your team.

11. **Do you have a vision of how the book should look and feel?** Do you have a vision of yourself succeeding with it? The creation of a book can be incredibly draining—it's easy to sometimes wonder why you are on this path.

12. **Will you listen to your colleagues and follow through on their suggestions?** There's a lot of work to this thing called authorship. The professionals you will be working with have earned their stripes and should welcome your input, but you should embrace theirs. There must be a high level of trust that they will bring the right team together, guide you through the book publishing maze, and help you stay sane during the process.

Caution: If for some reason you interrupt the process—put the book on hold, decide you want to do a massive rewrite, whatever—your coach, consultant, or book shepherd will need to go through a restart, sometimes going back to the beginning to get his or her head around you and your book once again. Expect additional costs.

The best book shepherds have walked the walk, not just talked the talk. They are a combination of a maestro with a magnificent orchestra and a creative director of an ad agency. They are good at fine tuning: fading soloists and groups in and out; adding the snap, crackle, and pop to your writing and book presentation; and at all times overseeing the entire process.

Nothing is free. Make sure you have a clear understanding of how any advisor gets paid, what their timeline is, and whether they have expertise in your specific genre or niche. Getting references is important. Not every coach, consultant, or shepherd is a fit for your book.

Do your homework. Ask for a brief discussion about your book. Is there chemistry between the two of you?

If the professional doesn't think your book rocks, it's the wrong fit. There needs to be some enthusiasm.

Don't get duped

There are many who call themselves book coaches, consultants, or shepherds who merely have some knowledge of publishing, or authoring, or marketing, or publicity, or blogging, or [fill in the blank]. Someone with a little knowledge and the right jargon can be downright dangerous.

No one will write your book for you, but they should keep you from making senseless mistakes; guide you through the meticulous publishing process; and watch over your journey. When it's over, you should feel that it has been one of the best investments you've ever made.

Your costs

Coaches, consultants, and book shepherds provide a variety of services and charge a wide range of fees. At one end of the spectrum are those who work like book packagers. They literally take over the development of the book—rewriting or ghosting; editing; and handling cover and interior design, printing, marketing, and in some cases, PR. Your investment will range from $10,000 to $50,000 or more—a lot of money.

At the other end of the range, you can work with someone who charges on an hourly basis on specific parts of your book project. Others charge on a per-project basis or ask for a monthly retainer. Depending on the time involved, your investment could be a few hundred to several thousand dollars.

Caution: Any publishing professional should absolutely tell you whether they are getting kickbacks from people they refer you to.

Be as clear as you can about what you need. Get the arrangement in writing. What is this person really going to do for you? What are the expectations on both sides? And be willing to accept that if either of you feels it's not working, it's not working. Sometimes the team just doesn't click; sometimes what was promised isn't materializing; sometimes you feel it's not the right fit for you. If this happens, end it. There's no reason to continue your agony or mistrust. Make sure there's an escape clause in your agreement that is based on the consultant/shepherd's performance, including time frames for the completion of your project. Your advisor should bring passion, persistence, perception, planning, and professionalism to the table.

How it works

You need to ask some questions: Will all the work be done by phone? Should you schedule time to work in his or her office? What about coming to your office? If you hire someone who lives far from you, it will most likely be a remote relationship: phone, texting, email, and Skype.

Don't try to do it all yourself. If you do, the end product—that book you wanted and believed in—will look like a do-it-yourself project.

Summing up

Book publishing consultants and coaches may just focus on publishing—creating a book and getting it out there— whether by a traditional publisher or by self-publishing. They will likely identify a variety of methods to use. Some book coaches overlap with writing coaches—guiding the author through the manuscript phase to the finished product. Both will usually recommend other publishing professionals to support your needs.

Book shepherds should combine the two roles—helping you create a quality manuscript that leads to a finished book that in turn leads to publication. And during the process, they will work with you to create an overall game plan covering pre-, during-, and postpublication.

When an author has a comprehensive plan, the cost of using any consultant is reduced. The savvy author views publishing as a business, not a whim. She's committed. It takes money—with the huge number of books being published every year, the adage "If you can't do it right, don't do it at all" holds up. Schlocky-looking books can't compete with spiffy covers and interiors that flow and have strong eye appeal.

If you are going to compete in the multibillion-dollar publishing business, the quality of your presentation shouts volumes. Covers, interiors, and editing augment the power of your words. Each speaks loudly.

Trying to publish on a shoestring usually shows, as does embracing RTP syndrome: Rush to Publish. Publishing is riddled with obstacles, and sometimes they are nightmares for the author. You don't need problems—you want solutions. This is a process that takes time and effort. Having the right advisor on your team can make all the difference for your peace of mind and the success of your book.

Judith Briles
The Book Shepherd (www.thebookshepherd.com)

Judith Briles is known as The Book Shepherd® and creates successful authors with practical publishing guidance. She's the author of thirty-five books, nineteen of them with major publishers and the remainder with her own imprint. Judith is the founder of Author U (author.org) and understands the authoring experience and the demands of being both author and publisher.

Author's Voice Publishing – McPherson, KS 620-245-0009
OR 410-259-0299 jan@authorsvoicepublishing.com,
http://authorsvoicepublishing.com/ "Jan Hurst offers
publishing assistance, editing, book design & promotion
services"

Beagle Bay, Inc. – Reno, NV 775-827-8654
http://www.beaglebay.com/ "JC Simmonds offers publishing
consulting, book packaging & production services"

Beren, Peter – San Francisco, CA 510-821-5539
info@peterberen.com, http://www.peterberen.com/ "A very
experienced publishing consultant & book shepherd who is also
a literary agent"

The Book Shepherd – Aurora, CO 303-885-2207 judith@briles.com,
http://thebookshepherd.com "Judith Briles, a very experienced
book shepherd who has published over twenty of her own
books"

Bookless, Kim – Chicago, IL 312-972-1613 kim@kimbookless.com,
http://kimbookless.com "guides & assists self-publishing
authors through the process of publishing"

BookTrix – New York, NY 203-903-5176 david@booktrix.com,
http://www.booktrix.com/live/index.php/about-booktrix
"founder David Wilk + team offer comprehensive consulting
services to help indie authors bring their book to fruition,
connect to its audience & promote sales; from coaching, to
author websites, to social media marketing/branding strategies"

Budd Publishing – Ottawa, Ontario Canada 613-824-9707
ev@buddpublishing.com, http://buddgraphics.com/consulting/
"Evelyn Budd connects authors to experienced & quality writers,
editors, printers, marketing gurus"

Concierge Marketing Inc – Omaha, NE 402-884-5995
lisa@conciergemarketing.com,
http://www.conciergemarketing.com/ "Lisa Pelto makes top
quality books for self-publishing authors"

EditFor.me – Dallas, TX 661-524-5573 blake@editfor.me, http://www.editfor.me "Blake Atwood provides copyediting, ghostwriting, & book consultation services."

McGinnis, Marti – San Miguel de Allende, Mexico (also USA) 956-242-6777 martimu@gmail.com, http://martimcginnis.com "author website design + maintenance, social media/marketing strategies, MS to PDF design/formatting & book trailers; specializing in illustrated/photo-heavy books"

PeopleSpeak – Laguna Hills, CA 949-581-6190 pplspeak@att.net, http://www.detailsplease.com/peoplespeak "Sharon Goldinger, book shepherd, offers content/copyediting, proofreading, manuscript evaluation, research + fact checking & publishing consulting"

Publish with Connie – Franklin, MA 508-446-1711 publishwithconnie@gmail.com, http://publishwithconnie.com "Connie Dunn offers book writing & publishing coaching for both non-fiction & fiction writers"

Side by Side with the Wonderlady – Novato, CA 415-515-9003 ruth@thewonderlady.com, http://thewonderlady.com "Ruth helps authors take their book from finished manuscript all the way through to having it up on Amazon & available to bookstores through IngramSpark"

Illustrators & Cartoonists

The quest for illustrators, cartoonists, and other creative professionals

---

Greetings, fellow indie publishing adventurer! Fancy meeting you here in the creative services market. So you would like to hire some creative people to join your expedition into the publishing wilderness? Well, you've come to the right place, as you can find many fine additions to your team right here. But maybe you don't know who to hire and for what. Well, not to worry, friend! I'll help set you on the right path to ensure you avoid that nasty quicksand of buyer's remorse.

First of all, dear adventurer, here are . . .

Five things you need before you embark on your quest for a creative professional:

1. **Make sure your book, novel, or manual is 100 percent finished before you seek creatives to help enhance it.** There's nothing worse than commissioning a fantastic piece of art, only to realize it no longer fits your project.

2. **Know what type of creative services you need.** There's no point in finding a fantastic cartoonist if what you really need is a cartographer.

3. **Collect examples of the styles or types of work you're looking for so you can compare potential creative professionals and help narrow your search.** Pinterest

boards are great for this, and you can even share the boards with your artist(s) after you select them.

4. **Know what type of format you need and what the requirements for the job will be.** Don't expect your creative professional to know the exact specs that would work best for your project. Do your research to avoid unnecessary pitfalls and headaches.

5. **Know your budget for the project.** It's a waste of your time and resources to consider a top creative professional if your budget would never allow you to actually hire that person.

Now that you have completed your manuscript, collected samples, and know what you need and can afford, here are . . .

Five places to seek out those elusive creative professionals:

1. **BookWorks** (www.BookWorks.com). The Self-Publishers Association also maintains an up-to-date, curated list of publishing and creative professionals, as well as a forum where you can post your work-in-progress and a robust blog for indie authors and their service providers.

2. **99designs** (99designs.com). This company boasts it is "the #1 marketplace for crowdsourced designs," and since their services are used by industry powerhouses like Joanna Penn and the guys of the Self-Publishing Podcast, I'm inclined to believe them.

3. **Bibliocrunch** (bibliocrunch.com). This site is a community-based marketplace where you can hire vetted, trusted book publishing professionals to add to your production team. They also host the #indiechat live Twitter chat every Tuesday evening and maintain a blog of helpful tips and advice.

4. **Google** (www.google.com). Google the service you are seeking. Seriously, this is what it was designed for, and if you struck out at the previously mentioned sources, your creative professional might be waiting for you out there in this directory of knowledge.

5. **Ask a fellow indie.** You're not the first author to require the services of a creative professional, and many of your peers probably already have a list of great people waiting to join your team.

Now that you know where to find these elusive creative professionals, how do you know whose services you will need? Well, my friend, here are . . .

Five creatives whose services you might need—and what they do

1. **The illustrator.** If cover art, promotional art, art for book trailers, or interior illustrations are what you seek, this is the creative professional to add to your publishing team.

2. **The cartoonist or comic artist.** If you are looking for small black-and-white illustrations, line art, chapter header art, or comic inserts, this is the right creative professional for you.

3. **The typographer or title designer.** If custom font graphics or beautiful and unique title treatments like those of Harry Potter, the Grisha books, and my own Bride of the Harvest Wolf series are what you seek, then this is the creative professional you're looking for.

4. **The cartographer or map maker.** If the main location of your story is particularly hard to describe, if you write historical fiction, or if your story spans a great distance, then a map is what you seek, and you should add this creative professional to your team.

5. **The graphic artist.** These creatives are the jack-of-all-trades in the field of art and design; if your project needs a wide range of artistic extras, this is probably the best route to go.

Now that you have familiarized yourself with what is available to you in the creative services marketplace, here are . . .

Three things to consider when selecting a creative professional:

1. **Pick a creative professional who does the type of work you are looking for.** Not all graphic artists have the same skill set, and asking a typographer to illustrate a photorealistic fantasy painting is like asking a baker to build a car engine.

2. **Pick someone who is available.** Unless you absolutely must have a particular creative professional on your team and no other will do, there really is little sense in waiting months (or years!) for an overbooked creative's schedule to free up. Life happens, and you may find you've waited all that time for nothing.

3. **Do your due diligence.** Google the creative professional you are considering before adding them to your team. You may uncover some ugly truths they've been trying to keep hidden, and lots of heartaches and headaches can be easily avoided with only a few minutes of research ahead of time.

I hope I have given you a few things to ponder and helped put your fears at ease. But let me offer these last few words of advice, dear adventurer, from one who has traveled these roads before.

Avoid the following at all costs:

1. Never ask a creative professional to imitate or re-create another person's style, *especially* if they do not normally use that style. It is unbelievably offensive and disrespectful and will most likely *not* result in the outcome you are hoping for—or, worse, could land you in legal troubles.

2. Avoid using such phrases as "Just do what you think looks good," "Use your best judgment," or "My spouse/mother/cat looked at it and suggested you change/add/remove . . ." This kind of chat has never ended well for anyone, and the only guaranteed result is that one or both of you will be unhappy in the end.

3. Never work without a written agreement or contract. We all like to give those we work with the benefit of the doubt; however, there is nothing worse than finding that your creative team has not only failed to deliver the goods, but they've also run off with your funds.

Don't let these words of caution deter you from embarking on your indie publishing adventure. Though the publishing journey is sometimes perilous, it is also a rewarding and exciting one. I wish you well on your expedition, and safe travels!

Kat Vancil
KatGirl Studio (www.katgirlstudio.com)

Kat Vancil writes imaginative coming-of-age sci-fi and fantasy fiction and instructional nonfiction from her home in the San Francisco Bay Area. When not crafting new adventures to inflict on her characters, she can usually be found running amuck in the imaginary worlds within her head or frolicking in general geekiness.

Agudelo, Fernando – Hollywood, FL 954-433-9074
http://www.coroflot.com/fernandoart "illustrator, designer
+ fine art painter specializing in nature, animals & fantasy for
publishing/editorial/advertising"

Association of Medical Illustrators (AMI) – Lexington, KY 866-
393-4264 hq@ami.org, http://www.ami.org "more than 800
professional illustrators worldwide specializing in medicine,
research, life sciences, education & communication"

Auerbach, Adam – Queens, NY 347-721-2107
adam@adamauerbach.com, http://www.adamauerbach.com
"illustrator + graphic artist for children's books & editorial"

Batra, Nancy – nancydesigner05@gmail.com,
http://nancybatra.weebly.com/ "illustrator for children's
literature, graphic novels, and concept art. Proficient in
sketching + coloring in Photoshop & Illustrator, story-boarding,
2D animation.Variety of styles including realistic, cartoon,
caricature & stylized categories"

Bersea, Dianne – BC, Canada dianne.islandartist@gmail.com,
http://www.islemuse.com "fine artist + illustrator for book
covers/interiors, whose work is a colorful, often whimsical
interpretation of the natural world"

Cabib, Leila – Potomac, MD 301-299-2659 leila@leilacabib.com,
http://www.leilacabib.com "cartoons, humorous illustration +
animation, specializing in children's publishing & editorial"

Carol Bancroft & Friends – Danbury, CT 203-730-8270
cb_friends8270@sbcglobal.net, http://www.carolbancroft.com
"represents more than 27 international illustrators, most of
whom specialize in the children's market"

Cartoon Images for Licensing – Chassell, MI
dan@danscartoons.com, http://danscartoons.com "custom
cartoons/humorous illustrations + stock images available for
licensing for publishing or advertising"

Cornell & McCarthy – Westport, CT 203-454-4210
contact@cmartreps.com, http://www.cmartreps.com
"represents 30 artists specializing in children's book illustration
across a wide range of styles"

Creative Freelancers, Inc. – Tallevast, FL 800-398-9544
cfinc@freelancers1.com, http://www.freelancers1.com
"online resource for freelance website designers + illustrators,
photographers, graphic designers, etc."

Daly Art – Camden, ME 207-236-8834 dan@dalyart.com,
http://www.dalyart.com "artist, painter + illustrator specializing
in outdoors/nature/scenic landscapes for publishing & editorial"

David Kelley Design – Falmouth, MA 508-457-1183
dfkelley@pair.com, http://www.davidkelleydesign.com "Dan
Daly, artist, illustrator, designer with background in publishing
provides images including photography + infographics for
books, websites & advertising"

De Muth Design – Cazenovia, NY 315-655-8599 rdemuth@syr.edu,
http://www.demuthdesign.com "Roger De Muth, artist,
illustrator + designer, offers original work or available images for
licensing, with a style appropriate for adults & kids"

DogFoose – Wichita, KS 316-264-4112 mikey@dogfoose.com,
http://dogfoose.com "artist Michael Kline specializes in
infotoons & infographics for kids' publications"

Franson, Leanne – Martensville, SK Canada 306-382-1696
inkspots@videotron.ca, http://www.leannefranson.com "artist
& illustrator with a specialty in children's books; will work with
experienced, informed self-publishing authors"

International Mapping Associates – Ellicott City, MD 800-761-6944/
443-367-0050 info@internationalmapping.com,
http://internationalmapping.com "professional cartographers
offering custom map design services including 3-D, interactive
& animation for the publishing industry"

Itzhack Shelomi Design – Scarsdale, NY 212-689-7469
studio@ishelomi.com, http://www.ishelomi.com "illustrator/
designer for trade books + textbooks (especially medical), also
offers cover design, interior design/formatting, art direction,
production & editorial services"

Janice Phelps, LLC – Harbor Springs, MI 614-309-0048
queries@janicephelps.com, http://www.janicephelps.com "Janice
Phelps Williams, illustrator, artist + designer for book covers/
interiors including page/eBook formatting & editorial services"

Melissa Turk & the Artist Network – Suffern, NY 845-368-8606
melissa@melissaturk.com, http://www.melissaturk.com
"represents 22 artists & illustrators offering a broad range of styles"

Minor, Wendell – Washington, CT 860-868-9101
wendell@minorart.com, http://www.minorart.com "artist and
illustrator specializing in children's books"

Parrot Graphics – Stillwater, MN 651-430-8127
info@parrotgraphics.com, http://www.parrotgraphics.com
"specializes in technical & educational illustration including
maps, charts, graphs, diagrams, etc."

Robert Pizzo Illustration/Design – Redding, CT 203-938-0663
rp@robertpizzo.com, http://www.robertpizzo.com "illustrator/
designer specializing in graphic illustrations + infographics for
book covers/interiors & promotional materials"

Purington, Nancy – Iowa City, IA 319-337-7865
nancy@nancypurington.com, http://nancylpurington.com
"fine artist + illustrator"

Pushpin Inc. – New York, NY 212-529-7590
seymour@pushpininc.com, http://www.pushpininc.com
"Seymour Chwast, award-winning illustrator & graphic designer"

Smith, Lori Joy – Charlottetown, PE Canada lori@lorijoysmith.com,
http://lorijoysmith.com "artist + illustrator with a style well-
suited to the children's book market"

Tusan, Stan – Phoenix, OR 541-535-6791 stantoon@charter.net,
http://www.stantoon.com "humorous illustration, cartoons +
graphic designs, both custom & licensing"

Wendy Edelson Studios – Johnson, VT 212-475-0440 (agent)
wendy@wendyedelson.com, http://www.wendyedelson.com
"artist & illustrator of children's books including image licensing"

Wilkinson Studios Inc. – St. Charles, IL 630-549-0504
chris@wilkinsonstudios.com, http://www.wilkinsonstudios.com
"international agents representing more than 50 artists &
illustrators offering a wide range of styles"

Translators

Translators and translations for indie authors

We live in a global economy. Everybody knows that. The big question for indie authors is whether it makes sense to have your books translated into languages other than English so they will be attractive to many more people in this worldwide marketplace—people who primarily speak Spanish, French, German, Polish, Russian, Arabic, or Japanese, for example.

Here's how translation rights usually work. If your book were being represented by a literary agent and published by a traditional publisher, either the agent or the publisher would control those rights, and you wouldn't have to do anything about getting your book translated into other languages. The agent or publisher would submit your book to the appropriate foreign publishers, and, with luck, several publishers would buy the rights to translate and publish your book in the language spoken in their country. So your book could be translated into Spanish, French, German, Mandarin, and a dozen or so other languages, and the publisher in each country where it is being distributed would pay for the translation. You would then receive a royalty from, say, the Spanish publisher on all the Spanish-language books distributed and sold by that publisher.

Self-publishers can use the same procedure to sell foreign rights to their own books. Of course, it's helpful if you know specific publishers who might be interested in your book so you can approach them directly. If you sign a contract with one of these publishers, the process will work exactly the same as it does for traditional publishers. And if your books have strong overseas appeal, you may want to find and engage a foreign rights agent to handle this for you.

If your book is being published by a subsidy publisher, they will make the same kinds of arrangements with foreign publishers. In some cases they may offer to have the book translated for you, usually for an additional fee. Again, you will receive a royalty on each translated book sold.

Self-publishers can consider another path that may be a smart marketing move: make your own arrangements to hire a freelance translator to translate your book for you. You can then make the arrangements to have your translated book distributed through a company such as Ingram, which has a substantial overseas business, distributing to more than 130 countries. This is more work and can be expensive, but you have more control and get to keep a larger percentage of the revenue from each book sold.

Check the following list or try a Google search if you are looking for freelance translators in languages that are somewhat obscure.

When you select a translator, be sure to pin down the following:

- What will the translation cost?
- What are the terms of the payment?
- How long will it take?
- How will the agreement be canceled if either party wants out?
- What other books have they translated?
- Are they a native speaker of the language?

- Who can you check with for references?
- Who will own the copyright to the translated work?
- Will they help you market your book?

Translations are not cheap, but they can open up a whole new market for your book as well as increase your global visibility.

Betty Kelly Sargent
BookWorks (www.BookWorks.com)

American Literary Translators Association – Richardson, TX
972-883-2092 maria.suarez@utdallas.edu OR
altacentral2014@gmail.com, http://www.utdallas.edu/alta
"association for translators specializing in literary works,
including a directory of member profiles listing their language
proficiencies"

American Translators Association – Alexandria, VA 703-683-6100
M-F 9a-5p EST ata@atanet.org, https://www.atanet.org
"association of professional translators + interpreters, including
search tools & directories to help you find the right person for
your needs"

Book Translation Service – www.booktranslationservice.com
"online job board to find translators for books or documents,
offering free price quotes"

CBTS (Comprehensive Book Translation Services) – Melbourne, AU
+61 4 0812 4498 matt@bookwebtranslation.com AND
matt.sundakov@gmail.com, www.bookwebtranslation.com
"large team of qualified, experienced translators for books,
documents & websites in the language of your choice"

Com Translations – New York, NY (+ other locations worldwide)
888-636-3341 info@comtranslations.com,
www.comtranslations.com "international agency of more
than 4,000 certified translators to help authors reach global
readership; offering instant quotes, 1st page translation + full-
book plan"

Torres, José Ramón – Cambridge, UK +44
7952597097 info@eslanguagexpertise.com,
http://www.babelcube.com/user/dr-jose-ramon-torres-aguila
"English-Spanish translation, Spanish editing/proofreading;
Latin American, Iberian & neutral Spanish variants"

Traduguide – Germany info1@traduguide.com,
www.traduguide.com "international online job board; post
your request to receive quotes from competent freelance
translators"

Verbal Ink – Los Angeles, CA 877-983-7225
info@verbalink.com, http://verbalink.com "Verbal Ink has
hundreds of transcriptionists & translators on its staff & is one
of most trusted leaders in transcription & translation services in
the world"

Verbumsoft, LLC – Burbank, CA 818-748-6235
www.translatorsbase.com "online marketplace of freelance
translators; post your book/project to obtain free quotes"

For those interested in selling foreign rights to their book abroad,
check out PubMatch.com

PubMatch – New York, NY 212-377-5500 rights@pubmatch.com,
http://pubmatch.com "Industry-facing marketing outlet to
show your book to publishers and agents around the world to
help you sell your foreign rights and expand your book's reach,
with loads of built in marketing tools"

Writing Software

Writing really requires only a few tools. Most of the books we treasure were written longhand, and penmanship for many centuries was a key skill for authors.

The Industrial Revolution transformed the act of writing with the typewriter, a mechanical device that freed writers from the time-consuming drudgery of copying over their own manuscripts.

When digitization rewarded us with word processors, it seemed writers had reached a kind of word-wrangling apotheosis, as our stodgy piles of paper morphed into dazzling, mutable, endlessly editable computer files.

Sure, these new files were disturbingly easy to lose, but when it came to redrafting, editing, and correcting a manuscript, writers had been freed from almost all the drudgery.

Since then, software tools for writers have evolved and proliferated. The basic text editor is so ubiquitous now that many programs come with the text editing function built in.

And the capacity of today's word processors is truly astonishing. Not content with merely processing words, sentences, and paragraphs, you can now use your word processor to format an illustrated trade book, create collateral material like fliers, embed spreadsheet cells, and run automated processes with the help of user-defined scripts, just to scratch the surface.

Writers and Word Processors

Writing is a very personal, mostly solitary activity. We move our ideas, stories, or narratives slowly from mind to screen. This is such an intimate and idiosyncratic process that the tools we use during this transfer must align with our individual ways of working.

Luckily, we now have a plethora of software, with programs that are geared to different writing styles and stages of the writing process. There are so many it's almost an embarrassment of riches.

Since I write every day as part of my job, I've discovered my own favorite programs for each step of my creative process. For instance, I often work on first drafts in a low-distraction environment. I use iA Writer for this, but there are many other programs that work roughly the same—removing the menus, buttons, scroll bars, and all the other detritus that litters our screens, distracting us from the hard work of writing.

Once I've finished my draft, if I need to do further research for the project, I might move the draft straight to the Word-Press editing screen, if what I'm writing is destined for my blog.

If it's part of a book I'm working on, I'm likely to instead move it to Scrivener, a program that helps writers organize and output their work in a unique and very productive way.

Scrivener has revolutionized the writing process for thousands of writers by putting powerful, easy-to-use organizational tools in our hands. In this program you can accumulate the articles you're using for research, the images you've captured, the media files you'll be referring to, and just about anything else you might need. Everything is easy to move around and sequence with the tools built into the program. And when you're finished, you can export e-book files right from Scrivener.

But probably the word processor I use most—unsurprisingly—is Microsoft Word. Both loved and reviled by millions of writers, Word has grown from its humble roots into a massive, multifunctional workhorse. It's the default word processor for corporate America and has come installed on many of the computers we buy.

Many of us grew up with Word, using it to write papers in school, memos at work, recipes to swap with friends, or whatever we needed, usually in Times New Roman.

To this day, most of the manuscripts I receive from authors and editors arrive in Word. That's a good thing, because it allows the many people working on a book to share files without worrying about whether *my* file will open on *your* computer.

Word's DOC and DOCX file formats are compatible with almost all word processors, so your files never have to be orphaned due to software incompatibility. Word is fast, will allow you to manipulate graphics to some extent, and can help you add an index, footnotes, endnotes, and a bibliography to your book. It's really very capable.

However, many people have come to view Word as cumbersome, bloated, and inefficient, complaining about not being able to *find* all those great features under the layers and layers of dialog boxes. They hate the way critical functions change names, locations, and functions from one version of the program to another.

Those people aren't wrong, but Word's advantages still tend to outweigh its disadvantages.

What Word Processor Will You Use?

With so much great software to choose from, and with many programs free or available at very reasonable prices, how do you decide?

Since I work with words for my livelihood, I've got a lot invested in this question. Using an inefficient tool can cost time and, therefore, money. Using software that doesn't function properly can make your workday miserable. So what should you do?

First, you'll need to break the habit of always clicking the same icon every time you sit down at your computer to write. You don't use the same knife for every task in your kitchen, do you?

I think of writing as separate tasks, each of which might need a different tool, rather than trying to figure out how to do every single thing with the same program.

Consider these task-based scenarios:

- **Outlining or identifying the basic building blocks of the piece and their relationships?** I'll probably reach for mind-mapping software like Mindjet MasterMind, rather than a word processor, but that's just me.

- **Ready to start on the first draft?** I like to work at this stage with the absolute minimum of distraction, because the raw ideation process takes so much sustained, attentive focus. A program like iA Writer works well.

- **Putting together all the pieces of a longer work as you complete them and adding your research?** The only program I know that excels at these tasks is Scrivener.

- **Generating a draft for proofreading and then correction?** I'm going to use Word for its Markup and Track Changes functions, which save an incredible amount of time.

- **Putting together an eye-pleasing media kit?** I might use Apple's Pages, a capable word processor that doubles as an easy-to-use layout program for graphically oriented documents.

- **No money to spend?** Try OmmWriter, a browser-based program that comes complete with mood music and lovely backgrounds and creates a low-distraction environment a writer can really sink into.

This really is a golden age for writers of all kinds, with more ways to quickly get our work in front of an audience than ever before.

Part of what makes this golden age possible is the astonishing variety of software available to authors. I encourage you to experiment with the many programs in these listings and find the ones that are just right for you. It will make your writing life more productive and more enjoyable at the same time.

Joel Friedlander
The Book Designer (www.thebookdesigner.com)

Atlantis Word Processor (Windows) – support@atlantiswordprocessor.com, http://www.atlantiswordprocessor.com/en "word processing"

AutoCrit (online) – https://www.autocrit.com "manuscript editing for linguistic errors, overused words, repeated words/phrases, clichés, writing faults"

Buzzword (Mac & Windows) – http://www.adobe.com/uk/acom/buzzword "word processing based on Flash, collaborating, accessing documents online"

Byword (Mac, iPhone & iPad) – byword@metaclassy.com, http://bywordapp.com "distraction-free writing, editing, auto-saving, exporting, publishing"

Character Name Generator (Windows) – http://www.characternames.org "free name generator"

Character Writer (Mac & Windows) – support@typingchimp.com, http://www.characterpro.com/characterwriter/index.html "tools for character development, story generating, editing, organizing"

Clean Writer Pro (Mac) – http://cognitivebits.com/clean-writer-pro.html "distraction-free writing program, text editing"

ConnectedText (Windows) – http://www.connectedtext.com "wiki system, researching, project managing"

CopyWrite (Mac) – http://www.bartastechnologies.com/products/copywrite "writing, full screen editing, text editing, note taking, versioning, auto backup, exporting"

DEVONThink (Mac) – http://www.devontechnologies.com/products/devonthink "database for researching, organizing, basic text editing"

Dramatica Pro (Mac & Windows) – http://dramatica.com "writing tool to help with character development, plot, story structure, dramatic themes"

EditMinion (online) – http://editminion.com "copy editing, grammar checker, language faults"

FocusWriter (Mac & Windows) – http://gottcode.org/focuswriter "distraction-free, full-screen word processing, auto-saving, timers"

Gingko (cloud) – https://gingkoapp.com/p/about-us, https://gingkoapp.com "word processing, organizing, structuring, collaborating"

Grammarly (online) – www.grammarly.com "grammar checking, automated proofreading"

iA Writer (Mac & iPad) – http://www.iawriter.com/mac "distraction-free writing environment"

Jer's Novel Writer (Mac) – http://jerssoftwarehut.com/jers-novel-writer/download-jers-novel-writer "annotating, outlining, editing, note-taking, storing"

Judoom (Windows) – info@badwolfsoftware.com, http://www.judoom.com "tabbed word processing, document managing"

Learn Scrivener Fast – joseph.michael@scrivenercoach.com, http://learnscrivenerfast.com "training course for Scrivener created by Joseph Michael"

Liquid Story Binder XE (Windows) – contact@blackobelisksoftware.com, http://www.blackobelisksoftware.com "word processor, editing, tracking, gallery for organizing pictures, journaling feature, store and review research, labeling"

MacJournal (Mac) – http://marinersoftware.com/products/macjournal "journaling & blogging tool"

NewNovelist (Windows) – http://www.newnovelist.com "templates, analysis and advice for novel writing, organizes writing into twelve parts"

A Novel Idea (iPhone & iPad app) – https://itunes.apple.com/us/app/a-novel-idea/id421948244?mt=8 "organizing, plotting, jotting down ideas"

OmniOutliner (Mac & iPad) – info@omnigroup.com, http://www.omnigroup.com/omnioutliner "storing, collecting, outlining"

OpenOffice (Mac & Windows) – https://www.openoffice.org/product/index.html "word processing, free alternative to Microsoft Word"

Org mode (Mac & Windows) – http://orgmode.org "note taking, writing, editing"

Outline 4D (Windows) – http://www.learnoutline4d.com "outlining, storyboarding"

PageFour (Windows) – http://www.softwareforwriting.com "distraction-free writing, editing, organizing, word processing, outlining capabilities, versioning"

ProWritingAid (online) – http://prowritingaid.com "proofing tool, grammar checking, repeated words/phrases, clichés"

Q10 (Windows) – http://www.baara.com/q10 "editing"

Quip (Mac, iPhone, iPad, Android, Windows) – https://quip.com/about, https://quip.com "word processor across platforms, note taking, organizing, collaborating"

Scrivener (Mac & Windows) – https://www.literatureandlatte.com/scrivener.php "word processing, project management, index card storyboarding, outlining, full-screen editing, organizational tool for first drafts"

SmartEdit (Windows) – http://www.smart-edit.com "editing tool to use with a writing program, includes 20+ checks for grammar and repeated phrases/words"

Storybase 2 (Windows) – http://www.storypros.com/Storybase.html "story & character development, narrative prompts, brainstorming"

Storyist (Mac, iPad & iPhone) – support@storyist.com,
http://storyist.com/index.html "writing, index cards, plot,
character and setting sheets, text editing, organizational tool"

StoryMill (Mac) – http://marinersoftware.com/products/storymill
"full screen, distraction free, annotating, organizing by scene,
chapter and character, progress meter"

StyleWriter (Windows) – http://www.stylewriter-usa.com "style
and usage checker, identifies writing faults, clichés, flags poor
grammar"

SuperNotecard (Mac & Windows) – info@mindola.com,
http://www.mindola.com/supernotecard "electronic note cards
for organizing writing ideas"

TextRoom (Mac & Windows) – http://textroom.sourceforge.net
"full-screen text editor, distraction-free"

Ulysses (Mac) – http://www.ulyssesapp.com "full-screen view for
text editing, brainstorming, drafting, revising"

WhiteSmoke (online) – http://www.whitesmoke.com "manuscript
editing for writing faults, clichés, jargon, grammar, thesaurus"

WhizFolders (Windows) – http://www.whizfolders.com
"organizing, outlining for notes, editing"

WriteItNow (Mac & Windows) –
http://www.ravensheadservices.com "hierarchical organizing,
researching tools, storyboarding, thesaurus, name generating"

WriteMonkey (Windows) – http://writemonkey.com/index.php
"writing space, text development, editing"

WriteRight (Mac) – http://www.writerightapp.com "text editing,
grammatical suggestions, thesaurus"

WriteRoom (Mac & iPhone) –
http://www.hogbaysoftware.com/products/writeroom "full
screen, distraction-free writing program, write time tracking"

Writer's Blocks (Windows) – support@writersblocks.com,
http://www.writersblocks.com "visual index card system"

Writer's Café (Mac & Windows) – writerscafe@anthemion.co.uk, http://www.writerscafe.co.uk "writing, structuring, note taking, journaling, scrapbooking"

WriteWay Pro (Windows) – http://www.writewaypro.com "organizing into acts, chapters and scenes, text editing"

yWriter (Mac & Windows) – http://www.spacejock.com/yWriter5.html "word processing, organizing into chapters and scenes"

Writers' Conferences & Workshops Offering Scholarships

Three reasons writers need conferences more than ever

Now is the best time ever to be an author and publisher. Self-publishing has become the salvation of the book industry. Indie authors now publish more books each year than traditional houses. The spirit of independence is huge. The changes brought about by new technology are one of the most positive effects of the whirlwind transformation of the book publishing business. Self-publishing allows for the democratization of writing. It's also next to impossible.

Publishing is a complex enterprise that incorporates commerce as well as art. Self-publishing requires a team of collaborators who provide the skills and services you lack. The priest and writer Ronald Knox once called a baby "a loud noise at one end with no sense of responsibility at the other." But your book is your baby. You give birth to it twice: once when you write it and once when you bring it into the world on publication. And even if you decide you'd rather write than share custody of your baby with a publisher, your book still needs all the nurturing you can give it.

O say can you C?

Writers' conferences give authors an excellent opportunity to gain perspective on their work and learn about the publishing process. "A Celebration of Craft, Commerce and Community" is the guiding principle of the San Francisco Writers Conference.

Craft, commerce, and community are the holy trinity of what it takes to succeed, and they are needed more than ever. A conference can give you:

- Clarity about your literary and publishing goals and how to achieve them
- The perspective you need on writing, publishing, and building your career
- The understanding that, at their best, writing, publishing, agenting, promotion, bookselling, and reviewing are labors of love

Here's an overview of the three Cs.

Craft

Technology is turning the publishing pyramid upside down. More than ever, content is king. Readers are replacing the Big Five, the big media, and the big chains as reviewers and gatekeepers. Word of mouth can make any book a best seller, regardless of who publishes it or how. Now we have word of mouse to help self-published e-books hit the *New York Times* best-seller list.

But this takes craft. Sales of genre and commercial fiction may be based more on the authors' storytelling ability than on their craft. But it's more vital than ever that, no matter what you write, your books be as well-conceived and well-crafted as you can make them. Every word you write is an audition for the next. Every line must compel your readers to read on. If your work doesn't inform, entertain, enlighten, inspire, or otherwise delight readers, they'll stop reading—fast.

A conference gives you the opportunity to learn about the craft of writing and get feedback from literary agents, editors, and writing teachers, as well as other writers.

Commerce

Before the advent of technology, writers had one job: writing books. Technology has added a second challenge and opportunity in one: communication, or reaching the people you need to succeed.

You have to think of yourself both as a writer with something to say and an author with something to sell. When more than a million books are published each year, you need state-of-the-art information on how publishing works and how to cut through the noise of other books and authors. The web is a bottomless, continuously enriched ocean of information, but learning and interacting in person with writers and publishing professionals can have more lasting impact than words on a screen.

Community

One paradox of technology is that the more technology connects us to the world, the more it isolates us. Writing is a solitary act, but that's the only part of the process you have to do alone. You need to build communities of people who want to help you because they know, like, and trust you.

Only a community of knowledgeable readers, and perhaps a freelance editor, can help you ensure your work is as good as you want it to be. You'll be too close to it to know. A conference is the best way to establish relationships with aspiring writers, published authors, literary agents, freelance editors, and other publishing professionals who can give you the objective feedback you need.

Craft or commerce: What kind of conference do you need?

Conferences embody the vision of the people who start them. I and my wife, Elizabeth Pomada, had been literary agents for years. We wanted to create a conference that would be informative, enjoyable, and inspiring while helping attendees achieve their goals. Our hope with the San Francisco Writers Conference is also to encourage a spirit of fun and community for the three hundred writers from thirty states and abroad who attend every year. But conferences vary a great deal in their size, their goals, their programs, and how they are run, so be sure to check out the ones you are interested in carefully.

Ten commandments to help guarantee your success

1. **Love what you do.** Make your work and how you communicate about it a labor of love for your craft and your readers.

2. **Know your goals.** Have clearly defined literary and publishing goals that keep you inspired.

3. **Create content your readers love.** The holy trinity of salable prose:

    a. Read to set your goals and find models for your books and career.

    b. Write enough drafts to make your work 100 percent.

    c. Share your work with a community of knowledgeable readers.

4. **Serve your communities.** Build and maintain networks of people eager to help you because they know, like, and trust you.

5. **Build your platform.** Develop continuing visibility with potential book buyers.

6. **Test-market your book.** Prove it works in as many ways as you can.

7. **Eliminate failure as an option.** Commit yourself to your goals by devoting your life to your craft and your career.

8. **Share your passion for your work.** Communicate with your communities.

9. **Be a contentpreneur.** Run a creative, innovative business that creates, sells, and repurposes your content to build your brand and generate diverse income streams.

10. **Make people and the planet as important as profit.** This will help you create a literary ecosystem that will build synergy as long as you sustain it with content and service.

If this vision of being a writer and publisher feels right to you, look for a conference that provides this kind of guidance. You have a spectrum of conferences to choose from. Many focus on craft, others on commerce, and still more try to balance the two. Elizabeth and I wanted a conference that balances the art and commerce so attendees can make their books both as good and as successful as they want them to be.

Choosing the right conference for you

Here are ten suggestions for finding the right conference for you:

- Be clear about what you need from a conference.
- Determine your budget for the conference and the other expenses involved.

- Decide where you'd like to go to a conference.

- Ask your community of writers and members of writers' organizations you belong to about conferences they've been to.

- Check ShawGuides to Writers Conferences (<u>writing.</u> <u>shawguides.com</u>), a list of conferences around the country (and a few in other countries as well).

- Research the speakers and programs of conferences on their websites.

- See how much of the conference is devoted to independent publishing.

- Decide what size of conference you will be comfortable at.

- Look at their newsletter and testimonials from attendees.

- Read the cancellation policy.

If you choose the right conference, and your heart and mind are open to the people you meet and what you learn, a conference can transform your writing, your career, and your life.

Michael Larsen

San Francisco Writers Conference (<u>www.sfwriters.org</u>)

Michael and his wife, Elizabeth, cofounded Larsen-Pomada Literary Agents in 1972. The agency seeks nonfiction writers with talent, a platform, and a promotion plan for books with social, esthetic, or practical value. He is the author of *How to Write a Book Proposal* and *How to Get a Literary Agent* and co-authored *Guerrilla Marketing for Writers*. Michael is the codirector of the San Francisco Writers Conference.

22nd Annual Winter Poetry & Prose Getaway – January 16-19, 2015 - Galloway, NJ 888-887-2105/609-823-5076 info@wintergetaway.com, http://www.wintergetaway.com "challenging and supportive workshops, insightful feedback, and an encouraging community for fiction, nonfiction, memoir, screenwriting & poetry; scholarships available"

Algonkian Writers Conferences – year-round, various locations – 800-250-8290/703-403-4280 algonkian@algonkianwriterconferences.com, http://algonkianconferences.com "writer conferences and novel workshops teach writing craft and provide opportunities for professional connections to writers at all stages on the writing path: scholarship available"

American Literary Translators Association (ALTA) Annual Conference – (2015 dates to be announced) - Milwaukee, WI 972-883-2093 maria.suarez@utdallas.edu, http://www.alta2014.org "genres in poetry, fiction, creative nonfiction and playwriting; scholarships available"

Ann Arbor Book Festival Writer's Conference – June 20, 2015 - Ann Arbor, MI 734-764-3166 info@aabookfestival.org, http://aabookfestival.org "festival sessions include writing in a variety of genres, the writer-editor & writer-agent relationships, crafting pitch letters and more; half-price student rate is available with some scholarships also available"

Antioch Writers' Workshop – July 11-17, 2015 - Yellow Springs, OH 937-769-1803 info@antiochwritersworkshop.com, http://www.antiochwritersworkshop.com "teaches writing craft & provides opportunities for professional connections to writers at all stages on the writing path; scholarships available"

Association of Writers and Writing Programs, Conference & Bookfair – April 8-11, 2015 – Fairfax, VA 703-993-4301 events@awpwriter.org, https://www.awpwriter.org, https://www.awpwriter.org/contests/wcc_scholarships_overview "celebrates the authors, teachers, students, writing programs, literary centers and publishers of that region; offers two annual cash scholarships to emerging writers who wish to attend a writers' conference, center, retreat, festival or residency"

AuhtorU Extravaganza – September 15-17, 2017 – Denver, CO 303-885-2207 info@authorU.org, http://authoru.org/ "a nonprofit membership association for authors who want to be seriously successful. AuthorU provides free webinars, coaching, podcasts, meetings, and more. Membership is $99 per year and includes discounts for AuthorU members"

Bear River Writers' Conference – May 28-June 1, 2015 - Boyne City, MI 734-936-2271 beariver@umich.edu, http://www.lsa.umich.edu/bearriver "workshops in poetry, fiction, and creative nonfiction, as well as readings, discussions, nature walks, and time for writing; scholarships available"

Bread Loaf Orion Environmental Writers' Conference – June 1-7, 2015 - Middlebury College, VT blorion@middlebury.edu, www.middlebury.edu/blwc/blorion "week-long writers' conference designed to hone the skills of people interested in producing literary writing about the environment and the natural world; scholarships available"

Bread Loaf Writers' Conference – August 13-22, 2015 - Middlebury College, VT 802-443-5286 blwc@middlebury.edu, http://www.middlebury.edu/blwc "workshops in fiction, poetry & nonfiction are at the core of the ten-day conference; scholarships available"

Community of Writers at Squaw Valley: Poetry Workshop – June 20-27, 2015 - Squaw Valley, CA 530-470-8440 info@squawvalleywriters.org, http://www.squawvalleywriters.org/poetry_ws.htm "when poets gather in a community to write new poems, each may break through old habits and write something stronger and truer than before; financial aid available"

Community of Writers at Squaw Valley: Writers Workshops in fiction, narrative nonfiction, memoir & screen writing – July 6-13, 2015 - Squaw Valley,

CA 530-470-8440 info@squawvalleywriters.org, http://www.squawvalleywriters.org "these workshops assist serious writers by exploring the art and craft as well as the business of writing; financial aid available"

Conference of the Great Mother and New Father – year-round - Nobleboro, ME 401-497-0310 traceydillon@mac.com, http://greatmotherconference.org "the conferences consider a wide variety of poetic, mythological & fairy tale traditions; some scholarships available for new attendees"

Eckerd College Writers' Conference: Writers in Paradise – January 17-25, 2015 - St. Petersburg, FL 727-864-7994 wip@eckerd.edu, http://writersinparadise.eckerd.edu "intimate workshop classes, roundtables, panel discussions, readings, book signings & receptions; scholarships available"

The Frost Place Conference on Poetry – (2015 dates to be announced) - Franconia, NH 603-823-5510 frost@frostplace.org, http://www.frostplace.org "a week at intensive poetry camp with writers who are deeply committed to learning more about the craft of writing poetry; scholarships available"

The Frost Place Conference on Poetry & Teaching – (2015 dates to be announced) - Franconia, NH 603-823-5510 frost@frostplace.org, http://www.frostplace.org "hard-working classroom teachers and highly skilled poet/teachers share their experiences of how poetry is most effectively presented in the classroom; scholarships available"

Gettysburg Review Conference for Writers – June 3-8, 2015 - Gettysburg, PA 301-331-1351 getrev@hbp.com, http://www.gettysburgreview.com/conference/2015-conference-for-writers "small workshops focused on the critique of work-in-progress; scholarships available"

Glen Workshop West – August 2-9, 2015 - Santa Fe, NM 206-281-2988 mccabe@spu.edu, http://www.glenworkshop.com "an innovative and enriching program combining the best elements of a workshop, arts festival & conference; scholarships available"

Hampton Roads Writers – September 17-19, 2015 - Virginia Beach, VA 757-639-6146 hrwriters@cox.net, http://www.hamptonroadswriters.org/2014conference.php "workshops cover fiction, nonfiction, screenplays, memoir, poetry, and the business of getting published, with bookshop, book signings & many networking opportunities; need-based (documentation required) full & partial scholarships"

Highlights Foundation – offers workshops for writers year-round. Please check their website (www.highlightsfoundation.org) for the 2015 schedule. A sampling from the 2014 roster:

> ***Autumn Poetry Retreat and Workshop** – Honesdale, PA 877-288-3410 jo.lloyd@highlightsfoundation.org, http://www.highlightsfoundation.org "brings poets together to delve into all elements of poetry; to play with words, images and sounds; and to polish their poetry skills; scholarships available"

> ***Building a Novel: From Sentence to Scene** – Honesdale, PA 570-253-1192 jo.lloyd@highlightsfoundation.org, http://www.highlightsfoundation.org "workshop will offer strategies for improving your manuscript by exploring what makes a scene in a novel, how scene and summary serve the overall narrative arc, and how scenes build toward a dramatic climax; scholarships available"

> ***Everything You Need to Know About Children's Book Publishing: A Crash Course** – Honesdale, PA 570-253-1192 jo.lloyd@highlightsfoundation.org, http://www.highlightsfoundation.org "a comprehensive look at how the children's book publishing industry works; scholarships available"

> ***Fact into Fiction: Writing the Historical Novel** – Honesdale, PA 570-253-1192 jo.lloyd@highlightsfoundation.org, http://www.highlightsfoundation.org "learn how to remain

true to the facts without letting your story get bogged down by them; scholarships available"

*Finding Your Voice – Honesdale, PA 570-253-1192 jo.lloyd@highlightsfoundation.org, http://www.highlightsfoundation.org "this intensive activity and writing-based workshop has been developed to break writers through to their authentic voices; scholarships available"

*From Pose to Picture to Published: Writing a Marketable Picture Book – Honesdale, PA 570-253-1192 jo.lloyd@highlightsfoundation.org, http://www.highlightsfoundation.org "guides you through the process of creating a sellable picture book; scholarships available"

*Poetry for the Delight of It – Honesdale, PA 570-253-1192 jo.lloyd@highlightsfoundation.org, http://www.highlightsfoundation.org "from budding poet to published veteran, we learn and teach at every stage; scholarships available"

*Rekindling the Fire – Honesdale, PA 570-253-1192 jo.lloyd@highlightsfoundation.org, http://www.highlightsfoundation.org "this workshop is designed to leave you inspired and equipped with skills to integrate a flourishing writing practice into your current lifestyle; scholarships available"

Hunter College Writers' Conference – June 6, 2015 - New York, NY 212-772-4292 lfrumkes@hunter.cuny.edu, http://www.hunter.cuny.edu/thewritingcenter-ce "one-day fiction and nonfiction conference; scholarships available"

Jack Kerouac School of Disembodied Poetics Summer Writing Program at Naropa University – June 14-July 11, 2015 - Boulder, CO 303-245-4862 swp@naropa.edu, http://www.naropa.edu/swp "month-long colloquium of students, poets, fiction writers, scholars, translators, performance artists, activists, Buddhist teachers, musicians, printers, editors and others working in small press publishing; scholarships available"

Juniper Summer Writing Institute & Institute for Young Writers – June 21-28, 2015 - Amherst, MA 413-545-5503 juniperinstitute@hfa.umass.edu, http://www.umass.edu/juniperinstitute "a week of intensive writing workshops, craft sessions, Q&As, readings, and manuscript consultation for poetry, fiction, creative nonfiction & memoir; scholarships available"

Kachemak Bay Writers' Conference – June 12-16, 2015 - Homer, AK 907-235-7743 iyconf@uaa.alaska.edu, http://writersconference.homer.alaska.edu "creative writing workshops, readings, open mic, panel discussions, consultations plus time for writing; scholarships available"

Mendocino Coast Writers Conference – (2015 dates to be announced) - Fort Bragg, CA 707-485-4031 info@mcwc.org, http://www.mcwc.org, http://www.mcwc.org/mcwc_schol.html "offers a place where writers find encouragement, expertise and inspiration; scholarships offered for a variety of applicants"

Napa Valley Writers' Conference – July 26-31, 2015 - St. Helena, CA 707-967-2900 x4 writecon@napavalley.edu, http://www.napawritersconference.org "the conference has remained a place to convene for fellowship and serious work with a focus on craft; scholarships available"

New York State Summer Writers Institute – June 29-July 24, 2015 - Saratoga Springs, NY 518-580-5593 summerwriters@skidmore.edu, http://www.skidmore.edu/summerwriters "features creative writing workshops in fiction, nonfiction & poetry; scholarships open to students enrolled full-time in undergraduate or graduate programs who are nominated by their creative writing instructors"

North Carolina Writers' Network 2014 Fall Conference – (April & November, 2015) - Charlotte, NC 336-293-8844 ed@ncwriters.org, https://www.awpwriter.org/programs

conferences/wcc_entry_view/1317/www.ncwriters.org "a weekend full of activities that include lunch and dinner banquets with readings, keynotes, tracks in several genres, open mic sessions, and the opportunity for one-on-one manuscript critiques with editors or agents; scholarships available for poets who teach full-time"

Odyssey Writing Workshop - June 8 – July 17, 2015 - Mont Vernon, NH 603-673-6234 jcavelos@sff.net, http://www.odysseyworkshop.org "the six-week workshop is a serious, demanding program for developing writers whose work is approaching publication quality and for published writers who want to improve their work; scholarships available"

Postgraduate Writers' Conference – (2015 dates to be announced) - Montpelier, VT 802-828-8835 pgconference@vcfa.edu, http://www.vcfa.edu/writing/pwc "emphasis on process and craft through small-group workshops limited to 5 or 6 participants, creating a supportive and non-hierarchical writers' community; scholarships available"

Rocky Mountain Fiction Writers Gold Conference – September 11-13, 2015 - Westminster, CO 303-331-2608 conference@rmfw.org, http://rmfw.org/conference "a full weekend of writerly camaraderie, exciting programming, plus opportunities to pitch projects to the industry's top agents and editors; scholarships available"

San Diego State University Writers' Conference – January 22-24, 2016 - San Diego, CA 619-594-3946 sdsuwritersconference@mail.sdsu.edu http://www.ces.sdsu.edu/writers/ "designed to help every writer at every writing level. Learn how to improve your writing skills, develop your marketing awareness, & meet one-on-one with top editors and agents to facilitate the next step in your publishing career"

San Francisco Writers Conference – February 12-15, 2015 - San Francisco, CA 415-673-0939 sfwriterscon@aol.com, http://sfwriters.org "more than 100 panels & sessions, along with keynote addresses, give new and experienced writers information about the world of publishing and polishing their craft; a limited number of one-day scholarships available to San Francisco Bay Area high school students"

Sewanee Writers' Conference – July 21-August 2, 2015 - Sewanee, TN 931-598-1654 swc@sewanee.edu, http://www.sewaneewriters.org "provides instruction and criticism through workshops and craft lectures in fiction, poetry & playwriting; scholarships available"

Sitka Symposium – (2015 dates to be announced) - Sitka, AK 907-737-3794 peter@islandinstitutealaska.org, https://www.awpwriter.org/programs_conferences/wcc_entry_view/1261/ www.islandinstitutealaska.org "by exploring story, place and community, the Symposium engages writers, readers and thinkers in the social, environmental & ethical challenges of our time; scholarships available"

Slice Literary Writer's Conference – (2015 dates to be announced) - Brooklyn, NY editors@slicemagazine.org, http://slicemagazine.org/conferences/slice-literary-writers-conference "walks writers through the professional publishing process, from the writer's desk to the bookstore shelf; scholarships available to students"

Southampton Writers Conference – July 8-19, 2015 - Southampton, NY 631-632-5030 southamptonarts@stonybrook.edu, http://www.stonybrook.edu/writers "forum for authors of all genres to study and discuss the craft of writing; scholarships available"

Taos Summer Writers' Conference – July 12-19, 2015 - Albuquerque, NM 505-277-5572 taosconf@unm.edu, http://www.unm.edu/~taosconf "week-long and weekend workshops in fiction, poetry, nonfiction & screenwriting; scholarships available"

Tin House Summer Writer's Workshop – (2015 dates to be announced) - Portland, OR 503-219-0622 lance@tinhouse.com, http://www.tinhouse.com/writers-workshop "combines morning workshops, each limited to 12 participants, with afternoon craft seminars and career panels; scholarships available"

Tinker Mountain Writers' Workshop – year-round - Roanoke, VA 540-362-6229 cpowell@hollins.edu, http://www.hollins.edu/tmww "week-long workshop with small classes, readings, in-class critiques, manuscript reviews, individual conferences & more; scholarships available"

Wesleyan Writers Conference – (2015 dates to be announced) - Middletown, CT 860-685-3604 agreene@wesleyan.edu, http://www.wesleyan.edu/writing/conference/scholarship.html "welcomes new writers, established writers, and everyone interested in the writer's craft; seven scholarships and a teaching fellowship awarded"

Willamette Writers Conference – August 7-9, 2015 - West Linn, OR 503-305-6729 wilwrite@teleport.com, http://www.willamettewriters.com "brings to Portland, Oregon, three days of workshops, authors' signings, receptions, and opportunities to meet with literary agents, editors & Hollywood producers; teacher/student scholarships available"

Grants & Funding for Writers

Indie publishing is empowering. You hold all the cards in your hands, and you are the boss. The book is yours to do with as you wish. But you also face one of the largest challenges created by the differences between indie publishing and traditional publishing, and that is paying for publication.

As editor of FundsforWriters.com (fundsforwriters.com), a website and newsletter that reaches thirty-four thousand readers each week, a resource that's been around for sixteen years, I keep my eye on the manner in which authors fund their careers.

Most authors initially seek a simple grant, thinking there are philanthropic gods out there who love doling out money to new writers. Sorry: they do not exist. There isn't a grant I know of that pays new or part-time indie writers to publish books. When I explain that to those who query me daily, I hear the air whoosh out of their sails. They think it's the end of the world because they have no idea how or where to find the money to make their book dream come true.

That's when I tell them to use that creativity that molds great stories and think about how to seek, earn, or win money for their project.

First, the hard cold facts:

- No grant exists to pay new indie authors. Face it and move on to the rest of this article. Trust me, there are still ways to make this project of yours work.

- No money source happens quickly. Finding money takes advance thought and planning, just as your story and marketing strategy do. Don't finish the book and then scramble for the money, thinking you'll have it in a couple of weeks. It's not difficult to plan in advance.

- No money you acquire for your book is nontaxable. Whatever you gather to publish your dream—grant, contest winnings, crowdfunding, or retreat—it is taxable, so just keep that in mind. However, an author has tons of items to write off, too. Just keep track of your income and expenses for tax time.

Come on, you say. What are the funding sources?

Grants

Yes, I said no grants are available for newbies. However, you need to understand them because occasionally one arises, particularly once you publish a few books and build a brand and platform.

A grant is money given for a specific purpose, with no intention of repayment. Grants are not as common as they once were. A weak economy over the past decade or so has eroded a lot of grant opportunities.

Most grants come from government agencies and non-profits sometimes known as foundations. Because of the United States tax code, these organizations give grants to other organizations or nonprofits more than to individuals, making the grant arena complicated.

Some groups that offer individual grants are:

- **State arts commissions.** Find yours at the National Assembly of State Arts Agencies (www.nasaa-arts.org).

- **Local arts councils.** Google your town/county and "arts council."

- **Local governments.** Locate the government website and do a search for grants.

While I'd love to tell you how to apply to each one of these grants and advise you how to win them, I cannot, since each office or organization has a different standard and set of rules for how they select grant recipients. The best ways to learn about anyone's grant structure are:

- Call a representative and ask to meet with them about what they expect;
- Sign up for their newsletter or e-mail updates; and
- Offer to serve on a grant panel.

The last option sounds ominous, but these grant groups need a diversity of minds to help them make appropriate grant selections. You'll learn not only about how grants work, but also which grants get selected. Plus you'll get to know the people who manage the grants so that when you apply, your name will ring a bell.

But let's say you win one of these grants. Expect the amount to be from a couple of hundred dollars to a couple of thousand; the rare exceptions grant up to $10,000 to authors who can prove themselves with significant bodies of work.

Crowdfunding

These days, when someone asks me where the grants are, I tell them to consider crowdfunding instead. Crowdfunding sites include Kickstarter, Indiegogo, Unbound, RocketHub, and many other lesser-known sites.

Here's how they work. You are given a place on the crowd-funding site to post your campaign, which means your book, and to explain the funds you need for whatever purpose: research, travel, publishing, editing, or even promotion. From there, you are given a deadline during which you solicit funding from the general public, building supporters as you go. You can ask for as little as a dollar or as high as thousands, and anything in between.

In your campaign, you request these funds with the promise of a gift. Sometimes it's as simple as a $5 donation for an e-book in return. It could mean that for a $1,000 donation you'll have dinner with someone's book club. Twenty-five dollars might earn a supporter a paperback. One hundred dollars might earn them their name in the book. There are no rules here. Creativity is paramount to attract attention.

The best way to learn how to develop a successful campaign is to study the successful ones. They stay up on the crowdfunding sites for a long time after the deadline passes. Even consider donating to one or two to get a feel for how the game is played.

Remember that in determining how much money you need, you must take into account the cost of running the campaign. Such costs include the administrative fee that the site will take from your earnings, the cost of whatever devices you use in your promotion (e.g., a video, a slideshow), the cost of the rewards you give to your supporters, and any possible tax liability from the money you raise.

The administrative fees vary from site to site, with some having multiple options. With some you have to meet your monetary goal or you receive nothing, while others give you whatever is pledged, even if you don't meet your goal. The fees differ based on the site and the type of administrative option you choose.

Feel free to contact successful crowdfunding authors, too. Most will open their arms and give you ample advice on setting up your own campaign. Anne Belov held not one but three successful fundraisers for her book series, **Your Brain on Pandas**. Here's a link to the Kickstarter campaign for one of them: https://www.kickstarter.com/projects/arttraveler/your-brain-on-pandas-book-1-of-the-panda-chronicle. She's warm and genuine and would be glad to point you in the right direction.

Freelancing

Crowdfunding is more empowering than a grant, and freelancing is more empowering than crowdfunding. Why? Because more of your success is in your control.

Any writer can freelance. By freelance, I mean write for someone else (magazine, business, newspaper, newsletter, blog) in exchange for compensation. Sooner or later, you will be asked to write a blog post, an article, or a journalistic piece about what you do. It's all part of self-promotion. So why not be proactive and write pieces in advance—for money?

For the most part, magazines pay from five to fifty cents per word for articles. Avoid those that want you to write for free. Right now you are seeking funding for your book, so income is key. Try to pitch twenty magazines or publishing opportunities a week. Yes, you'll be rejected until you get the hang of it, but if you're lucky enough to land several gigs, that means more money in your coffers. It does not take many $100 pieces to build the funds you need to publish your book.

A great side effect of this effort, besides the income, is that you are putting your name out there to the public. Chances are your byline on a magazine article or paying blog site will reach more people in a weekend than your new book will reach in a year. This is how you build credibility and name recognition as a writer. Each publication, no matter what it is, adds a rung to your ladder. So when you finally publish that book, you will have readers in tow.

Make sure you have a personal blog or website that takes note of your successes. Link to where you are published. Another goal is to be googleable. The more articles you have published, and the more you post on your website, the more easily readers will be able to find you.

Also make sure the money you earn goes into your savings account for the book, and remember to write off your freelancing expenses on your taxes.

Resources to find freelancing gigs and magazines:

- FundsforWriters (www.fundsforwriters.com)
- WritersMarket.com (www.writersmarket.com)
- Freelance Writing (www.freelancewriting.com)
- Worldwide Freelance (www.worldwidefreelance.com)
- All Indie Writers: "38 Websites and Blogs That Pay Writers $100 Per Article and More" (http://allindiewriters. com/blogs-pay-writers-100-per-article/)
- Minterest: "Make Money Writing Articles" (http://www. minterest.org/how-to-make-money-writing-articles/)

Sponsors

This tool isn't advertised much across the blogosphere. A century or two ago, authors often had sponsors who funded their work. A charismatic and savvy author can still do the same.

You can either ask people to purchase ownership shares in your book, in which case you must be prepared to show them your marketing plan to confirm you intend to earn a decent income from the sales, or ask them to support your book in exchange for an advertisement as your sponsor.

This latter option is used more often. You can partner with a nonprofit group, business, entrepreneur, club, sports team, or even individual, and tell them you will mention their sponsorship in the back of your book, on your website, and on all of your promotions. This option sometimes scares people, but actually it's one of the fastest ways to earn money. You just need to be passionate about your book and have an organized marketing plan to show them where you intend to promote and make sales happen.

Fiscal sponsorships

This type of funding is a marriage of grant and sponsorship with a dash of crowdfunding. Find a nonprofit that is willing to apply for a grant on your behalf. They have access to group funding, whereas you only have access to individual funding. So they get the grant, keep an administrative fee of roughly 10 percent (it varies), and you get the rest to pursue your project.

Why would they do this for you? First, for the administrative fee. Second, you have to show them that your book goes along with the nonprofit's mission, and if you do well, it makes them look as though they are doing well. For instance, an animal shelter might be willing to be your fiscal agent for your cozy mystery about a dog. You promote them for being your agent, and they get the administrative funds to help run their organization. There have to be parallel goals between the nonprofit and you.

No, they don't get part of your royalties. Yes, you turn in evidence of your success to the nonprofit for their records so they can show you used the money properly. It's not difficult.

For more information on how a fiscal agent works, see these sites:

- Fractured Atlas (https://www.fracturedatlas.org/site/fiscal)
- Creative Capital (http://www.creative-capital.org/)
- New York Foundation for the Arts
  (www.nyfa.org/Content/Show/Fiscal%20Sponsorship)

Foundation Center (http://foundationcenter.org/getstarted/tutorials/fiscal/index.html)

Contests

While this sounds almost like buying lottery tickets, contests are much more than playing a game.

While you are writing, feel free to enter chapters, short stories, poetry, or other portions of your work into paying contests. The competition is fierce, which is great because that competition makes you write your best. Also, contests can be wonderful barometers for you to judge how well you are writing. I didn't publish my first mystery novel, *Lowcountry Bribe*, until I'd placed or won in several contests for its opening line, first chapter, and entire unpublished manuscript.

There will be fees. Some novice writers assume that when a contest charges, it is a scam. Frankly, I wonder about the contest when it does not charge a fee. How is the prize money paid? Who pays for the advertising or the honorariums to the judges? I've seen contests go broke. I prefer a contest with a fee.

A rule of thumb to use in paying a fee is this: it should be no more than 5 percent of the first prize amount. If you feel very compelled to enter a specific contest that exceeds this rule, then absolutely limit the entry fee to 10 percent of the first prize money. Any fee larger than that is greedy.

Some contests also offer publishing as part of the award. Isn't that what you want anyway? But wait, maybe this is traditional publishing, and you want to remain an indie author. I still argue that for you to win a contest, receive funds, and acquire a traditional publishing contract is worth the sacrifice of some royalties. This could be a huge shot in the arm for your career and launch you as an author.

Some contests, however, may only pay, or only wish to publish a chapter of your work. Assuming they are a credible contest, by all means let them. But how do you find a credible contest?

FundsforWriters.com is known for vetting contests, and contests make up the majority of the paid subscriptions it manages. We've been watching and screening contests for more than a decade. You'll also find many of these contests on the website.

The Poets & Writers website (www.pw.org) also posts some of these contests. NewPages (www.newpages.com/classifieds/big-list-of-writing-contests) is another internationally reputable site for contests.

You have options. Finding money for your book means simply thinking like an entrepreneur. You are a creative soul, gifted at making up stories, finding twists, and painting with beautiful words. The same brainpower can be used to think about how to earn money for your book. Create a one-year business plan describing how you will not only write, but also earn the money to bring it to life in print.

Yes, you can do this. With diligence and focus, you can create your book.

C. Hope Clark
FundsforWriters (www.fundsforwriters.com)

C. Hope Clark is the founder of FundsforWriters.com. Her work has been published in *Writer's Digest, The Writer, Writer's Market, Guide to Literary Agents*, and more. She speaks nationally and publishes a newsletter to 34,000 writers. Hope is also a mystery novelist with two series and five books under her belt, and has another due out in Summer 2016.

Fiscal Agents – http://www.foundationcenter.org, www.nyfa.org
"many of these agents are part of sponsorship groups"

Funds for Writers – http://www.fundsforwriters.com

Libraries – "most large libraries and presidential libraries offer
research grants for writers"

Local Arts Council – "find out what's going on in the arts
community in your town; many offer research and/or travel
grants"

National Endowment for the Arts – http://arts.gov

State Arts Commission –
http://www.statelocalgov.net/50states-arts.php "every state
has one"

Universities and Private Schools – "learn which ones in your area
offer scholarships and residences for writers"

Women Arts –
http://www.womenarts.org/funding-resources/index

Professional & Trade Associations

Why indie authors need trade associations

Trade associations have played a role in business as far back as the nineteenth century. Also known as industry trade groups or professional associations, they are organizations that operate in a specific industry for the benefit of their members. And that's what they do in the publishing industry—offer advice and support to their members.

The trade organizations in our industry promote their members' businesses, offer news about the industry and its activities, and provide education on a variety of topics that will help their members. While associations may have paid employees, the majority of groups are set up as nonprofits and are run by volunteers.

I have been a member of the Independent Book Publishers Association (IBPA, formerly known as PMA) for more than twenty years. I've often attended IBPA's annual conference, Publishing University, and I was so impressed by the range of information provided that I volunteered to help organize many panels for the association. I have also advertised my services in the association's magazine, *Independent*. The issues are filled with members' stories, experts' advice, and the latest information about the publishing industry.

On a local level, I have been an officer and/or board member of the local IBPA affiliate chapter, Publishers Association of Los Angeles, since its inception in 2003. I've helped run meetings, set up programs, bring in guest speakers, and work on our catalog and directory. I have learned a tremendous amount and met wonderful people who have helped me— whether by teaching me something I didn't know, providing me with a valuable professional service, or becoming an important member of my professional network. All my experiences have been worth every minute of the time I have volunteered.

Trade organizations are a great place to ask those questions that you didn't know whom to ask. For example, you might want to know the difference between an interior book designer and a cover designer. Or you might want a clear definition of the differences between content editing, copyediting, and proofreading. Then again, you might want help figuring out if your local book fair would be a good place to advertise or exhibit, whether you'd need postcards and bookmarks, how to find your target readers, and what else you should be doing to promote your book. Associations are also a safe place to admit that you don't know what you don't know.

More often than not, a self-publisher must wear all the hats of a self-publishing company: writer, editor, designer, book producer, accountant, marketing director, publicist, and sales rep. It is hard to do each job equally well. For example, although you may be a brilliant writer, you may loathe bookkeeping and know absolutely nothing about PR. Joining trade and professional associations can help put you in touch with the many experts you can hire to help you with the skills you don't have, don't have time to learn or do, or dislike.

In the publishing industry, the goal of trade and professional associations is to bring together like-minded, like-goaled individuals and companies. Within the self-publishing community specifically, that involves providing a way for self-publishers and industry professionals who work with self-publishers to meet one another. Members include a diverse group of people: about-to-be-published authors, one-book publishers, one-book-a-year publishers, people who publish both their own work and other authors' works, and industry-related professionals (for example, editors, designers, indexers, printers, and marketing consultants).

I've already touched on a few of the benefits of joining a professional or trade organization. I started networking in these organizations before I had my own business, and it's been a great experience for many reasons.

The first reason is *networking*. Having the opportunity to meet others like myself, who have "been there and done that," has been invaluable. My colleagues have willingly shared their resources, tips, good and bad experiences, and so much more throughout my tenure in every group. The people in your network may also be able to help spread the word about your books by arranging speaking engagements or connecting you with their friends in other organizations.

The second reason is *education*. Most organizations offer programs. Many are monthly meetings over a meal; others are teleseminars or webinars, full-day workshops, or several-day conferences. I believe that knowledge is power—no matter the industry. The more knowledge I gain, the more value I can create for my business, projects, and clients. The more knowledge an author or publisher gains, the better the decisions he will make, the more opportunities he can take advantage of, and the better prepared he'll be when problems arise.

The third reason is *resources*. Many self-publishers work alone, and if this is a new industry to them, they don't know all the places, people, and companies that can help make their book better. Organizations can assist with this in many ways: newsletters, networking, and resource directories, to name just a few.

The fourth reason is *saving money*. Members may be able to take advantage of discounts on conferences or memberships in other organizations. Most organizations that offer benefits (such as a yearly conference or free shipping) usually do so at a discounted price unavailable to nonmembers.

Now let's address the issue of competition. Sometimes people ask, "Why would others in this business want to help me? Aren't they in competition with me?" The publishing industry is interesting in that having two identical books is extremely rare. Certainly there are books on the same subject or in the same genre, but are they really identical? Do both books have the same point of view; do both authors have the same experiences, stories, and case studies to share with their readers; do they offer the exact same advice? It's very, very rare to have a situation like this. So in reality, publishers are not competitors. A publisher who has published a business book can easily share her tips about designers, a trade show, a marketing program, or a publicist with another publisher who has published a self-help, travel, or health book. And, in the best of all possible worlds, publishers can run marketing ideas by each other, participate in cooperative advertising and marketing programs, or meet for brainstorming sessions.

And the negative side of joining a trade or professional association? I can't think of one. Just in case you were thinking about the hassle of driving in traffic or having to carve time out of your busy schedule to attend a meeting, my response is that the benefits far outweigh these minor inconveniences.

The publishing industry has some terrific associations, including the ones listed in the following pages. I encourage you to check them out, as well as those in your area. Visit them as a guest and get more information about their goals, mission statements, and programs. Attend a few meetings before you decide whether the group is a good fit. I also encourage you to look into groups outside your geographical area—specifically those that offer teleseminars, webinars, or conferences you could attend.

Join an organization. Listen, learn, and share. You can't go wrong.

Sharon Goldinger
PeopleSpeak (www.detailsplease.com/peoplespeak)

Sharon Goldinger is a book shepherd, editor, and publishing and marketing consultant specializing in nonfiction books. With an eye for details, she leads authors through the often-complicated publishing process (writing, editing, design, printing, marketing, distribution) to help them produce and sell exceptional, award-winning books.

Academy of American Poets – New York, NY 212-274-0343 academy@poets.org, http://www.poets.org "to support American poets at all stages of their careers & to foster the appreciation of contemporary poetry"

Alliance of Independent Authors – London, UK press@allianceindependentauthors.org, http://allianceindependentauthors.org "global nonprofit association of author-publishers, offering connection, collaboration, advice & education, to further the interests of self-publishing writers everywhere"

American Booksellers Association – White Plains, NY 800-637-0037/914-406-7500 info@bookweb.org, http://www.bookweb.org "trade organization for independently owned bookstores; access ABA's Membership Directory free online to find bookstores in your area"

American Christian Fiction Writers – Palm Bay, FL admin@acfw.com, http://www.acfw.com "professional organization devoted to Christian fiction through developing the skills of its authors, educating them in the market & serving as an advocate in the publishing industry"

American Society of Journalists and Authors – New York, NY 212-997-0947 http://www.asja.org/about/contact.php, http://www.asja.org "the nation's professional organization of independent nonfiction writers"

Association of Independent Authors – info@independent-authors.org, http://www.independent-authors.com "body representing, advancing, promoting & supporting independent, self-published authors globally"

Association of Publishers for Special Sales – Colorado Springs, CO 719-924-5534 OR Avon, CT 860-675-1344 Kaye@bookapss.org, OR BrianJud@bookapss.org, http://www.spannet.org "provides high-quality, functional, innovative sales & marketing resources that enhance content producers' efforts to grow their businesses profitably"

Association of Writers and Writing Program – Fairfax, VA 703-993-4301 awp@awpwriter.org, https://www.awpwriter.org "fosters literary achievement, advances the art of writing as essential to a good education while serving the makers, teachers, students & readers of contemporary writing"

Authors Guild – New York, NY 212-563-5904 staff@authorsguild.org, http://www.authorsguild.org "the nation's leading advocate for writers' interests in effective copyright protection, fair contracts + free expression since it was founded as the Authors League of America in 1912; providing legal assistance & a broad range of web services to its members"

AuthorU – Aurora, CO 303-885-2207 info@authorU.org, http://authoru.org/ "a nonprofit membership association for authors who want to be seriously successful. AuthorU provides free webinars, coaching, podcasts, meetings, and more. Membership is $99 per year and includes discounts for AuthorU members"

Bay Area Editors' Forum – San Francisco, CA http://www.editorsforum.org/contact.php, http://www.editorsforum.org "association of in-house & freelance editors from a variety of publishing settings"

Bay Area Independent Publishers Association – San Rafael, CA membership@baipa.org, http://baipa.org "educational organization dedicated to independent author-publishers, whose members include creative people involved in various aspects of publishing; linking writers with the services they need to publish & sell their work"

Book Promotion Forum – San Francisco, CA membership@bookpromotionforum.org, http://www.bookpromotionforum.org "organization devoted

to education about publicity, promotion, marketing +
distribution of books throughout Northern California & beyond"

BookWorks – New York, NY 855-878-2435 info@bookworks.com,
http://www.bookworks.com "the Self-Publishers Association is
a worldwide community dedicated exclusively to helping self-
publishing authors prepare, publish & promote their books"

The Catholic Writers Guild – Indianapolis, IN
http://www.catholicwritersguild.com "helping build a vibrant
Catholic literary culture by offering educational programs that
teach Catholic writers about their craft as well as how to sell &
market their work"

Christian Small Publishers Association – Charlotte, NC
704-277-7194 cspa@christianpublishers.net,
http://www.christianpublishers.net "represents, promotes &
strengthens the small publisher in the Christian marketplace"

Colorado Independent Publishers Association – Lakewood, CO
970-315-2472 admin@cipacatalog.com,
http://www.cipacatalog.com "nonprofit association of
independent book publishers, authors, future authors & related
publishing service providers"

Connecticut Authors & Publishers Association –
http://www.aboutcapa.com "nonprofit organization with a
mission to help authors, publishers + support services increase
their sales, revenue & profits"

Erotica Readers and Writers Association –
erwa.website@gmail.com, http://www.erotica-readers.com
"international community of men + women interested in the
provocative world of erotica & sensual pleasures"

Florida Authors & Publishers Association – Longwood, FL
member.services@floridapublishersassociation.com,
http://www.floridapublishersassociation.com "dedicated
to providing the highest quality of information, resources +
professional development to those interested in the writing &
publishing profession in the state of Florida"

Gemini Ink – San Antonio, TX 210-734-9673 http://geminiink.org "small volunteer reading series for local writers, committed to addressing the dynamic needs of San Antonio writers & readers"

Historical Novel Society – 14 local chapters throughout the US & UK http://historicalnovelsociety.org "a literary society devoted to promoting the enjoyment of historical fiction"

Horror Writers Association – Sherman Oaks, CA 818-220-3965 hwa@horror.org, http://horror.org "organization of writers + publishing professionals around the world, dedicated to promoting dark literature & the interests of those who write it"

Independent Book Publishers Association – Manhattan Beach, CA 310-546-1818 info@IBPA-online.org, http://www.ibpa-online.org "nonprofit membership organization serving + leading the indie publishing community through advocacy, education & tools for success"

Independent Publishers of New England – Arlington, MA 339-368-5656 talktous@ipne.org, http://www.ipne.org "provides networking, resources, education & cooperative marketing for New England's independent publishing community"

International Association for Journal Writing – Sarasota, FL 941-227-4410 http://www.iajw.org "group of 30 of the best-known journal experts, offering real solutions & practical guidance"

International Digital Publishing Forum – Seattle, WA 530-988-8405 membership@idpf.org, http://idpf.org "global trade standards organization dedicated to the development + promotion of electronic publishing & content consumption"

International Thriller Writers – Eureka, CA membership@internationalthrillerwriters.com http://thrillerwriters.org "represents professional thriller authors from around the world, a society of authors, both fiction + nonfiction that seeks to provide a way for suc-cessful, bestselling authors to help debut & midlist authors advance their careers"

The International Women's Writing Guild – New York, NY 917-720-6959 iwwgmembernews@gmail.com, http://www.iwwg.org "network for the personal & professional empowerment of women through writing, open to all regardless of portfolio"

Islamic Writers Alliance, Inc. – momtotsan@yahoo.com, http://www.islamicwritersalliance.net "nonprofit, tax-exempt, US-based professional Muslim organization with an international membership"

Literarymarketplace.com – Medford, NJ 800-300-9868 custserv@infotoday.com, http://www.literarymarketplace.com "for more than 50 years, LMP has been the resource directory for American & Canadian book publishing, consulted by publishing professionals, authors, industry watchers & those seeking to gain entry into the world of publishing: one-week + annual subscriptions"

Maine Writers & Publishers Alliance – Portland, ME 207-228-8263 info@mainewriters.org, http://mainewriters.org "nonprofit statewide organization working to enrich the literary life + culture of Maine, through supporting/promoting Maine's writers, publishers, booksellers & literary professionals"

MidAtlantic Book Publishers Association – Washington, DC http://www.midatlanticbookpublishers.com "professional trade association helping independent publishers/self-publishers become more profitable + successful by learning how to produce quality books, promote them effectively & navigate the rapidly changing book publishing industry; a regional affiliate of the Independent Book Publishers Association (IBPA) serving Delaware, Maryland, New Jersey, Pennsylvania, Virginia, & Washington, DC"

Midwest Independent Publishers Association – St. Paul, MN 651-917-0021 http://www.mipa.org/contact, http://www.mipa.org "serves the Midwest publishing community by sharing publishing, production & promotion/marketing information + providing support & encouragement to authors who want to learn about the myriad publishing options emerging in this dynamic digital world"

Mystery Writers of America – New York, NY 212-888-8171 (11 regional chapters throughout the US) http://mysterywriters.org "the premier organization for mystery writers, professionals allied to the crime-writing field, aspiring crime writers & those devoted to the genre"

National Association of Independent Writers and Editors – Ashland, VA 804-767-5961 director@naiwe.com, http://naiwe.com "professional association for writers & editors dedicated to helping members succeed through a focus on creating multiple streams of writing income"

National Association of Memoir Writers – Berkeley, CA 877-363-6647 customersupport@namw.org, http://www.namw.org "membership organization that invites memoir writers from all over the world to connect, learn & become inspired about writing their stories"

National Writers Association – Parker, CO 303-841-0246 natlwritersassn@hotmail.com, http://www.nationalwriters.com "nonprofit organization to enhance the future of writers by fostering continuing education through scholarships, no- or low-cost workshops & seminars; an ethical resource for writers at all levels of experience"

National Writers Union – New York, NY 212-254-0279 membership@nwu.org, https://nwu.org "the only labor union that represents freelance writers"

New Mexico Book Association – Santa Fe, NM 505-660-6357 http://www.nmbook.org "statewide nonprofit serving all book professionals; book creators, writers, editors, publishers, illustrators, librarians, booksellers, book designers, typesetters, printers, literacy advocates, agents, reviewers + avid readers all sharing the common goal of preserving & promoting the book"

Northern California Publishers & Authors – Sacramento, CA 916-934-8434 http://www.norcalpa.org/pages/contact.html, http://www.norcalpa.org "alliance of independent publishers, authors + publishing professionals in Northern California, whose purpose is to foster, encourage & educate"

Novelists Inc. – Manhattan, KS ninc@varney.com, http://www.ninc.com "Ninc is the only writers' organization devoted exclusively to the needs of multi-published novelists"

Pacific Northwest Writers Alliance – Issaquah, WA 425-673-2665 pnwa@pnwa.org, http://www.pnwa.org "organization dedicated to helping writers in the Northwest connect to other writers, publishers, agents & editors across the country"

PEN American Center – New York, NY 212-334-1660 info@pen.org, https://www.pen.org "working to ensure that people everywhere have the freedom to create literature, convey information/ideas, express their views + make it possible for everyone to access the views, ideas & literature of others"

Poetry Society of America – New York, NY 212-254-9628 http://www.poetrysociety.org "mission is to build a larger, more diverse audience for poetry, encourage a deeper appreciation of the vitality of poetry in the cultural conversation + support poets through an array of programs & awards"

Poets & Writers – New York, NY 212-226-3586 http://www.pw.org "the nation's largest nonprofit organization serving creative writers"

Publishers and Writers of San Diego – San Diego, CA http://publisherswriters.org "nonprofit trade organization with the mission to help independent publishers + authors understand the many facets of the industry & publish successfully, while upholding professional standards in a constantly changing business"

Publishers Association of Los Angeles – Manhattan Beach, CA 949-581-6140 info@pa-la.org, http://www.publishersassociationoflosangeles.com "PALA welcomes authors, publishers + affiliated publishing professionals, with the goal of providing education, networking & resources"

The Publishing Triangle – New York, NY publishingtriangle@gmail.com, http://www.publishingtriangle.org "open to anyone interested in the growth of LGBT writers, literature, publishers, editors, agents, marketing, sub-rights, publicity, salespeople, booksellers, designers, librarians & general book lovers"

Romance Writers of America – Houston, TX 832-717-5200 info@rwa.org, http://www.rwa.org "dedicated to advancing the professional interests of career-focused romance writers through networking & advocacy"

Science Fiction and Fantasy Writers of America – Enfield, CT http://www.sfwa.org "professional organization for authors of science fiction, fantasy & related genres, with excellent *Writer Beware* blog"

Sisters in Crime – Lawrence, KS 785-842-1325 admin@sistersincrime.org, http://www.sistersincrime.org "authors, readers, publishers, agents, booksellers + librarians bound by affection for the mystery genre & support of women who write mysteries"

Small Publishers, Artists and Writers Network – Ojai, CA 805-524-6970 http://www.spawn.org/blog/?page_id=698, http://www.spawn.org "provides information, resources + opportunities for everyone involved in or interested in publishing, whether you are an author, freelance writer, artist or own a publishing company"

Society of Children's Book Writers and Illustrators – Los Angeles, CA 323-782-1010 scbwi@scbwi.org, http://www.scbwi.org "nonprofit 501(c)3 & one of the largest professional organizations for writers and illustrators for children + young adults in the fields of literature, magazines, film, television & multimedia"

St. Louis Publishers Association – St. Louis, MO, 314-301-8767
http://slpa.memberlodge.com "provides education/networking
opportunities that empower authors + publishers to create,
market & sell their books"

Upper Peninsula Publishers & Authors Association – Saline,
MI membership@UPPAA.org, http://uppaa.org "nonprofit
association of publishers & authors residing or doing business in
Michigan's Upper Peninsula"

Western Writers of America – Pierre, SD
membership-chair@westernwriters.org, http://westernwriters.org
"promotes the literature of the American West & bestows Spur
Awards for distinguished writing in the Western field"

Women's National Book Association – New York, NY
info@wnba-books.org, http://www.wnba-books.org "national
nonprofit, 501(c)3 organization of women + men who work
with/value books; WNBA exists to promote reading & support
the role of women in the community of the book"

Writers Guild of America, East – New York, NY 212-767-7800
kobrien@wgaeast.org, http://www.wgaeast.org "labor union of
thousands of professionals who are the primary creators of what
is seen or heard on television & film in the US, as well as the
writers of a growing portion of original digital media content"

Writers Guild of America, West – Los Angeles, CA 800-548-4532/
323-951-4000 http://www.wga.org "labor union representing
TV + film writers in Hollywood & Southern California"

Writers' League of Texas – Austin, TX 512-499-8914
wlt@writersleague.org, http://www.writersleague.org
"nonprofit professional forum for information, support + sharing
among writers; to improve their skills, market their work as well
as promote the interests of writers & the writing community"

Best Books on Writing

"If it sounds like writing, I rewrite it." That's what Elmore Leonard says in *Elmore Leonard's 10 Rules of Writing*—a must-read, in my opinion. I was lucky enough to have been the editor of several of Leonard's novels, and working with him was a joy. I learned much more from Leonard than he did from me. He taught me how important it is to keep it simple and not clutter up a story with lengthy descriptions of characters, places, things, and especially the weather. He didn't like adverbs, exclamation points, or using any word other than "said" to carry the dialogue. He was a master, eager to share his wisdom with other writers.

Another great teacher on the art and craft of writing is William Zinsser. In his celebrated *On Writing Well: The Classic Guide to Writing Nonfiction*, he says, "The secret of good writing is to strip every sentence to its cleanest components." He also points out that "Clear thinking becomes clear writing: one cannot exist without the other." In one final jewel of wisdom, he says, "If the reader is lost, it's usually because the writer hasn't been careful enough." Interesting that these two fine writers, Leonard and Zinsser, have such similar points of view.

Writing is both an art and a craft. Some people say it can't be taught. You either have the gift or you don't. I disagree. Michelangelo learned to paint by studying in the studio of Domenico Ghirlandaio; Johnny Cash developed his singing style by listening to Jimmie Rodgers on the radio; and authors can learn to write well by reading everything they can get their hands on in general and in their genre in particular, and by studying some of the best books on writing, many of which are listed here.

Betty Kelly Sargent
BookWorks (www.bookworks.com)

The Art of Styling Sentences by Ann Longknife Ph.D. and K.D. Sullivan, Barron's Educational Series, Fifth Edition (2012) – "reviews the fundamentals of correct sentence structure and presents 20 basic sentence patterns that encompass virtually every effective way in which simple, compound and complex sentences can be structured"

The Artist's Way by Julia Cameron, Tarcher (2002) – "write every day, explore a new subject each week, unleash your creativity through discipline and persistence; don't keep that novel you've always dreamed about inside you; do the work and make it happen"

The Chicago Manual of Style, 16th Edition, The University of Chicago Press (2010) – "the essential guide for writers, editors and publishers"

The Elements of Editing by Arthur Plotnik, Collier/Macmillan (1982) – "a guide for journalists and editors"

The Elements of Style, Fourth Edition by William Strunk Jr. and E.B. White, Longman (1999) – "everything you need to know about grammar, style and composition"

Elmore Leonard's 10 Rules of Writing by Elmore Leonard, William Morrow (2001, 2007) – "witty, charming advice about the essence of writing well, how to show not tell and stay more or less invisible if you are the author"

On Writing by Stephen King, Scribner (2010) – "part memoir, part master class, a brilliant, revealing and practical view of the writer's craft as well as some essential tools of the trade"

On Writing Well, 30th Anniversary Edition by William Zinsser, Harper Perennial (2006) – "a charming, practical guide to writing nonfiction (though much of the advice applies to fiction as well); keep it simple, clear, uncluttered and watch out for those adverbs"

Self-Editing for Fiction Writers, Second Edition: How to Edit Yourself into Print by Renni Browne and Dave King, William Morrow (2004) – "chapters on dialogue, exposition, point of view, interior monologue, and other techniques take you through the same processes an expert editor would go through to perfect your manuscript, illustrated with examples"

Technique in Fiction by Robie Macauley and George Lanning, St. Martin's Griffin (1990) – "an imaginative approach to writing fiction with lots of helpful examples"

Twelve Keys to Writing Books that Sell by Kathleen Krull, Writer's Digest Books (1989) – "a guide to evaluating the strengths and weaknesses in your writing"

The War of Art by Steven Pressfield, Black Irish Entertainment (2012) – "great value to frustrated writers struggling with writer's block"

Woe Is I: The Grammarphobe's Guide to Better English in Plain English by Patricia T. O'Conner, Riverhead (2010) – "an entertaining and informative look at grammar"

The Complete Handbook of Novel Writing, by the Editors of Writer's Digest Books, Writer's Digest Books (2002) – "a clear, down-to-earth instruction on how to write a novel"

The Writing Life by Annie Dillard, Harper Collins (1989) – "don't fall in love with your words, be tough; writing is hard work but it is probably the most rewarding work there is"

Writing the Heart of Your Story: The Secret to Crafting an Unforgettable Novel by C. S. Lakin, Ubiquitous Press (2014) – "Learn the secret of how to write the heart of your story! This writing skills book, full of fiction writing technique, is like no other"

Writing Tools: 50 Essential Strategies for Every Writer by Roy Peter Clark, Little, Brown (2008) – "tools not rules, with many examples from literature and journalism to illustrate the concepts; short, entertaining and a must read for beginning writers"

Zen in the Art of Writing by Ray Bradbury, Bantam Books (1992) – "helps the writer seek out the joy in art, 'if you are writing without zest, without gusto, without love, without fun, you are only half a writer'"

Helpful Links

Here are some links to resources you will need while you create and market your book. For instance, we always recommend that you purchase your own ISBNs from Bowker Identifier Services (the ISBN agency for the United States; for other locations, see the link to the International ISBN Agency) so that your imprint will be shown as the "publisher of record."

You'll also find links to services that can supply you with Cataloging in Publication data, the U.S. Copyright Office and Library of Congress, and several other sites that you'll want to have at your fingertips.

Joel Friedlander
The Book Designer (www.thebookdesigner.com)

Bar Codes – http://www.createbarcodes.com OR
http://www.barcodegraphics.com

Bibliocrunch – http://bibliocrunch.com/

BISAC Subject Codes – https://www.bisg.org/bisac-subject-codes

Bowker Identifier Services – https://www.myidentifiers.com

CIP Data Blocks – http://www.cipblock.com

Copyright Office Information – http://www.copyright.gov

International ISBN Agency – https://www.isbn-international.org/

ISBN (US) – http://www.isbn.org

ISBN (Canada) –
http://www.collectionscanada.gc.ca/isn/041011-1000-e.html

Library of Congress – http://www.loc.gov/publish

Reedsy – https://reedsy.com

Quality Books P-CIP Program –
http://www.quality-books.com/faq.html

PUBLISH

Once you've made your book the best it can be, with the help of freelance book-publishing pros, it will be time to convert your manuscript into an e-book, a print book, and even an audiobook, if that's your goal. This can be a bit confusing for authors new to self-publishing, so we have tried to break it down into easy-to-understand options.

E-book Conversion

More than half of American adults today own a tablet or e-book reader. According to a Pew report: "More than two-thirds (69 percent) of people said they had read at least one printed book in the past year versus 28 percent who said they'd read an e-book and 14 percent who said they had listened to an audiobook. Eighty-seven percent of e-book readers and 84 percent of audiobook listeners also read a print book in the past twelve months."

The people who buy your e-book may own a single-purpose e-book reader like a Kindle or a Kobo as well as a multi-purpose tablet—perhaps an iPad, Kindle Fire, or a Samsung device. People also read on their mobile devices and computer screens. More than a few of your potential customers have discovered that they can pick up where they left off on one device and continue reading on another. The point of all this is that your book should look great on all devices, and it can.

For most novels and creative nonfiction, e-book conversion is simple and affordable. If you know how to use Microsoft Word or WordPress styles, you can easily format (convert) your manuscript to an e-book on your own. However, it's so affordable that I usually hire someone to do it for me so I can spend more time writing and marketing—the two things I do best and enjoy the most.

The more complex the book, the more difficult and expensive it can be to format, so if your book includes subtitles and special text treatments, expect to pay more. You'll definitely need a professional to help you build a beautiful e-book if it includes tables, sidebars, formulas, and complex layouts. These kinds of books are designed to be read on a tablet computer like the iPad or Kindle Fire, and it can cost more than a thousand dollars to have one designed correctly.

Formatting and conversion explained

Formatting your book: The act of applying styles to your manuscript so it can be read by e-book readers and apps is called book formatting. Correct styles lead to correctly formatted books that are displayed beautifully in e-book readers. You can do this yourself or hire someone to format your book, as I mentioned.

Paragraph format: Here, format refers to the style applied to each and every paragraph in your manuscript. To format your manuscript in your Word document, Mark Coker of Smashwords recommends starting by selecting the entire document to apply the "Normal" style (from the Styles menu) to every paragraph. Then apply the "Title" style to each chapter head. You can modify these styles to change the font, font size, and amount of space (leading) between the paragraphs. You should never use spaces, tabs, or carriage returns. Change the style, not the individual paragraph, to create a correctly formatted manuscript that the e-book reader will be able to display properly.

Paragraph style: As in the above example, use Word styles to format a Word document. If you're using an HTML publishing tool like PressBooks, you'll also apply formats to paragraphs. Under the hood, these formats are controlled by something called CSS (Cascading Style Sheets). You can apply various CSS templates to change the entire look of your manuscript at will. Styles and formats exist so your changes can be applied to your whole manuscript at once, preventing tedious, repetitive edits.

Every text-editing program uses styles and formats, which is the programming that tells the e-book reader how to display chapter headings, paragraphs, and special text like drop caps. Using styles and formats will save you lots of time and money in the long run.

Conversion: The act of taking a final, formatted manuscript written in the original program (Word, Pages, Scrivener, etc.) and converting it to EPUB and MOBI formats, which enables it to be read in e-book readers.

About the PDF, MOBI, and EPUB e-book formats

There are three basic types of e-book formats. EPUB is the format for all e-books except Amazon Kindle, which uses MOBI. PDF is the standard format for print, but, even though you can read a PDF on your computer or device, it's awkward and mostly used for samples, white papers, and other professional documents.

Here are details on each of these formats:

EPUB

EPUB is to books as MP3 is to the music industry. EPUB is an open standard, meaning that no single company can control the format. Most major devices use this format. There are two types of EPUB: reflowable and fixed layout.

Reflowable EPUB: Standard reflowable EPUB is great for publications where there are some images but most of the content is text. The text reflows to fit the screen of the e-book reader, whether it is a large computer screen or a mobile device. E-book buyers can determine the size and even style of the font. Someone with poor eyesight can increase the font size on their e-book reader, which means that the text becomes larger and easier to see. But larger text also means there are fewer words on each page. This is why there are no page numbers on e-books.

Fixed-layout EPUB: The size of the text on a fixed-layout EPUB book, on the other hand, does not reflow or change in size, no matter what device is being used to read it. When viewed on a tablet, books in fixed-layout EPUB will look great, but they are generally too small to be read easily on a mobile device. Fixed-layout e-books are best for books where images tell the story.

Use fixed-layout formats for graphic-heavy books like comic books, graphic novels, graphic-laden textbooks, and children's books. You might experiment with a tool like Apple iBooks Author to reach iPad users, or Kindle Kids' Book Creator for the Kindle Fire, but generally fixed-layout books require a deeper level of expertise to create and should be handled by a professional e-book designer. Hiring someone who really understands how to make a quality fixed-layout e-book will save you lots of headaches and is well worth the extra money.

Kindle

MOBI and Kindle Format 8 (KF8) are used by Amazon to deliver e-books to Kindle devices and applications. KF8 is slowly replacing MOBI, but we'll concentrate on MOBI for simple books.

Many of the same services that create EPUB books for you will also create a Kindle-formatted e-book. Or you can convert your EPUB (or HTML) formatted e-book by using a free program called KindleGen available from Amazon. It doesn't do a great job, so don't make that your final version, but it's great for advance reader and review copies.

Fixed-layout e-books for Kindle tablets are created using KF8, similar to fixed-layout EPUBs as described above.

PDF

PDF is another format used for print books, but people deliver documents in PDF for all kinds of reasons. It's not a great format for e-book readers because it doesn't reflow. But PDF docs look great on computer screens, and a lot of people print them out.

You might give away or sell your book or parts of your book in PDF format—sample chapters, for example, or review copies. Personally, I like to receive review copies in EPUB or Kindle format because I don't like reading on my computer screen. It feels too much like work!

To create a PDF, simply choose SAVE AS PDF from your Microsoft Word (or other program) toolbar, or PRINT AS PDF. It's that easy!

Cost

I'm going to go out on a limb and say that it shouldn't cost more than about $100 to create an EPUB and Kindle version of a very simple novel. It's when you start adding elements like drop caps and pull quotes, flourishes and images, subtitles and footnotes that the price starts to go up. What you're paying for is technical skill, reliability, and reputation. Your e-book conversion/formatting specialist needs to make sure that your book looks great on every e-book reader.

Some authors prefer to do it themselves using Smashwords' free tool, charmingly called the Meatgrinder, to convert their properly formatted Microsoft Word file and distribute it to online retailers. Smashwords converts the manuscript into EPUB, MOBI, PDF, plain text, and HTML.

The key term in that sentence was "properly formatted." You must use proper Word styles to mark chapter titles, body text, subtitles, pull quotes, etc. for Meatgrinder to work correctly. Creating a Word document that can be successfully uploaded to Smashwords and included in their premium catalog for distribution to retailers can be tricky, and many authors give up.

Luckily, you can find specialists to format your manuscript for Smashwords, or for uploading to IngramSpark, Amazon Kindle Direct Publishing (KDP), and other retailers and aggregators, for less than $100.

If your book requires a complex layout, such as with a cookbook, textbook, or children's book, you're going to need an entirely different kind of specialist—someone who uses a tool like Adobe InDesign—to create a fixed-layout EPUB or KF8 file for Kindle Fire. This person should help you make critical decisions on which format you need. If you think most of your readers own iPads, you should choose EPUB; if you think most own Kindle Fires, choose KF8. This formatter also functions as a designer, and knows, for example, what elements of your book should give the reader the ability to zoom in. Your formatter can embed multimedia correctly and make sure images are sized for maximum impact. This formatter is going to be more expensive and act as an advisor on the design and delivery of your e-book. I rely on the e-Book Architects website (ebookarchitects.com) to keep me up to date on what's happening with fixed-layout e-books, and you should too. Try to learn everything you can before you have a conversation with a professional formatter.

E-book readers and apps

There are too many e-book readers to count these days! Your customer will read your e-book on a dedicated device or tablet computer, or by using an app on their mobile device or computer. For example, the free Kobo app lets iPad/iPhone/iPod Touch users read Kobo books (which the publisher delivers in EPUB format). Apple device owners can also read Amazon Kindle books by downloading Amazon's Kindle app.

By the way, the word Kindle may refer to any of the following:

- the Kindle e-book reader itself (the Kindle Paperwhite or the Kindle Fire)
- the Kindle e-book format (technically, the MOBI or AZW format)
- the Kindle app that your customers can download to their other devices

There are many, many apps, but the most popular are Kindle, Kobo, Ibis Reader (HTML5 format), EPUB Reader for Firefox, Adobe Digital Editions, and Stanza (for Apple).

The most popular e-book readers today are the Apple suite (iPad, iPhone, iPod Touch), Amazon's Kindle and Kindle Fire, Android-powered mobile devices, any web browser (Firefox, IE, Safari, Chrome), Kobo, and Nook.

Online retailers

An online e-book retailer is an online store that sells e-books. The four major online e-book retailers are Amazon (which commands the majority of the market), Kobo (with its wide international reach), Barnes & Noble (Nook), and Apple. There are many, many others, but most of your customers will shop at these four.

You could rather tediously sign up for each retailer's publishing programs, enter your automatic payment information, and upload your e-book to each of these stores separately. But many authors find that using an e-book aggregator is much more efficient, giving us more time to do what we love, which is write.

Even so, many authors begin with Amazon Kindle (KDP) to reach the Amazon store and use an aggregator to distribute everywhere else. All you need is a Kindle-formatted e-book file to upload it yourself.

E-book aggregators

E-book aggregators distribute your book to the various on-line retailers for you and collect a percentage of your sales, paying you at intervals. Many authors feel that the small percentage (15 percent is typical) is a fair trade for the wide distribution, which also includes centralized accounting and payment services.

Once you upload your formatted book to the aggregator, they'll deliver it and it will appear in the online stores. This can take a few days or a few weeks, depending on the retailer's cycle.

Smashwords provides e-book distribution just about everywhere except to Amazon. They offer lots of perks and features, including library distribution, preorders, author self-interviews, gifting, and discount coupons. Smashwords also allows you to upload an EPUB file, if you already have one, via Smashwords Direct. If you can't manage to format your Word file or don't want to buy a book template, you can hire someone to do it for you, as I've said. The maximum file size for Smashwords is 10MB, so it's not a viable option for books with a lot of images. If you have a big e-book with lots of formatting, you might look to a book creation and distribution service or hire one of the pros listed here.

IngramSpark is owned by Ingram (the largest book distribution company in the world), so they have a very wide reach. Most of the other book distributors and aggregators hook in to Ingram's distribution service, so you don't have to use Spark to get distributed by Ingram. However, Spark is the only service that offers both e-book and print book distribution in a single dashboard. Centralizing your activities in one place is a great reason to use IngramSpark. They don't have book creation tools, but if you use one of the professionals here (or Pressbooks, Scrivener, etc.) to create your EPUB to upload to IngramSpark, they will convert your EPUB to Kindle format for you and send it to Amazon.

Other services that distribute/aggregate your print/e-book include Blurb, with their DIY tools (especially Book-Wright), and BookBaby, which does everything for you. I really like those services, but I also value the one-on-one, personal relationship of working with an e-book conversion specialist. I know you'll find a good one here.

Carla King
Self-Pub Boot Camp (http://authorfriendly.com)

Carla King is an adventure travel author and technical journalist who has been self-publishing since 1995. In 2010 she founded Self-Pub Boot Camp, an educational program of books and workshops that teaches authors how to self-publish. In 2015 she created Author Friendly to assist authors who don't want to do it all themselves.

A to Z eBook Conversion – Pondicherry, India +91 413-2237678 http://www.atozebookconversion.com "eBook conversion, distribution & author website design"

Code Mantra –Boston, MA 617-273-8217 http://www.codemantra.com "publishing software/services to manage + deliver digital content across all electronic platforms & devices"

Create My EBooks – http://www.createmyebooks.com "eBook conversion for the Amazon Kindle format"

Digital Divide Data – New York, NY 212-461-3700 info@digitaldividedata.org, http://www.digitaldividedata.com "digital services including eBook conversion, via social impact outsourcing (skilled training/education/employment for individuals in the developing world)"

Digital Pubbing Ebooks – San Francsico, CA sabrina@sabrinaricci.com, http://ebooks.digitalpubbing.com/ "eBook conversion for MOBI & EPUB"

eB Format – info@ebformat.com, http://www.ebformat.com "conversions from most file formats to MOBI, EPUB, PDF, CreateSpace & Smashwords Style Guide specifications"

eBook Adaptations – Akron, OH info@ebookadaptations.com, http://www.ebookadaptations.com "eBook conversions for EPUB & MOBI with quick turnaround"

eBook Architects – Austin, TX 978-225-2758 joshua@firebrandtech.com, http://ebookarchitects.com "eBook conversion, design + creation, including children's books, fixed-layout nonfiction & enhanced eBooks"

eBooks by Design – Northampton, UK http://www.ebooksdesign.com "eBook design + conversion for EPUB & Kindle, also copyediting, proofreading, cover design"

ePubDirect – New York, NY (also in UK) 646-568-7797 conversions@epubdirect.com, http://www.epubdirect.com "eBook conversion, distribution & analytics"

Firsty Group – Newbury, Berkshire, UK 01635 581185
info@firstygroup.com, http://firstygroup.com/ebooks "eBook
conversion + apps"

Formatting an eBook in 10 Easy Steps - Part 1 – by James
Calbraith http://jamescalbraith.com/2012/09/29/formatting-an-
ebook-in-10-easy-steps-part-1

Formatting an eBook in 10 Easy Steps - Part 2 – by James
Calbraith http://jamescalbraith.com/2012/10/04/formatting-an-
ebook-in-10-easy-steps-part-2

Henkel, Guido – bizdev@guidohenkel.com,
http://guidohenkel.com/ebook-services "eBook formatting,
tutorials & cover design"

Make My eBook – http://www.makemyebook.com "eBook
formatting + conversion for all popular formats & devices"

Polgarus Studio – Hobart, Tasmania, AU
contact@polgarusstudio.com, http://www.polgarusstudio.com
"eBook/print formatting + eBook conversion to MOBI, EPUB,
Smashwords, CreateSpace & Lightning Source"

Primedia eLaunch – 469-232-7943 info@primediaelaunch.com,
http://www.primediaelaunch.com "eBook conversion,
distribution & marketing"

Publish Green – Minneapolis, MN 612-436-3954
https://www.publishgreen.com "eBook formatting, conversion,
editing, marketing & distribution with 100% royalty to author"

Stillpoint Digital Press – Mill Valley, CA 415-381-1408
editor@stillpointdigital.com, http://stillpointdigital.com "David
Kudler and team offer eBook conversion, distribution & more"

Print-on-Demand (POD) Printing & Distribution Services

What is book distribution, anyway?

When we talk about book distribution, there are two distinctly different models you need to understand:

- Full-service distribution
- Wholesale distribution

Full-service distributors are companies that provide a variety of services on behalf of traditional or well-established authors and publishers, usually with proven sales records. These services can range from sales representation directly into stores, libraries, and wholesalers to warehousing, marketing, and publicity; order fulfillment; and back-end office functions such as paying royalties and providing collections services. Examples of these companies are Ingram Publisher Services (IPS), Publishers Group West (PGW), Independent Publishers Group (IPG), and Midpoint Trade Books, to name just a few. Some specialize in genre-specific, academic, or religious content. Typically a new indie author or publisher may not have sufficient sales or a proven track record to support a full-service distribution partner.

So let's focus on wholesale distribution, since that's likely to be the model that fits most indie author/publishers. In this model, the author/publisher makes their book available to a distributor like Ingram, which in turn makes that book available to retailers and libraries so they can order it. The wholesaler is not typically promoting or selling that book; the author/publisher is doing that. Since Ingram is the world's largest book wholesaler, it's an advantage for booksellers to be able to purchase books from many different publishers from a single source. It makes no difference whether the stores and libraries are built of brick or live entirely online, or whether they sell print or e-books—it is all called wholesale distribution. Ingram and Baker & Taylor are the two dominant book wholesalers in the United States today.

When it comes to e-books, Ingram is also the dominant distributor. They partner with some seventy online retailers, including the big four (Amazon Kindle, Apple iBooks, Barnes & Noble Nook, and Kobo). For you, the indie author, it can be cumbersome to upload directly to each of these retailers, especially when you consider that every change you eventually might like to make in your book would require separate uploads again to each retailer. That's why a service like IngramSpark is handy as a one-stop solution.

Why booksellers like distributors

With IngramSpark, print on demand (POD) is tied directly to Ingram's global network to make for a seamless and inexpensive way to distribute books. With no inventory on hand, print books are manufactured (POD) or distributed (e-book) as retailers place orders. The publisher is paid for the sale minus the cost of printing (POD only), so there are no up-front inventory costs other than a nominal fee to set up your title in the IngramSpark platform.

The reason distribution is so important for indie author/publishers is that most booksellers and certainly libraries would rather not order a single title directly from the author/

publisher because it's just too time consuming. It's far more convenient for retailers and libraries to order from a single supplier. This is exactly the role that Ingram plays in the industry—it is the central hub of the very complex publishing wheel revolving between publishers and retailers.

When you set up your title in the IngramSpark platform, you provide the completed digital files (PDF for print and EPUB for e-books) along with the metadata (book informa- tion). In this metadata, you will also include your list price and the discount you want to offer to the retailers and libraries that might want to purchase your book. The discount represents the profit that both the bookseller (retailer) and Ingram make transacting the sale. The standard trade discount is 55 percent of the list price, but you can set a range anywhere from 30 percent to 55 percent in IngramSpark. Applying a discount of less than 55 percent may limit the sale of your book to booksellers, but this may be the right choice for some author/publishers depending on their sales strategies.

The same holds true for choosing to make your book "returnable" or "non-returnable." Most booksellers, including chains like Barnes & Noble, will not even consider stocking your book without the returnable option. If you make your POD title non-returnable, it may be special ordered but probably will not be stocked by a bookstore. So I would suggest you make your POD title returnable, just as it would be if it had been traditionally printed. That said, you can always change your price, the discount, and the returnable options later, so do what makes you feel most comfortable now. If your book isn't selling and you are actively marketing, you might want to try adjusting your pricing, the discounts, or the returnable option to see if that helps move the needle.

IngramSpark also encourages publishers to place orders for their own books so they can be shipped to them or drop shipped directly to their customer. This is known as a "publisher direct or drop ship order." In the case of these orders, the author/publisher only pays print and shipping fees (no discount is applied). The beauty of this service is that author/publishers don't need to worry about a print inventory or have books stacked in their garage. They don't have to invest in warehousing, packing supplies, or the actual packing of orders. If you'd like to learn more about IngramSpark, go to https://www.ingramspark.com/.

The benefits of POD tied to distribution

In the old days, booksellers would often consider a title tagged POD as inferior. Today, in the Ingram book-ordering system, POD books look like any other title. So where POD may not factor into the bookstore's buying decision, discounts and the returnable status of your book will. If you make your POD title non-returnable, it may be special ordered but probably will not be stocked by a bookstore. So I would suggest you consider making your POD title returnable, just as it would be if it had been traditionally printed. It's a decision you should weigh carefully, and in my opinion, making your POD returnable should become part of the overall publishing strategy for your book.

Publishers large and small use POD today as part of their overall business plan. They test the demand for a new author or genre using POD and then print traditionally if a title takes off. Publishers of academic or low-demand content use POD for all of their current, front list titles.

POD reduces the publisher's financial risk in bringing a book to market. Before POD, a publisher had to predict what the demand for a particular book would be over time and then print (offset), warehouse, and ship the number of copies they predicted could be sold. Often their predictions were wrong and they ended up with either too many copies of the book or too few. A surprise best seller with too few copies printed created almost as many headaches as a title that was languishing in the warehouse because they had printed too many copies.

Ingram's POD platform now includes the choice of hardcover or paperback as well as a wide variety of trim sizes and options for color interiors. And when you tie POD in directly with distribution, as Ingram has done with IngramSpark, customers get POD service bundled with e-book distribution to 39,000 retail outlets and libraries.

Probably the best thing about POD is that a title can be easily updated or corrected. Imagine getting a great endorsement or review or spotting an embarrassing typo on the first page (it happens). If you had boxes of printed books stacked in your garage, you wouldn't be able to add the review or correct the typo until you had sold through that inventory. With POD, updating content is as easy as uploading new files.

POD is not a viable option for books designed with foldouts, pop-ups, or nonstandard trim sizes or for titles you know will sell more than two thousand copies per year. That figure is going up, though, as the cost of POD is coming down. If you have invested in print inventory and have at least ten titles, it is possible to get Ingram distribution for your books, but the titles have to be approved through an application process. To learn more about how it works, visit Ingram Content Group at http://www.ingramcontent.com/.

Robin Cutler
IngramSpark (www.ingramspark.com)

Robin is senior manager for independent publishing at Ingram Content Group. She was formerly vendor manager with Amazon/CreateSpace, CEO of Summerhouse Press, and assistant director of the University of South Carolina Press. She lives, writes, reads, and works in New Mexico.

360 Digital Books – Madison Heights, MI 866-379-8767 info@360digitalbooks.com, http://wbsusa.com/index.php/digital-books "short run digital printer (25-1,000) offering multiple binding/trim sizes in B/W, 4/C from PDF files, plus warehousing & fulfillment through author/publisher's website"

Aventine Press – Chula Vista, CA 866-246-6142 M-Th 9a-5p, Fri 9a-3p PST http://www.aventinepress.com "full-service POD (paperback/hardcover) + eBooks including cover/interior design/layout, distribution & optional marketing services"

Blurb – San Francisco, CA 888-998-1605 M-F 3a-6p PST http://www.blurb.com "specializes in POD photo + eBooks with free BookWright conversion tool & distribution options"

BookBaby – Portland, OR 877-961-6878 M-F 9a-8p EST book@bookbaby.com, http://www.bookbaby.com "full service publishing + distribution packages; offering cover design, editing, conversion/formatting, ISBN's as well as promotional tools for both print (POD) & eBooks"

BookLocker – Bradenton, FL http://www.booklocker.com "POD (hardcover/paperback in 4/C, B/W) + eBooks with no long-term contracts, quick turnaround & fair rights distribution"

Bookmasters – Ashland, OH 877-312-3520 http://www.bookmasters.com/ "Bookmasters offers offset printing and binding, short-run digital printing & binding, & print-on-demand with high quality, fast turn-around, & competitive pricing"

CreateSpace – https://www.createspace.com "trade paperback + Amazon Kindle uploads, in-house editing, cover design, marketing, ISBN purchasing & distribution"

DiggyPOD – Tecumseh, MI 877-944-7844/734-429-3307 M-F 9a-5p EST https://www.diggypod.com "POD perfect bound printed books (hinge binding, 4/C covers) + online publishing & optional cover design"

eBookIt – Sudbury, MA 855-326-6548/978-440-8364
http://www.ebookit.com/index.php "POD + eBook conversion,
distribution, audiobook production + promotional services; free
content not allowed; no DRM"

Equilibrium Books – Mandurah, WA Australia +61 4 1895 4470
info@equilibriumbooks.com, http://www.equilibriumbooks.com
"softcover print publishing + Kindle eBook formatting,
specializing in genre fiction primarily for, & with distribution
only in, Australia"

FastPencil – Campbell, CA 408-540-7571 support@fastpencil.com,
http://www.fastpencil.com "full-service POD + eBook
publishing packages under their or your imprint, including
editing, cover/interior design, promotion & distribution to all
major retailers"

Foremost Press – Cedarburg, WI 262-377-3180
mary@foremostpress.com, http://www.foremostpress.com
"self-publisher of trade paperbacks with finished size 6"x 9"/108-
500 pages including light editing, typesetting, ISBNs, POD,
optional eBook & distribution"

Ingram Spark – La Vergne, TN
ingramsparksupport@ingramcontent.com,
https://www1.ingramspark.com "publishing platform with fully
integrated print, digital, wholesale + distribution services to
every major/emerging eBook retailer worldwide"

Inkwater Press – Portland, OR 503-968-6777 M-F 8a-5p PST
info@inkwater.com, http://inkwater.com "full-service self-
publisher of paperback/hardcover print (digital POD, offset) +
Kindle eBooks including image scanning, indexing, editorial,
marketing & distribution services"

Lightning Source – La Vergne, TN 615-213-5815
inquiry@lightningsource.com, https://www1.lightningsource.com
"printed books (hardcover + paperback, 4/C) with print-to-order,
print-to-publisher & print-to-warehouse distribution"

Mill City Press – Minneapolis, MN 612-455-2294 info@millcitypress.net, https://www.millcitypress.net "full-service short run digital (1-500) + offset printing (minimum 500); also cover design, editorial, eBook formatting, marketing, distribution/fulfillment & ISBNs"

Self Publishing Inc. – Tuckahoe, NY 800-621-2556 http://www.selfpublishing.com "full service self-publisher for print + eBooks offering editorial, design, ISBNs, coaching, marketing services, plus POD, warehousing/fulfillment, distribution to wholesalers & retailers through their partner divisions"

Volumes – Kitchener, ON Canada 888-571-2665/519-571-1908 sales@volumesdirect.com, http://www.volumesdirect.com "POD packages including cover design, interior formatting, ISBN, e-commerce distribution, tracking & payment of royalties"

Wheatmark – Tucson, AZ 888-934-0888/520-798-0888 9a-5p MST info@wheatmark.com, http://www.wheatmark.com "selective self-publisher offering manuscript evaluation, editorial, design, marketing + distribution (via Ingram) services for POD (hard/softcover) & eBooks"

WingSpan Press – Livermore, CA 866-735-3782 info@wingspanpress.com, http://www.wingspanpress.com "basic packages/à la carte services including ISBNs + distribution for hard/softcover (4/C, B/W) print & eBooks"

POD Printing – (No Distribution Services)

48 Hour Books– Akron, OH 800-231-0521 info@48hrbooks.com, http://www.48hrbooks.com "fast turnaround POD including multiple cover/binding/dust jacket options + ISBN/bar codes for print & eBooks"

Alexanders – Lindon, UT 801-224-8666 M-F 8a-5p MST info@alexanders.com, http://alexanders.com "full-service print + marketing firm offering digital POD (1-2,000) warehousing & fulfillment; also marketing strategies, PR, SEO, analytics, events"

TheBookPatch – Scottsdale, AZ 480-941-8355/480-773-4447 M-F 8a-5p MST info@thebookpatch.com, http://www.thebookpatch.com "paperback books in full range of sizes from PDF files, with free templates + optional cover design, text formatting, file conversion & ISBNs as add-on services"

Snowfall Press – Monument, CO 719-487-1864 support@snowfallpress.com, http://www.snowfallpress.com "network of digital printers, offering POD in perfect binding with multiple trim sizes & fast turnaround"

Virtualbookworm.com Publishing – College Station, TX 877-376-4955 http://www.virtualbookworm.com "printed books (hardcover/paperback in 4/C, B/W) + eBooks; author retains full control over retail price"

Subsidy Publishers

Is there a difference between vanity and subsidy publishing?

Some fee-charging publishers will try to convince you that there is. They'll claim that subsidy publishing is more respectable because subsidy publishers don't publish everything that's submitted to them, or that they provide "quality" editing and design and give their authors personal attention. Others employ a variety of euphemisms intended to suggest that they're only charging you part of the cost of publication: "joint venture," "co-op," "partner," "equity," and "hybrid" are all terms you may encounter.

Don't be fooled. Even if a vanity publisher is selective (and many are), their gatekeeping processes are minimal (since their business model is built on author fees, they can't afford to be too picky). Those "quality" services may contribute to a staggering cost—or not be quality at all, to avoid cutting into their profits. As for the publisher investing its resources alongside yours . . . it's a lot more likely that your money will cover not only the whole cost of publication, but the publisher's overhead and profit as well.

The pitfalls of vanity/subsidy publishing

For projects where the number of books to be printed is small and marketing and profit aren't a concern (for instance, memoirs or genealogies or recipe collections intended for family and friends or to be given as gifts), an honest, straightforward vanity or subsidy publisher can be an acceptable way to go.

It can also be a valid option for writers with niche non-fiction projects where they're able to reach their audiences directly, or for people who can exploit "back of the room" situations—for instance, lecturers who can sell books at their appearances. Again, though, with the many self-publishing options available these days, a vanity publisher is an unduly costly choice.

If you want to establish a career as a writer, however, or if you actually want people you don't know to buy and read your book, vanity/subsidy publishing is a bad idea.

For one thing, as I've noted, the expense can be enormous. In order to ensure their profit, vanity/subsidy publishers charge far more than the actual production cost of a book. For another, it's very difficult for authors to recoup this invest-ment, since vanity/subsidy publishers rarely offer meaningful distribution or marketing. They have no economic incentive to do so, since their principal source of income isn't the sale of books to the public but the sale of services to authors. If you publish through one of these houses, you will probably lose money.

There's also a stigma attached to fee-based publishing. This has eroded over the past few years, thanks to the growth of self-publishing options, but it still exists, and if you try to market your vanity/subsidy-published book, you'll likely run up against it. Reviewers and book bloggers may give you the cold shoulder. Bookstores may refuse to carry your book even if you offer it on consignment or agree to buy back any unsold copies (and if you're with a fee-based publisher that doesn't place its books into wholesale distribution, bookstores may not even be able to special-order it). As for building a writing resume, editors, publishers, and reviewers are unlikely to regard vanity-published books as professional writing credits.

Another important consideration: while there are honest vanity publishers that fulfill contractual promises, there are also many that engage in a wide range of unethical or fraudulent practices, including misrepresenting themselves as traditional publishers, grossly overcharging for their services, failing to fulfill contract obligations, producing shoddy books, providing kickbacks to literary agents who refer manuscripts ... the list goes on.

Vanity publishers in sheep's clothing

As writers become more aware of the pitfalls of vanity/subsidy publishing, many less-than-honest pay-to-publish operations are trying to dodge the vanity label by various sneaky means, such as failing to mention their fees on their websites or shifting their charges to areas other than production and printing. I often hear from writers who are confused because they've been offered a contract by a publisher that describes itself as "traditional" but wants its authors to make some sort of financial commitment in order to be published.

If asked, such publishers vehemently deny that they are vanity/subsidy publishers. After all, they don't accept everyone who submits! And they aren't asking their authors to pay for publishing—just to finance their own editing, or buy a certain number of printed books.

But whether you're paying for book production or for adjunct services, the bottom line is that if you don't hand over the cash, you won't be published. A publisher that turns its authors into customers has little incentive to get books into the hands of readers and is not likely to invest resources in marketing and distribution. Some of the "alternative" charges you may encounter from vanity publishers in disguise:

- **A setup fee or deposit**. Publishers that require a setup fee will tell you that you're not paying to publish—just contributing to the cost of preparing your book for printing or making a "good-faith investment" in your own success. Some publishers promise to refund the fee under certain conditions (usually carefully crafted so they'll almost never be fulfilled). The setup fee may not be large by vanity standards—often just a few hundred dollars—but since such publishers typically use digital technology to produce their books on demand, it likely more than covers the cost of production.

- **A fee for some aspect of the publication process other than printing/binding**. Some publishers ask you to chip in for editing, or for your book's cover art, or for publicity. Real publishers provide these things as part of the publication process, at their expense. These services may cost thousands of dollars, and are often minimal and not of professional quality.

- **Fees for "extra" services over and above the basics of publication**. The publisher may offer you the "opportunity" to pay for expedited editing, or special website placement, or inclusion in book fair catalogs, or enhanced marketing. These services are optional—so the publisher can claim it's not forcing authors to pay to publish—but there's often heavy pressure to buy them, and authors who don't pull out their credit cards are treated like dirt.

- **A claim that your fee is only part of the cost**. The publisher may tell you it will spend as much as or more than it's charging you on your book, or that the additional services it provides—warehousing, distribution, publicity—are worth far more than your "investment." At best, this is an exaggeration; at worst, it's a lie. Since most vanity publishers use digital technology, provide minimal editing and marketing, and access the same wholesale/retail distribution channels employed by self-publishing services, their production and distribution costs are minimal. Most of the time, your fee covers not just the entire expense of publication, but the publisher's overhead and profit as well.

- **A prepurchase requirement.** Some publishers include a clause in their contracts requiring you to buy a specific quantity of finished books—anywhere from a few hundred to several thousand copies, often at a paltry discount. This can be more expensive than straightforward vanity publishing.

- **A presale requirement.** A similar contract clause may require you to presell a certain number of books prior to publication or "guarantee" a minimum number of sales (usually exactly as many as are needed for the publisher to recoup its investment and make a profit). You don't have to buy them yourself, but if you don't deliver the sales, the publishing deal is off. This is a particularly tricky variation on the pay-to-publish scheme, because it allows the publisher to claim that it's not asking you for cash. But it's not an author's job to be a salesperson for his or her own books—that's what the publisher is supposed to do.

- **A sales guarantee.** If your book doesn't sell X number of copies within X amount of time, you must agree to buy the difference. Most authors have an overly optimistic vision of the sales they can achieve and figure they'll never have to pay up, but vanity publishers' substandard (or nonexistent) marketing and distribution ensure that those authors are usually wrong. In an especially sneaky version of this ploy, the publisher pressures authors to buy their own books for resale but doesn't count author purchases toward the guarantee—so authors are snagged twice, once during the honeymoon period (the weeks or months before the first royalty statement arrives), and again at the expiration of the guarantee period.

- **Withheld royalties.** You get no royalty income until the cost of production has been recouped. In this version of vanity publishing, you don't have to actually lay out any cash, but money that should be yours is kept by the publisher, which amounts to the same thing.

- **Pressure to buy your book yourself.** The publisher may not contractually require you to purchase your own book—indeed, it may make a big deal of telling you that you don't have to buy anything. Even so, it will put you under heavy buying pressure—for instance, providing an author guide that extols the financial benefit of buying your own book for resale or bombarding you with special incentives such as extra discounts or contests for the month's top seller. These are all signs of a publisher that relies on its authors as its main customer base, and therefore has little interest in selling books to the public. Unfortunately, if the publisher employs such tactics, you may not find out about them until you've already signed the contract.

- **A variety of other devious tactics.** Some examples from Writer Beware's complaint files: requiring authors to pay for publisher-sponsored conferences, lectures, or "publicity opportunities"; requiring authors to sell ads that are included in the company's books; hawking

company stock to authors, despite the lack of an appropriate license; and requiring authors to hire the publisher's staff to perform various services. The permutations
are endless.

Due Diligence

Writer Beware never recommends that writers use vanity/
subsidy publishers. With all the small presses out there, not
to mention the growing number of self-publishing options,
there's just no reason to pay an arm and a leg to a vanity publisher, even one that won't rip you off.

But if, after all the above, you still want to consider going
this route, take these precautions:

- **Order a couple of the publisher's books, so you can
assess quality**. Does the interior formatting look professional? Are all the pages in order? Is the cover art attractive? Are the books sturdy? Did the order process
go off without a hitch?

- **Research the publisher**. Have there been complaints?
If there are problems, a thorough web search may turn
them up. A good place to check is the Bewares, Recommendations & Background Check forum of the Absolute Write Water Cooler (absolutewrite.com/forums/
forumdisplay.php?22-Bewares-Recommendations-
amp-Background-Check). And you can always contact
Writer Beware (beware@sfwa.org).

- **Contact writers who've used the publisher's services**.
Are they happy with the quality of the books? Did they
receive the services they paid for? Do buyers have any
trouble getting hold of the books? Have there been any
broken promises?

- **Have a knowledgeable person look over the contract.** Vanity publishers' contracts, which usually aren't negotiable, can include unpleasant clauses and hidden fees. (Note: if you use a lawyer, be sure to find one who has experience with publishing contracts.)

- **Make sure the publisher distributes through a minimum of one wholesaler, such as Ingram.** That way, the books will be available online, and people can at least special-order them from bookstores.

- **Don't take the publisher's promises at face value.** If the publisher says it has an arrangement with a distributor, make sure it is telling the truth. If there are marketing promises, ask for sample marketing materials. Never rely on verbal promises that aren't included in the contract.

Warning Signs

When approaching vanity/subsidy publishers, use extreme caution. And if you encounter any of the following, consider walking away:

- **A vanity/subsidy publisher that poses as a real publisher.** Many vanity publishers don't mention their fees on their websites or in their publicity materials; authors find out that money is due only after signing up. The idea is to entice authors who wouldn't normally submit to a fee-charging publisher and may find an actual publication offer hard to refuse, fee or not. But a publisher that doesn't present itself honestly at the outset will probably not treat you honestly in the long run.

- **Terms like "co-op," "joint venture," "partner," "hybrid," or any other phrase that suggests the publisher will**

be matching your investment with its own. A vanity/subsidy publisher's profit comes from the fees its authors pay, not from book sales. The publisher, therefore, has a powerful incentive to publish as cheaply as possible.

- **A claim to share costs.** See above.

- **A referral from a literary agency or freelance editor.** Reputable literary agents and freelance editors do not work with fee-based publishers. Period. Those who do are either receiving a kickback, own the publisher themselves (possibly under another name), or are incompetent. Whatever the reason, it's bad news for you.

- **A promise (stated or implied) of a profit.** Some vanity/subsidy publishers provide nicely formatted sample sales projections showing how you can make thousands of dollars by selling X number of books. In fact, for the reasons outlined above, it's extremely difficult just to break even on a vanity-published book. An ethical vanity/subsidy publisher won't promise profits; in fact, it will warn you at the outset that vanity-published books rarely recoup authors' investments.

- **Refusal of reasonable requests for information.** You're paying for the service, so it's your right to have all your questions answered fully, honestly, and promptly. If a vanity/subsidy publisher refuses to provide you with references or hedges about details such as production schedules, marketing, and so on, be suspicious.

- **Refusal to provide a firm price.** The exact amount you are expected to pay should be stated at the outset (and specified in the contract), including any extras such as warehousing or marketing. Never deal with a vanity publisher that is vague about money—for instance, a publisher that tells you the final price can't be quoted until the books are printed (in which case you might wind up paying a substantial "differential"), or that warehousing will be charged "at the publisher's discretion" (in which case you could be hit with enormous additional fees).

- **Verbal promises that aren't duplicated in the contract.** Some dishonest vanity/subsidy publishers try to soothe nervous writers by promising various perks, such as a full or partial reimbursement of their costs if the book doesn't sell out within a specified time. However, if such promises aren't included in the contract, you'll have little recourse if they aren't fulfilled (which is exactly why unethical publishers don't write them down). If the publisher is willing to promise something, it should also be willing to include it in the contract.

- **Extravagant praise and/or promises.** This is nothing more than a sales tactic. Even if it's selective, a vanity/subsidy publisher has little reason to care how good your work is, since you're paying to publish it. And if a vanity/subsidy publisher says it can get you on national talk shows, or tells you it will organize speaking tours or national book signing campaigns, be seriously skeptical. Even the big publishing houses don't provide these perks for most of their authors.

- **A double standard.** Dishonest vanity/subsidy publishers sometimes entice writers by saying they can't risk a regular contract for a brand-new author but would be willing to split the costs of publication. Or they may say that they've used up their traditional publishing budget for the year but would be glad to work on a "co-op" basis. Or they may promise to publish your second book without charge if the first book does well. In all these cases, the implication is that the publisher is primarily a "real" publisher and is offering the fee-based contract as a special circumstance. But though some fee-based publishers do occasionally offer non-fee contracts, most are fee-charging only, and imply that they're not solely to acquire customers.

- **Pressure.** A disreputable vanity/subsidy publisher wants to hook you quickly, before you change your mind. Beware, therefore, if a publisher tells you that its offer is "limited-time only," or that circumstances require you to "act immediately." Like the permanent going-out-of-business sale, this is just another marketing ploy.

Victoria Strauss
Writer Beware
(www.sfwa.org/other-resources/for-authors/writer-beware)

Victoria is co-founder, with Ann Crispin, of Writer Beware, a publishing industry watchdog group sponsored by the Science Fiction and Fantasy Writers of America (SFWA) that provides information and warnings about the many scams and schemes that threaten writers. She maintains the popular Writer Beware website and blog (www.accrispin.blogspot.com), for which she won an Independent Book Blogger Award in 2012. She was honored with the SFWA Service Award in 2009 and is the author of nine novels.

Ardith – London, ON Canada 877-288-0114 9a-5p EST
info@ardith.ca, http://www.ardith.ca "full service including
editing, design, marketing, publicity, distribution & printing
services to US & Canada"

Aventine Press – Chula Vista, CA 866-246-6142 M-Th 9a-5p, F 9a-3p
PST http://www.aventinepress.com "packages include cover/
interior templates, ISBN/bar codes & POD, with custom options
available"

Beaver's Pond Press – Edina, MN 952-829-8818
info@beaverspondpress.com, http://www.beaverspondpress.com
"small subsidy publisher also offering mentoring/consulting
on all aspects of prepress preparation + post-press marketing
strategies"

Bookstand Publishing – Morgan Hill, CA 866-793-9365/408-852-
1832 M-F 8:30a-5:30p PST support@bookstandpublishing.com,
http://www.bookstandpublishing.com "multiple packages
including POD, distribution & ISBN/bar codes"

Creation House – Lake Mary, FL 800-599-5750/407-333-0600 x3621
creationhouse@charismamedia.com, http://creationhouse.com
"co-publishing services for Christian-themed works"

CrossBooks – Nashville, TN 866-768-9010
http://www.crossbooks.com "full-range publishing services for
Christian books"

Dog Ear Publishing – Indianapolis, IN 888-568-8411 9a-5p EST
help-me@dogearpublishing.net,
http://www.dogearpublishing.net "full service including covers
(hard/soft) + interior layout, editorial, marketing, distribution,
ISBN/bar codes, POD & eBooks"

Dragon Pencil – Savannah, GA 888-497-6831
admin@dragonpencil.com, http://www.dragonpencil.com "full
service POD for children's print, apps & eBooks"

E-BookTime – Montgomery, AL 877-613-2665
publishing@e-booktime.com, http://www.e-booktime.com
"eBooks + paper & hardcover print books including ISBNs"

Epigraph Publishing Service – Rhinebeck, NY 845-876-4861
http://www.epigraphps.com "full service including design,
editorial, marketing, distribution, eBook conversion & POD"

First Choice Books – Victoria, BC Canada 800-957-0561/250-
383-6353 M-F 8a-4:30 PST info@firstchoicebooks.ca,
http://firstchoicebooks.ca "full service for print + eBooks
including design, editing, marketing & ISBN/bar codes"

Foremost Press – Cedarburg, WI 262-377-3180
mary@foremostpress.com, http://www.foremostpress.com
"self-publisher of trade paperbacks with finished size 6"x 9"/108-
500 pages including light editing, typesetting, ISBNs, POD,
optional eBook & distribution"

Goose River Press – Waldoboro, ME 207-832-6665
gooseriverpress@roadrunner.com,
http://www.gooseriverpress.com "full service including
copyediting, production, ISBN/bar codes, distribution +
promotion for POD & eBook"

Inkwater Press – Portland, OR 503-968-6777 M-F 8a-5p PST
info@inkwater.com, http://inkwater.com "full service self-
publisher of paperback/hardcover print (digital POD, offset) +
Kindle eBooks including image scanning, indexing, editorial,
marketing & distribution services"

Innovo Publishing – Collierville, TN 888-546-2111
info@innovopublishing.com, http://www.innovopublishing.com
"full service Christian traditional, independent + co-publishing
for print, audio & eBooks"

JADA Press – Atlanta, GA 904-226-8876 M-F 10a-5p EST
jadapress@aol.com, http://www.jadapress.com "cover
design, copyediting, formatting, ISBNs + distribution for POD
paperbacks"

Just Self-Publish! – Newtown, PA 888-737-4770
info@justselfpublish.com, http://www.justselfpublish.com
"specializing in children's picture books (hard/softcover) for
print only"

Mill City Press, Inc. – Minneapolis, MN 888-645-5248/612-455-2294 info@millcitypress.net, https://www.millcitypress.net "full service including design, formatting, editorial, ISBN, marketing + distribution for POD & eBooks"

Morgan James Publishing – New York, NY 212-655-5470 http://morganjamespublishing.com "specializing in POD & eBooks aimed at entrepreneurs"

Morris Publishing – Kearney, NE 800-650-7888 http://www.morrispublishing.com "DIY (soft/hardcover) POD, offering limited cover design, ISBNs + printed promo materials, including a division that specializes in cookbooks"

New Book Publishing – Apopka, FL 877-311-5100 http://www.newbookpublishing.com "Christian self-publisher offering design, editing, marketing/publicity + ISBNs for print & eBooks"

Professional Press – Chapel Hill, NC 800-277-8960/919-942-8020 http://www.profpress.com "soft/hardcover POD including manuscript critique, editorial, design, marketing & promotion"

PublishNext – 206-922-0418 http://publishnext.com/ "design, distribution, editing, imprints, registration, marketing, & printing services"

Short Fuse Publishing – shortfuse@fuseliterary.com, http://www.fuseliterary.com/short-fuse/ "a digital-first provider of groundbreaking fiction & nonfiction across many genres"

UBuildABook – Camarillo, CA 855-828-4532/805-383-7272 M-F 8a-5p PST info@ubuildabook.com, http://www.ubuildabook.com "hard/softcover (B/W, 4/C) printing + POD in standard/custom sizes, using their software or yours, including custom cover options"

Virtualbookworm.com Publishing – College Station, TX 877-376-4955/979-693-1020 http://www.virtualbookworm.com "cover/ interior design, distribution, marketing + website design for authors of POD & eBooks that meet their selective criteria"

Volumes – Kitchener, ON Canada 888-571-2665/519-571-1908
sales@volumesdirect.com, http://www.volumesdirect.com
"POD packages including cover design, interior formatting,
ISBNs, e-commerce distribution, tracking & payment of
royalties"

Wasteland Press – Shelbyville, KY 502-437-
0860 webmaster@wastelandpress.com,
http://www.wastelandpress.net "print (hard/softcover in
B/W, 4/C) + eBook packages including covers, ISBN/bar codes,
marketing & distribution"

Wheatmark – Tucson, AZ 888-934-0888/520-798-0888 9a-5p MST
info@wheatmark.com, http://www.wheatmark.com "editorial,
design, marketing + distribution for POD (hard/softcover) &
eBooks"

WingSpan Press – Livermore, CA 866-735-3782
info@wingspanpress.com, http://www.wingspanpress.com
"basic packages + à la carte services including ISBNs +
distribution for hard/softcover (B/W, 4/C) print & eBooks"

Xulon Press – Maitland, FL 866-381-2665/407-339-4217 M-F 8:30a-
5p EST http://www.xulonpress.com "Christian self-publisher
offering editorial, ISBNs, marketing + distribution for paperback
& eBooks"

Yorkshire Publishing – Tulsa, OK 800-651-4959/918-394-2665
http://yorkshirepublishing.com "full service subsidy, author-
assisted + co-publisher offering cover design, editorial,
formatting/layout, ISBNs, marketing & distribution"

Short Run Printers

Short run printers for indie authors

Can you imagine how thrilled you'd be if every book you printed got bought, you (and the characters you wrote about) became famous fast, and you were suddenly wallowing in big bucks?

Smile! That new sun is starting to shine for self-publishers.

That's because the days of begging to be in print are over, as are the days of garages bulging with unsold boxes of books. No longer must self-publishers buy runs of books by the thousands to make the price of each book low enough to at least hint that you might sell it at a profit.

A pair of miracles flipped our destiny upside down in the past fifteen years. One was the emergence of accessible presses that could list and sell our books almost instantly—publishers like CreateSpace, Kindle, Nook, Smashwords, Lulu, Blurb, Scribd, and iBooks. They invited us in and only printed our books when people bought them! (Why hadn't we thought of that?)

The second miracle is the short run print shops, with their ever-improving digital presses able to change course and quantities in moments. At a decent price they provide the tools and capacity to print books in the batches we want (from 1 to 500) that are spotless, ready in minutes, on the paper we choose, colored as we wish, and with shimmering artwork that begs to be viewed.

How should we take advantage of these miraculous advances?

Let's focus on the short run book printers first—how can we find, choose, and extract the benefits they can provide us?

Short run book printers come in two forms. Some are the publishers I mentioned above, such as CreateSpace. You can submit your book to them in their format, price it, and let them sell it. They keep 65 percent of the income in exchange for setting up the marketing and accounting and selling it through their online venue. Because they print on demand, they never have a pile of books sitting around.

If you want to sell the books yourself (or through other vendors), you can keep your own pile far smaller by using CreateSpace's sell-back program, where you order copies of your book from them, which they will print and mail to you for a few bucks apiece. You buy what you need or what you know you can sell—anything from a few copies to many boxes—and keep a controllable surplus on hand. That's a boon for self-publishers who want to start out slowly or who have a limited, targeted (i.e., niche) market, or who want to replenish their dwindling stock with just enough books for the last straggling buyers. Ingram's Lightning Source provides the same quick service for bookstores or other commercial outlets.

The digital printing revolution

What bedeviled self- or small-quantity publishers before the 21st century was the pace and complexity of offset printing. In offset printing, photographic "plates" bearing the image of the page are used to transfer the ink first to rubber sheets or rollers and then to the paper. What that meant to me when I first published 3,000 copies of my book in 1983 was that I had to wait several weeks plus six more days for my plates to reach the press—and if anything was amiss, another thirteen days (and maybe another thirteen days after that) until I got it right!

The emergence of office printers suggested a glint of hope for those who wanted only a limited quantity of quality books with bright, fetching covers—books as good as offset could produce but many times faster. It took years more until the digital technology picked up the speed and improved the quality, but now it's here—digital techniques that print high-quality digital images and text directly from a computer onto paper. For self-publishers, that was a true revolution.

Every page you print now can be different because printing plates aren't required. It's far less expensive too, with affordable jobs ranging from one page to thousands. At last, small publishers could afford small quantities of printed materials how and when they wanted them. So when quality digital publishing emerged, got fast, and looked good, the short run potential put small publishers on competitive footing with the major publishing houses. That meant that almost anybody who could write a publishable book could see it in print and expect to turn a decent profit after printing costs.

Finding a short run print shop

How do you find and choose a good short run print shop? Find examples of quality books similar to those you want to publish. Check the acknowledgments and front matter, or even ask the author (if you can) who designed their book, or the cover, or whatever it is you admire about the book. If you like the way the book is printed, get in touch with the printer and ask if they would be interested in giving you a bid for your book. That's not new. I've spent almost 50 years in writing and publishing asking just those kinds of questions.

Open publishing

Some years ago I was running a workshop when a lady came up to me and said, "I've got twenty-two kids' books that I wrote and illustrated, but nobody wants to publish them. I'm making Kinko's rich! What should I do?" She handed me one of them, called *Louie Has Warts!* "This is the newest. If kids are curious about something, I write about it. The books all look pretty much alike—and they are very funny," she said.

She was right. It was first rate, the artwork looked professional, and it was *very* funny.

"I can sell twice as many as I can make," she said, "but I'm exhausted with all the copying, folding, stapling, and schlepping."

I asked her if she sold many copies, and she said about fifty a week, but explained that she could sell hundreds of each book within a twenty-mile radius. Since she wrote a new book every month, "open publishing" would soon put her on the kids' book publishing map!

It used to be that you had two choices to get your book printed and sold: 1) you could finance it all yourself, putting up $2,500 or more to get your words decently prepped for sale, plus spending many months of high-risk, hard-marketing time; or 2) you could write a book proposal (or mail a written manuscript to a dozen publishers, though they preferred to be "courted" one at a time, and many would not even accept unsolicited manuscripts) and either not get a go-ahead and not write the book or get the nod, write the book, and then have it rejected—a gantlet of a thousand to fifteen hundred applicants for each unagented book seeing the light.

Today the stranglehold of the presses is over. Open publishing is a much faster and easier way to produce any book you want. It's called "open" publishing because about a decade back a handful of publishers opened the door for anybody to write, proof, style, and submit their book (accompanied by a ready-to-use cover), and unless the book was too bizarre, dirty, linguistically unfathomable, or treasonous, they would create a digital or paperback version and put it up for sale to you, your mate, or your mother, or anybody who was willing to pay the price (set by you).

That means if you write a book and save it in a ready-to-print file, there are more than seven legitimate publishers who will eagerly convert that file into a professional-looking book. From the moment you submit the text file, a cover file, provide enough information to tell a potential buyer what the book says or promises, and approve the proof of how the book will look in print, if your book is an e-book it can be posted for sale in a few minutes. If it's a bound book (probably paperback, not hardcover), it will take a day or two.

How much will publishing a short run book cost you out of pocket? Absolutely nothing. (Or a pittance: $5 to $20 in postage for bound proofs before the book is released; e-books are totally free.) That assumes you have basic software (like Microsoft Word), type your own manuscript, lay out the contents, insert the artwork, create the cover (front only for e-books, front, spine, and back for paperbacks), and provide an ISBN number (many of the publishers supply one for each version of your book). If you pay others for any of the publishing processes—editors, cover designers, proofreaders (all recommended), promoters, and so on, your ante goes up.

The open publishers are respected, knowledgeable firms that produce books identical to those you see in the bookstore or on the Internet. They create the books, promote them (sort of), provide a selling mechanism, print them a day or two after they are ordered (or let the buyer immediately tap into the e-book's download link), and collect the money. Then they give you from 35 percent to about 75 percent of the book's sale price. No inky hands, no hauling boxes to the street corner, no stocking, no shipping. You get paid at the end of each month. Your magic words can be purchased from anywhere almost any time, mostly by computer.

Where else might people buy your book? Directly from those publishers, from you, online, at brick-and-mortar bookstores, from display tables or at the back of the room after one of your seminars, through association catalogs, and so on.

You are just one finished, submitted manuscript away from being a paid author! And you needn't learn more than a modicum about publishing, spend a dime creating the pages, squander years trying to get big-city houses to accept your manuscript, or set up tedious and expensive self-publishing structures. You really can be the first in print in your family or on your block. And now it can be done in a week. The doors (better, the presses) are finally wide open!

Gordon Burgett

Gordon Burgett's Website (www.gordonburgett.com)

Burgett has published more than 1,700 articles and 46 books and offered more than 2,000 professional paid presentations. During that time he has appeared extensively on radio and TV as a guest author and publishing specialist. Burgett is a long-standing member of the National Speakers Association, the American Society of Journalists and Authors, and the Independent Book Publishers Association. He currently speaks nationwide at conventions, retreats, associations, and colleges or universities offering keynotes, breakout sessions, and workshops about three topics: "How to Publish Your Own Book in 30 Days or Less," "Niche Publishing," and "How to Sell 75% of Almost Everything You Write." Gordon's most recently published book is *How to Get Your Book Published Free in Minutes and Marketed Worldwide in Days* (www.mybookpublishedinminutes.com).

Glossary of Printing and Graphic Terms –
http://www.printindustry.com/Glossary.aspx

A&A Printing – Tampa, FL 813-886-0065 M-F 8a-5p EST
billy@printshopcentral.com, http://www.printshopcentral.com
"indie author–friendly, short run digital (minimum 50) + offset
(minimum 500) printing in 4/C, B/W with multiple binding
options; also cover design & bar code/ISBNs"

Adibooks – Lowell, MA 978-458-2345 adibooks1@adibooks.com,
http://www.adibooks.com "indie author–friendly division of
King Printing offers short runs (minimum 100) from print-ready
PDF files in multiple sizes with interior/text pages digitally
printed & both hard/softcovers offset printed"

Angel Printing – Oceanside, CA 888-769-2643/760-967-0492
info@angelprint.com, http://www.angelprint.com "indie
author–friendly, offering short run digital + offset printing (100–
1,500) in multiple binding options; also editorial services"

Bang Printing – Brainerd, MN 800-328-0450 (also Valencia, CA 800-
323-3582) info@bangprinting.com, www.bangprinting.com
"short run digital (minimum 20+) + offset printing (500-
1,000,000) in multiple binding options; also eBook conversion &
fulfillment services"

Blitzprint – Calgary, AB Canada 866-479-3248/403-253-5151
books@blitzprint.com, http://blitzprint.com "full service digital
short run printing (minimum 50) + design, formatting, editorial
& indexing services"

Book1One – Rochester, NY 585-458-2101 helpdesk@book1one.com,
http://www.book1one.com "full service digital short run
printing (1-2,000) in 4/C, B/W with multiple binding options
from print-ready PDF files"

BookLogix – Alpharetta, GA 470-239-8547 sales@booklogix.com,
https://www.booklogix.com "indie author–friendly, offering
short run digital printing (25-3,000) in 4/C, B/W with multiple
sizes/binding options; also editorial, eBook conversion, ISBN/bar
codes, cover design & formatting services"

Bookmasters – Ashland, OH 877-312-3520
http://www.bookmasters.com/ "Bookmasters offers offset printing and binding, short-run digital printing & binding, & print-on-demand with high quality, fast turn-around, & competitive pricing"

BookPrinting.com – Minneapolis, MN 612-455-4301
https://bookprinting.com "full service short run offset printing (300–10,000+) in 4/C, B/W with multiple sizes/binding options + design, editing, marketing, distribution, fulfillment & eBook conversion services"

Brandt Doubleday – Davenport, IA 800-393-2399 M-F 8a-4:30p CST
http://www.brandtdoubleday.com "short run digital printing (minimum 50) in 4/C, B/W with multiple binding options"

CMYK Graphix – Austin, TX 800-698-2071/512-377-6855
http://www.cmykgraphix.com "indie author–friendly, offering short run digital + offset printing (100-10,000) in 4/C, B/W with multiple sizes, saddle stitched or perfect bound"

C-M Books – Ann Arbor, MI 888-295-7244/734-663-8554 8a-5p EST
http://www.cushing-malloy.com "indie author–friendly, offering short run digital (25-199) + offset printing (minimum 200) in 4/C, B/W with multiple sizes/binding options; also eBook conversion & fulfillment services"

Colorwise Commercial Printing – Rosewell, GA 888-664-8166
bestbook@colorwise.com, http://www.bestbookprinting.com "indie author–friendly, offering short run digital + offset printing (1-10,000) hybrid option (digital pages/offset covers) in 4/C, B/W with multiple sizes & binding options"

The Country Press, Inc. – Lakeville, MA 888-343-2227
info@countrypressinc.com, www.countrypressprinting.com "indie author–friendly, offering short run digital (11-5,000) printing in multiple sizes with perfect (softcover) or saddle stitch binding"

Data Reproductions Corporation – Auburn Hills, MI 248-371-3700
solko@datarepro.com, www.datarepro.com "short run digital

(1-500) + offset printing (minimum 500) in 4/C, B/W with multiple sizes & binding options"

Digital Publishing of Florida, Inc. – Oldsmar, FL 813-788-3735 M-F 8a-5p EST jill@digitaldata-corp.com, http://www.digitaldata-corp.com "full service short run digital printing (25–2,000) in 4/C, B/W with multiple sizes/binding options + cover design, formatting & ISBN/bar codes"

EC Printing – Eau Claire, WI 888-832-1135/715-832-1135 books@ecprinting.com, http://www.ecprinting.com "indie author–friendly, offering short run digital (minimum 100) + offset printing (minimum 1,000) in 4/C, B/W"

Edwards Brothers Malloy – Ann Arbor, MI 800-722-3231/734-769-1000 http://www.edwardsbrothersmalloy.com "full service short run digital (1-500) + offset printing (minimum 500) in 4/C, B/W with multiple sizes/binding options; also eBook conversion, distribution & fulfillment services"

Friesens – Altona, MB Canada 204-324-6401 book_info@friesens.com, http://www.friesens.com "full service short run digital printing (250-1,000) for self-publishing authors + fulfillment services"

Gasch Printing – Odenton, MD 301-362-0700 info@gaschprinting.com, http://www.gaschprinting.com "indie author–friendly, offering short run digital printing (1-2,500) in 4/C, B/W with multiple sizes & binding options"

Gorham Printing – Centralia, WA 800-837-0970/360-623-1323 info@gorhamprinting.com, http://www.gorhamprinting.com "full service, offering short run digital + offset printing (25-2,000) in 4/C, B/W with multiple sizes/binding options; also cover design, formatting & eBook conversion services"

Greenerprinter – Berkeley, CA 800-655-5833/510-647-2500 M-F 8:30a-5:30p PST csr@greenerprinter.com, http://www.greenerprinter.com "indie author–friendly printer offering short run digital (1-250) + offset (minimum 250) perfect bound books in 4/C, B/W & multiple sizes as well as fulfillment services"

The H&H Group – Lancaster, PA 866-338-7569 info@thehandhgroup.com, http://thehandhgroup.com "full service short run digital (1-750) + offset printing (minimum 750) in 4/C, B/W with multiple sizes/binding options; also design, editing & fulfillment services"

Litho Press – San Antonio, TX 210-333-1711 mmayfield@lithopress.net, http://www.lithopress.net "short run digital (20-500) + offset printing (500-20,000) in 4/C, B/W with multiple sizes & binding options"

Maple Press – York, PA 978-858-0900 http://www.maplepress.com "short run digital (25-2,000) + offset printing (250-200,000) in 2/C, B/W with multiple sizes/binding options; also fulfillment & distribution services"

Marquis Book – Montmagny, QC Canada 855-566-1937 http://www.marquisbook.com/us/products/marquis-printing-services "digital + offset printer offering a wide range of custom solutions from text only to art-book quality in multiple sizes/ bindings to suit your project & budget, with no minimum; from print-ready PDF files only"

Mennonite Press, Inc. – Newton, KS 800-536-4686/316-283-4680 M-F 8a-12p, 1-5p CST http://www.mennonitepress.com "indie author–friendly, offering short run digital (maximum 500) + offset printing (minimum 500) in 4/C, B/W with multiple binding options"

Mill City Press – Minneapolis, MN 612-455-2294 info@millcitypress.net, https://www.millcitypress.net "full service short run digital (1-500) + offset printing (minimum 500); also cover design, editorial, eBook formatting, marketing, distribution/fulfillment & ISBNs"

Morgan Printing – Austin, TX 512-454-6874 terry. sherrell@1touchpoint.com, http://www.morganprinting.org "short run digital (1-1,200) + offset printing (600-50,000) in 4/C,

B/W with multiple sizes/binding options; also cover designs & page layout services"

Printmediabooks.com – Garden Grove, CA 714-903-2500 M-F 9a-6p PST books@printmediabooks.com, http://www.printmediabooks.com "short run digital (100-1,000) + offset printing (minimum 1,000); also cover design, book layout & fulfillment services"

Publishers' Graphics – Carol Stream, IL 888-404-3769 contactpg@pubgraphics.com, http://www.pubgraphics.com "indie author–friendly, offering short run digital (1-1,000) + offset printing (1,000-500,000) in 4/C, B/W with multiple sizes & binding options"

Sentinel Printing Co. – St. Cloud, MN 800-450-6434/320-251-6434 M-F 8a-5p CST http://www.sentinelprinting.com "short run digital (minimum 25) + offset printing (minimum 500) in multiple sizes/binding options"

Sheridan Books – Chelsea, MI 734-475-9145 http://www.sheridan.com "short run digital (1-300) + offset printing (300-25,000) in 4/C, B/W with multiple sizes/binding options & distribution services"

Thomson-Shore – Dexter, MI 734-426-3939 http://www.thomsonshore.com "short run digital (1-200) + offset printing (200-100,000) in 4/C, B/W with multiple sizes/binding options; also eBook conversion, fulfillment & distribution services"

Tobu Print Group – Glendale, CA 818-550-0819 marcia@tobuprintgroup.com, http://www.tobuprintgroup.com "printer of high-quality design books, offering short run offset printing (minimum 1,000) & fulfillment services"

Book Production Software

What software do you need to produce your book?

The answer to this question is another question: What kind of author are you, and how complex do you need your software to be?

Many authors who are new to self-publishing say, "All I have is Microsoft Word (or Scrivener, or Pages, or some other word processor). I love what it does, so I will just upload my manuscript and let CreateSpace, Lulu, Kindle Direct Publishing, Smashwords, and/or Draft2Digital make the conversion for me."

Other authors are willing to pay several thousand dollars for a book shepherd or vanity press to convert the Word document for them.

Traditional publishers will normally produce your book using Adobe InDesign. That's the professional choice.

So what do you need? First you have to answer one more question.

Do you really want to give up control of your book design?

In the three options mentioned above, that's what you have done. You've allowed someone else to produce your book outside your control. You can certainly make comments on the proof and get some changes made, but you will quickly discover that real control of the book design is held by the on-demand distributors or the publishers.

The problem is that good book design requires a great deal of knowledge and skill. You need to understand typography, readability, font design, page layout, printing technology, photo manipulation, graphic production, and much more. If you don't understand these things, in most cases you'll have no idea what is even possible.

Can you produce a professionally designed book using Microsoft Word?

Not really. But you can come very close if you purchase a professionally designed Microsoft Word template. The best are well-designed, include the necessary fonts, and guide you through the process. Book Design Templates (http://www.bookdesigntemplates.com/) has an excellent reputation, for example.

This process will work well for novels and simple nonfiction. But all word processors are very limited typographically. Can you get a book published that will look professional to the average reader? Certainly. Does it make book production an affordable line item in an author's budget? Probably. Is there a large need for this type of product? Definitely. But it is not your best choice in many cases.

What do you need before you start production?

- **A fully edited manuscript.** It not only needs to be edited, but thoroughly copyedited and, for print books, proofread. Any changes made to the book after production starts will cost you time, at the very least, and often quite a bit of money.

- **A cover.** It must be designed so you can use it for the various print sizes at the correct resolution and colors. It also must be easily converted to a ratio that works for the various e-book distributors. They all have different preferred ratios. The cover design must also work well as a thumbnail.

- **Professional graphics for the illustrations.** In most cases this will be full-cover images that can be easily used as web graphics.

- **Descriptions, blurbs, back cover copy, keywords, metadata, etc.** They are required at upload and provide the main marketing information needed to sell your book.

Many of these materials require Adobe Photoshop, and Adobe Illustrator is also a good idea. For print, Microsoft Word has very limited capabilities. You need to be extremely careful throughout any book production workflow if you are using Microsoft Word. Scrivener is a good writing tool, and some swear by its e-book export capabilities. But exporting files from it to Microsoft Word is a treacherous process . And once you get to Word, you still need to go through the editing and proofreading process. All of this brings us to the only real choice for professional book production.

Adobe InDesign is the professional book designers' choice

This is the software designed to import your Microsoft Word document, format it very fast at a quality level impossible for any word processor, add your graphics at whatever quality/resolution/formats are required, make a professional table of contents, add an index, and then directly export the PDFs, EPUBs, and Kindle documents you need for 21st-century publishing.

InDesign makes the best-quality PDFs for print in the industry. It is also the only real choice if you need excellent fixed-layout e-books like EPUB FXL and Kindle Textbook (or children's book, graphic novel, and the like). Its EPUBs are the best quality you can get.

But it's so expensive and hard to use!

Good tools are always expensive. They always require knowledge and practice to attain the skill levels required.

Professional carpenters do not buy the cheapest tools available. They need something that will last, not break down in the middle of a job, and work with a precision that amazes and befuddles DIY remodelers. The same is true of professional chefs and their knives, pots, and pans. Adobe InDesign is the tool of choice for that level of book production. It includes all the capabilities you will ever need, no matter how complex your books become. It will become your trusted tool in hand, like the well-worn sword of a tested warrior.

Special capabilities

- The interface is completely customizable with custom keyboard shortcuts available for any command and custom workspaces for each type of book you produce.

- It allows you to tear type apart to make the titles on your book covers.

- It can handle any type of file Adobe Photoshop can produce.

- It can add any hyperlinks you need, quickly, with keyboard shortcuts.

- It can produce animations and add them to your e-books.

- It can insert video and sound in your books.

- It can add fully hyperlinked indices (again, produced with keyboard shortcuts) and tables of contents.

Basically it is the perfect tool for those of us who produce many books. Because I also write several books a year, I only produce a dozen or so per year now. But when I finish a book, the actual production takes a day or two, and the quality is far better than that of typical self-publishing efforts.

More than that, I can make versions to sell directly from my website through companies like Gumroad. I can produce what the iBooks Store prefers; make an edition designed within Kobo's more limited capabilities, or the Nook's even *more* limited capabilities; make a downloadable, interactive PDF; and make special editions, leader/teacher versions, or anything else I might need to produce, market, and sell a book in this digital age.

This level of production is what InDesign has been crafted to produce. Microsoft Word and Scrivener are superb writing tools. But a word processor is a poor choice for book production.

So what are my real choices?

There are several different routes you can take, depending upon what you need.

Simple fiction e-books

Here is where Microsoft Word and Scrivener are the software of choice. Many fiction authors only produce Amazon Kindle versions of their books. They might add Smashwords and/ or Draft2Digital, but the books are simple. These authors are greatly limited by their low budgets, which are strained by simply getting editing and cover designs.

Simple nonfiction and fiction e-books with print versions

For many authors, most of their sales come from print copies available at their seminars and presentations. Here Microsoft Word production carries a fairly strong quality deduction, but for nonprofits and the like the appearance of good stewardship helps your sales. Production using Word may still be your best option.

Complex nonfiction, illustrated books, and illustrated textbooks

Here you are quickly entering Adobe InDesign country. If you are using complex tables, lists, graphics with callouts, multiple head/subhead levels, interactive e-books, and all the rest, InDesign is probably your best choice. In fact, it is almost certainly your best choice.

Can you produce this type of book using Word? Yes, it is possible. But the likelihood is that you will regret it sooner, rather than later. The production problems with complex formatting in Word are the stuff of legendary horrors for professional designers and producers of books.

If your author platform requires quality, don't skimp on your software.

You can get a license for Adobe InDesign very inexpensively. You do need the Creative Cloud (CC) version for the EPUB export capabilities. Older versions of Photoshop are cheap on eBay, and they will work fine for you back to CS4. The CC versions are not required.

However, if your book is part of a video course you are teaching online, the CC package from Adobe, with all the popular (and usually best) software for print, e-book, website, and video production will probably be your best choice. You can get by with less, but you will pay for it with slower, much more labored production schedules and capabilities that are simply not up to professional standards.

David Bergsland
Radiax Press (www.bergsland.org)

A graphic designer until 1983, David became art director of one of the largest commercial printers in New Mexico. He developed a degree in commercial printing for a community college in Albuquerque, and in 1996 he released the first textbook with an all-digital printing workflow. He began self-publishing with PDFs and started using Lulu, then Cre-ateSpace, then Kindle, and since 2009, he has been writing and publishing full-time with his dba Radiqx Press.

Adobe InDesign (Mac & Windows) –
http://www.adobe.com/products/indesign.html "page layout, book design, typography, high-resolution images, PDFs for hard-copy printing, export to EPUBs"

Adobe Lightroom (Mac & Windows) –
http://www.adobe.com/products/photoshop-lightroom.html "database to manage, sort and organize images, some image editing capability"

Adobe Photoshop (Mac & Windows) –
http://www.adobe.com/products/photoshop.html "sophisticated image editing for professionals"

Apache OpenOffice (Mac, Windows & Linux) –
https://www.openoffice.org "free, open source office suite for docs, multimedia graphics & math"

Apple's iBooks Author (Mac) –
https://www.apple.com/ibooks-author "templates, page layout, create eBooks for iPad or Mac"

Apple's Pages (Mac) – https://www.apple.com/mac/pages "word processing, templates, page layout, print-ready PDFs for hard-copy printing, export to EPUBs"

Book Design Templates (MS Word and Adobe InDesign) –
http://www.bookdesigntemplates.com "book cover and interior templates for print and eBook"

Calibre (Mac & Windows) – http://calibre-ebook.com "converts a wide range of files into a wide range of eBook files (MS Word to EPUB), edits eBooks, rescales fonts in eBooks, formats and structures for eBooks"

Cover Design Studio (Photoshop) –
http://www.coverdesignstudio.com "book cover templates"

DIY Book Covers (MS Word) – http://diybookcovers.com "book cover templates"

DIY Book Formats (InDesign, MS Word & eBooks) –
http://www.diybookformats.com "templates to format book layouts"

Gimp (Mac, Windows & Linux) – http://www.gimp.org "free, open source image manipulation software"

Inkscape (Mac, Windows & Linux) – http://www.inkscape.org/en "free, open source vector graphics editor"

iStudio Publisher (Mac) – http://www.istudiopublisher.com "page layout, book design, templates, PDFs for hard-copy printing, export to EPUBs"

Jutoh (Mac & Windows) – http://jutoh.com "create books for EPUB or create PDFs for hard-copy printing, templates for book covers"

LibreOffice (Mac, Windows & Linux) – http://www.libreoffice.org "free, open source document software including graphics, charts & math functions"

Microsoft Publisher (Mac & Windows) –
http://office.microsoft.com/en-us/publisher "simple page layout, design, PDFs for hard-copy printing"

PagePlus (Windows) – http://www.serif.com/pageplus "page layout, desktop publisher, word processor, photo editing, templates, PDFs for hard-copy printing + export to EPUBs"

PressBooks (web-based) – http://pressbooks.com "writing tool, book designs, book themes, PDFs for hard-copy printing + export to EPUBs"

PubML (WordPress) – http://pubml.com "ePublishing software"

QuarkXPress (Mac & Windows) – http://www.quark.com "create and edit page layouts, book design, typography, PDFs for hard-copy printing + export to EPUBs"

Scribus (Mac & Windows) – http://www.scribus.net/canvas/scribus "desktop publishing, page layout, typesetting, PDFs for hard-copy printing"

Sigil (Mac & Windows) – https://code.google.com/p/sigil "EPUB book editor; WYSIWYG & code-based"

Best Books on Self-Publishing

If you're new to book publishing, one of the best things you can do for yourself is get educated. There are lots of ways to learn about what goes into preparing, producing, and marketing your books, but this list will get you started quickly.

There are books here that cover the entire process of self-publishing, and others that address a specific topic to help you home in on subjects that particularly interest you. You can find out the best practices for marketing your books, get educated about the legal requirements of running a book publishing company, or take a deep dive into the contracts you may encounter when dealing with vendors.

We've kept this list short so you won't get overwhelmed with choices. You can be assured that every book you find here will help you get up to speed on book publishing and add to your growing expertise as an independent author.

Joel Friedlander
The Book Designer (www.thebookdesigner.com)

APE: How to Publish a Book by Guy Kawasaki and Shawn Welch, Nononina Press (2013) – "APE stands for Author, Publisher, Entrepreneur; the nuts and bolts of the self-publishing process, rich with details and information presented in an organized and easy-to-understand way"

Author YOU: Creating and Building Your Author and Book Platforms by Judith Briles, Mile High Press (2013) – "interactive guidebook for authors, discover how to create a successful book plan & more"

Business For Authors: How To Be An Author Entrepreneur by Joanna Penn, Joanna Penn (2014) – "Guide that shows you how to go from being an author to running a business as an author"

Choosing A Self Publishing Service 2014: The Alliance of Independent Authors Guide by Jim Giammatteo, Mick Rooney, + Orna Ross, ALLi (2014) – "compares the most significant self-publishing services—from single service suppliers to package providers"

Crush It With Kindle: Self-Publish Your Books on Kindle and Promote Them to Bestseller Status by John Tighe, Strategic Positioning Press Ltd. (2012) – "a simple step-by-step system that shows you how to write, publish and promote your books on Kindle"

Dan Poynter's Self-Publishing Manual, Vol. 2: How to Write, Print and Sell Your Own Book by Dan Poynter, Para Publishing (2009) – "filled with helpful tips & resources"

The Fine Print of Self-Publishing: A Primer on Contracts, Printing Costs, Royalties, Distribution, E-Books, and Marketing (fifth edition) by Mark Levine, Bascom Hill Publishing Group (2014) – "explains self-publishing companies' services, contract terms, printing markups and royalty calculations"

From Word to Kindle: Self Publishing Your Kindle Book with Microsoft Word, or Tips on Designing and Formatting Your Text So Your Ebook Doesn't Look Horrible (Like Everyone Else's) by Aaron Shepard, Shepard Publications (2014) – "In this book, Aaron Shepard offers his own tips for moving your document from Word to Kindle"

How to Blog a Book: Write, Publish, and Promote Your Work One Post at a Time by Nina Amir, Writer's Digest Books (2012) – "how to create a blog book with a well-honed & uniquely angled subject & targeted posts"

Indie Author Survival Guide by Susan Kaye Quinn, Susan Kaye Quinn (2013) – "This book is for every author who's thinking about indie publishing or has already taken the leap"

Indie Publishing Handbook: Four Key Elements for the Self-Publisher by Heather Day Gilbert, WoodHaven Press (2014) – "handbook covering the four key elements every self-publisher must oversee for successful book publication: editing, creating cover art + blurbs, formatting + uploading books, & marketing"

Let's Get Digital: How to Self-Publish, and Why You Should: Updated Second Edition by David Gaughran, Arriba Arriba Books (2014) – "practical advice on every aspect of the business"

Make a Killing on Kindle: The Guerilla Marketer's Guide to Selling Your Ebooks on Amazon by Michael Alvear, Woodpecker Media (2012) – "the title says it all"

Marketing Your Words: The writer's guide to bestselling book promotion strategies, tips, and interviews by S.R. Johannes, Coleman and Stott (2014) – "tips, strategies, & key steps to market your books"

Publishing 101: A First-Time Author's Guide to Getting Published, Marketing and Promoting Your Book, and Building a Successful Career by Jane Friedman, MBA for Writers (2014) – "how to approach editors & agents with your work, while avoiding the common pitfalls of first-time authorship"

Self-Publisher's Legal Handbook: The Step-by-Step Guide to the Legal Issues of Self-Publishing by Helen Sedwick, Ten Gallon Press (2014) – "the first step-by-step guide to the legal issues of self-publishing"

A Self-Publishers Companion by Joel Friedlander, Marin Bookworks (2011) – "demystifies the process and answers all your questions"

Self-Publishing Boot Camp Guide for Authors: Step-by-Step to Self-Publishing Success by Carla King, Misadventures Media (2012) – "for print books, eBooks, multimedia books and book apps"

Top Self Publishing Firms: How Writers Get Published, Sell More Books, and Rise to the Top by Stacie Vander Pol, CreateSpace

Independent Publishing Platform (2011) – "evaluates 26 self-publishing firms that sell more books, pay the highest royalties, and provide the best overall value for authors"

Your First 1000 Copies: The Step-by-Step Guide to Marketing Your Book by Tim Grahl, Out:think (2013) – "book marketing expert Tim Grahl of Out:think shares the tools and steps to building an online marketing platform"

Secrets to Ebook Publishing Success by Mark Coker, Smashwords (2014) – "30 best practices to help authors publish with pride, professionalism and success"

Write. Publish. Repeat: The No-Luck-Required Guide to Self-Publishing Success by Sean Platt and Johnny B. Truant, Sterling & Stone (2014) – "explains the current self-publishing landscape and covers the truths and myths about what it means to be an indie author now and in the foreseeable future"

PROMOTE

Now that your book has been prepared with the help of professionals, as well as published, the next big challenge is to figure out ways to announce it to the world—or at least to your target readers. Book promotion and marketing for indie authors has become quite sophisticated in the past few years. Be sure to vet the people you decide to hire. Ask them to explain exactly what they plan to do for your book, what it will cost, how long it will take, and what kind of results you can reasonably expect.

Website Design for Authors

At this point, you've heard the endless refrain: *you need a website*. Probably for years now. I won't reiterate it. You know you need a website. It feels a little 2008 to even mention it.

What is worth considering, though, is not that you need a website, but *what your website needs*. The independent author sphere is saturated with bad design and marketing — from unintentionally hilarious book covers to websites that look like refugees from the wreckage of GeoCities—and you don't want to add to it. But it goes much deeper than that. Design isn't just how your website looks, but what it does (to very loosely paraphrase Steve Jobs), and you have to do more than just have something out there. It needs to be remarkable—just as remarkable as your book.

Building an excellent website is one of the first priorities for every business (and make no mistake, you are a business). You're not just selling a book now, you're building your brand, and the optics of everything you put into the public sphere affects the perception of your brand, and therefore your sales.

The hard truth is this: self-published authors are still fighting an uphill battle for acceptance, despite the sensational success of a few. Yes, the media (especially the self-publishing media) loves to crow about how many books are being self-published, how much some authors are making, how many indie author millionaires there are. But the vast majority of indie authors will sell a handful of copies to friends and family, where they will collect dust on a shelf.

Don't be that author. You may not be selling as much barely masked Twilight fan fic as E.L. James (yet!), but you can certainly look the part. Plus, by putting time and effort into building a great website, you'll have a firm foundation when those numbers do start skyrocketing.

Following is some insider knowledge from a working web design firm to help you ensure that no matter what path you choose to build your site, you'll finish with a top-notch product.

The golden rules of good websites

When building your website, just keep these four rules in mind, and you should be all right. When in doubt, contact a pro to make sure you're giving your site the attention it deserves.

Your website is the hub of your brand—treat it as such

It's where every part of your communication strategy comes together — clickthroughs from your search engine ads, folks who heard you on NPR and want to learn more (dream big, folks), reporters checking you out for a story, readers who clicked from your Facebook page for more information, or people who picked up your literature at that reading you did last week.

Everything runs through the web. For most people, first contact with a brand will be through the web, and many of those first contacts will be at the brand's website. Your site needs to make sure that those who stop in get a great first impression and find what they're looking for quickly and easily.

Your website is NOT a brochure; update it regularly

"Brochure site" is web industry jargon for a static site with no interactive features, just information dumped onto a page, often with the indifference of a lunch lady doling out sloppy joes. It also suggests that most of those sites are updated about as often as print pieces.

It does not have to be this way. In fact, it cannot be this way for your site to be successful. A well-made website is easy (and free!) to update—so update it! Add a new blog post, tweak your bio, add a new headshot. Do whatever it takes to make sure the site always feels fresh and cared for. Keeping your site updated will also help your chances of ranking higher on major search engines, which use frequency of updates as one of the criteria for boosting ranking.

You must be mobile

With mobile and tablet viewing averaging around 50 percent of traffic for websites, you can't afford to have a site that isn't optimized for viewing on all devices and viewports. Thankfully, most website-building tools now offer easy options for creating a mobile-friendly site. If you're working with a professional, that's even better. A good web designer will take the time to create designs specifically for mobile and tablet in addition to the standard desktop designs.

IT'S NOT ABOUT YOU

See how that's in all caps? That's because it is the most important thing you'll ever read about building a website. The greatest sin on the Internet is vanity, and most of the website owners we work with are guilty of it.

While most vanity is expressed on the Internet through absurd selfies posted to social media, when you run a brand on the web, vanity is the assumption that users are visiting your site to hear what you have to say, rather than coming for their own reasons.

To keep users on your site and turn them into customers, you have to think about what they want and why they are visiting, rather than focusing on what you want to talk about. For authors, this can be a real challenge, especially after writing something so intensely personal and so centered on your perspective as a book. Work past that, however, and you can create something that is hugely beneficial for your brand.

But remember: this does not mean being all things to all people. Your book has a target market. You should be talking to the people in that market. If middle-aged readers of faith-based fiction are not your market and never will be, don't sweat it when they come to your site, find nothing that interests them, and leave. You're looking for *qualified traffic*— readers for whom your brand resonates.

The website build process

A good website is developed in five phases. These apply even if you're doing the site yourself, and any professional worth her salt will have you go through some version of these phases. They help you iron out what you need, what your users need, and how to join those requirements in an effective website strategy.

Discovery

This phase lays out the basic knowledge that will form the building blocks of your site. If you're working with a web professional, this will help them understand your brand, your book, your personality, and your readers so they can design a website that helps you achieve your goals.

Discovery is equally important if you're working solo, because it will get you used to thinking like a business owner with a goal-oriented mindset. Good discovery focuses on determining your goals, defining your market, and understanding your users.

To start your discovery inquiry, ask questions about:

- **Your Company**

    - What is your unique selling proposition—i.e., what do you do better than others in your field?

    - Where do you see your business in three years? How would your website help make that happen?

- **Your Market**

    - Who are the "big guys" in your market? What do they get right, and what do they get wrong?

    - What are some businesses that are being disruptive in your market?

    - Who do you compete most closely with?

    - What is your position relative to your competitors? Bigger, smaller, lighter, more agile, friendlier, etc.?

- **Your Existing Website (If Applicable)**

    - What is your main reason for wanting a new site?

    - What are your current site's strengths and weaknesses?

    - Consider and list the content you would like migrated from your old site to your new. How will you migrate it?

- **Your New Website**

    - Describe your ideal website. What does it do for your users?

    - Who is your ideal user?

- When users visit your site, how do you want them to feel, and what do you want them to think about you and your offering?

- What are the three most important things a user should do when they visit your website? Buy your product online? Contact you? Share certain content?

- **Advertising and Promotion**

  - Do you have any advertising and promotion in place? What does the website need, if anything, to accommodate this?

  - What are your advertising and promotion goals?

- **Big Goals**

  - What does success online look like to you, and how does your website facilitate that?

You can find these questions, and a few more, in this <u>simple discovery questionnaire</u>.

Information Architecture

Information architecture is just a fancy way of saying "how you organize your website." You must decide how visitors to your site would like to see the information you want to present, and how to best meet their needs with the structure and content of your site.

Content

Now you get to do what you do best: write. Using your information architecture document from the previous phase, you will create content for your entire site.

Design

If you are working with a professional designer, they will generally give you a few different design directions to choose from, and you can combine and revise those directions into something that works for your brand.

If you've gone the self-serve route, such as a website builder or self-hosted websites that use templates, you get to be the designer.

Development

Your web professional or agency will then code a custom website. Website builders and self-hosted websites will have the templates already created; you'll just need to do the required setup to use the theme with your site. Processes for getting the theme installed on your site, as well as the amount of setup once the theme has been installed, vary.

Testing

This can't be stressed enough: once the site has been developed, test it. After every revision during the development phase, test it. When you're hours from going live, test it again. And don't only test things that have changed—test it all. Test each page, each link, each product. Test the site in the four major browsers (Firefox, Chrome, Safari, and Internet Explorer) to make certain that users can see your site and brand as you intended them to. Then grab your tablet and mobile device and start all over again. Testing is grueling but absolutely necessary.

Choosing your provider

There are myriad ways to build a site today—from excellent website builders like Squarespace to self-hosted WordPress templates—but the gold standard remains hiring a professional to plan, design, and build your site.

What to look for in a web designer

Anyone can say they are a web designer—there are no credentials or certifications required—but finding one that has the right mix of design sense, industry knowledge, and the ability to finish their projects on time and on budget can be a challenge.

When looking for a good designer, treat the process as if you were hiring an employee at a business.

Ask for references

Testimonials on the designer's website are great, but you should request direct references and actually call them. Even clients who love a particular designer will have something useful to say that can help you work successfully with him or her.

Study their work

Does their design style match what you're looking for? Do they have experience creating sites for authors? Do the sites they link to in their portfolio achieve their owners' goals? Are the clients' brands represented well?

The proof is in the portfolio. Don't merely glance at the work they've chosen to show there; look carefully at their whole portfolio.

Look for credentials

While web design is a profession that only requires a computer and some knowhow, good designers will often be recognized by third parties. Look on their sites to see what awards they've won, where they have been featured in media outlets, or whether they've earned some sort of credential, such as a certificate in one or more of their key skills.

Take the interview seriously

When you finally get past checking out designers' sites and move into the hiring phase, you'll be getting on the phone or corresponding via e-mail with a few different prospective providers. These exchanges should sound and feel like job interviews—because that's exactly what they are. You are interviewing someone for a job, and you're the boss. What questions would you expect to be asked if you were applying for this job?

Ask the designer how they work on their projects, and what steps they take when creating a website. Find out what work they are particularly proud of and why. Ask them what they feel their weaknesses are, and how they compensate for them.

Even if you decide to hire a professional to do the hard work for you, you'll need to have a lot of input into building your site. Remember that an author website is not just a component of modern marketing—it's a launch point or endpoint for most actions that your potential readers take when learning about your book. A poor site will stop them dead in their tracks.

Use the insider information provided here to start your website on the right foot, and to ensure that you get the product you and your brand deserve.

Tyler Doornbos
Well Design (www.welldesignstudio.com)

Tyler Doornbos is a partner with Well Design, a Michigan-based design studio that partners with businesses, nonprofits, and individuals to create branding, web, and communications solutions.

AuthorBytes – Boston, MA 617-492-0442 http://authorbytes.com "website design + content management, blogs, trailers, podcasts, online/social media marketing & promotion"

Author Design Studio – UK +44 01227 392566 contact@authordesignstudio.com, http://www.authordesignstudio.com "Aimee Bell offers website design, book covers, trailers & social media services"

Author Media – Austin, TX 888-432-7734 http://www.authormedia.com "website + plug-in developers & social media management for authors"

Authors on the Web – New York, NY 212-246-3100 http://www.authorsontheweb.com "website development + maintenance, newsletters & SEO"

Bizango – Seattle, WA 206-462-4020 http://www.bizango.net "web design + easy site updates"

Books and Branding – Jersey City, NJ 201-420-8205 sndi@verizon.net, http://booksandbranding.com "Susan Newman offers book/author website design, branding, marketing & publicity packages as well as book design services"

Clockpunk Studios – Lawrence, KS 970-237-0830 studio@clockpunkstudios.com, http://www.clockpunkstudios.com "WordPress web design + development for publishing professionals, including copywriting & social media services"

Creative Freelancers, Inc. – 800-398-9544 http://www.freelancers1.com "online resource for freelance website designers; also illustrators, photographers, graphic designers, etc."

Elance – Mountain View, CA 877-435-2623/650-316-7500 support@elance.com, https://www.elance.com "web-based freelance marketplace for freelance website designers, illustrators, graphic designers, & photographers"

House of Design – Austin, TX 512-924-7674 info@myhouseofdesign.com, http://myhouseofdesign.com

"Shaila Abdullah designs websites for authors, book covers, collateral, as well as logos & branding materials"

Monkey C Media – San Diego, CA 619-955-8286 info@monkeycmedia.com, http://monkeycmedia.com "book cover &interior designs"

Outbox Online Design Studio – Portland, OR 503-610-2486 kate@outboxonline.com, http://www.outboxonline.com "Kate McMillan designs + maintains author WordPress websites; also logos, branding & marketing materials"

Section 101 – New York, NY 888-974-9950 M-F 9:30a-6:30p EST yourbrand@section101.com, http://section101.com "author website platforms including customer care, training, email marketing tools, reporting/analytics; either basic DIY or Premium with web-hosting & set-up support"

Silver Knight Author Websites – http://silverknightauthorwebsites.com "WordPress website design + optional maintenance packages"

Smart Author Sites – karin@smartauthorsites.com, http://smartauthorsites.com "website design + development including SEO & social media strategies"

Tamal Anwar – +880-1966-849881 hello@tamalanwar.com, https://www.tamalanwar.com "custom website design, website hosting, email marketing, & more"

Xuni.com – queries@xuni.com, http://xuni.com "author website design + management & social media branding"

Web Design Relief – Wood Ridge, NJ 866-405-3003 http://www.webdesignrelief.com "author website design, hosting + site technical support, as well as marketing guidance for writers"

Social Media Consultants

The dos and don'ts of social media

Many aspiring and newbie authors are confused by book marketing: Is it necessary? How do I go about it if I don't really understand marketing? How will I ever find the time? Should I hire someone to do it for me?

These are all valid questions, and ones that, as an author myself, I fully appreciate. It certainly helped that I had seventeen years of corporate marketing under my belt when it came time to market my book—marketing is marketing, right? Well, kind of.

Here's the issue: not only do we have *lives* outside our writing, we also have to write! Figuring out how to market our work effectively can be a massive learning curve, one that many authors simply don't have the time or desire to master. How can one person do everything that needs to be done, and do it all well?

This is where someone like me comes in: a social media/marketing consultant. Let's deconstruct.

Who needs a social media consultant?

Selling vs. connecting

Does the thought of selling your work on social media terrify you? Then hiring a social media consultant is probably the right choice for you, because selling your work on social media is one of the most ineffective ways to generate sales of your book.

Let's back up a little bit.

Social media is social, not selling. Social media is just one small part of creating your author platform (on which more in a moment). The main goal of using social media is to build relationships with readers, book bloggers, and reviewers—not to generate sales.

Here are the biggest mistakes I see new or aspiring authors make on social media:

- The hard sell
- Spamming book links
- The mistaken belief that everyone on social media is their demographic

New authors make these mistakes because they haven't taken the time to learn the culture of each social media channel. *You want to be where your readers are, not where you feel most comfortable.* This is where a consultant can really help you tailor your messages so you can find and connect with your ideal readers.

For example, let's say you write YA, yet you spend most of your day on Facebook. According to a study by the Pew Research Center (http://www.pewinternet.org/2007/12/19/teens-online-activities-and-gadgets/), 93 percent of teenagers are online (likely your demographic), and their use of the Internet is intensifying. Much of their time is spent on Snapchat, YouTube, and Instagram, posting photos and videos. If you're hanging out on Facebook, you're not reaching this audience.

Learning how to connect with your readers is critical. You'll need to create a marketing or social media plan—which is something most authors don't do.

Planning vs. spontaneity

Another way to look at social media is as organic posts versus planned posts. A consultant can help you figure out the best combination of these, which is especially helpful when you're busy writing or, you know, living. It's not possible to be on social media all the time (and you don't want to be; you'll burn out).

There are many tools available (Hootsuite is one example) to help you schedule evergreen content, blog posts, and other shares that will free you up to focus on writing while still allowing you to interact live when you have a spare moment. Your social media consultant can set up this tool, import your accounts, and show you how to compose your tweets and shares for each social media channel.

What is your author platform?

If the term "author platform" seems nebulous and scary, you may want to take a look at this article on my site, BadRedhead Media (BadRedheadMedia.com), which defines the term and why it matters. Here's a quick summary:

> Your platform consists of how visible you are, your authority on a particular topic(s), proven reach, and knowing your demographic (source: Jane Friedman).

Most authors I work with have or know maybe *one* of these. How do you figure out the rest? If you're a self-starter and understand marketing basics, you'll know that your author platform consists of far more than spamming links on Twitter. If not, you'll need to learn how to establish the following:

- An SEO-optimized website
- An active blog (once-weekly postings are ideal)
- Consistently posting and interacting on Twitter and Google+ (both are indexed by Google)

- A Facebook author page (since you cannot use your personal account to promote your work), Pinterest, Instagram, or Snapchat (depending on your demographic), with consistent growth and interaction
- An e-mail newsletter with a big subscriber list
- Reviews
- Book blogger connections
- And more

When to start marketing your book on social media

Many authors wait until their book comes out to start a blog or begin building their social media relationships, thinking they don't have anything to promote until they publish it, so why bother? They're wrong.

Here's the reason why: in publishing, we market the author, not the book.

Read this comment from author and marketing guru Seth Godin:

"The best time to start promoting your book is three years before it comes out. Three years to build a reputation, build a permission asset, build a blog, build a following, build credibility, and build the connections you'll need later."

(You can read the rest of his post here: http://sethgodin. typepad.com/seths_blog/2006/08/advice_for_auth.html. It's great.)

While three years is probably difficult for most authors, it worked for me. I started my blog in 2008, began building my social media presence in 2009, and released my first two books in 2011. By the time my books came out, I had built those critical relationships with potential readers, book bloggers, and reviewers, who were extremely generous in sharing and reviewing my work.

If you don't have three years in your back pocket, try for six months. Working with a consultant, you can devise ways to mete out focused content that will resonate with your ideal reader. The issue with waiting until after your book comes out is that you risk coming across as disingenuous. *"You waited until now to sound interested? Clearly, you're self-serving"* is how people will see you, even if that's not your intent.

How do I find a professional social media consultant?

There are a lot of people out there claiming to be professional consultants, so buyer beware. Here are a few tips I look for to see if someone is the real deal.

- Check their website. Do they list their services clearly? Do they have client testimonials or offer references? Do they blog regularly with original content?

- What's their Alexa ranking? If it's under 500K, great. Under 100K, even better.

- Are their social media icons prominent and linkable? If not, big red flag!

- A large social media following means little these days—people can easily purchase fakes. Take a look—are their Twitter followers' profiles full of pictures of eggs? That's a sure sign of fakes. (Don't assume they bought their own fakes, however; anyone can purchase followers for anyone else for a mere $5.)

- How do their social media profiles look? Are they professional, clear, and informative?

- Are their updates helpful or simply links to other people's content? You want to see a balance of their own original content, others' content, and non-links (e.g., quotes or tips).

- What's the tone of their updates? Are they calling people out in a negative way online? A professional will always move negativity offline.

- Do they write for respected online publications like The Huffington Post, BookWorks, IndieReader, Mashable, BuzzFeed, or Social Media Today? Those outlets don't hire just anyone—writers must demonstrate their expertise to be brought on as a columnist.

- What's their experience? You want a good consultant who brings many years of real-life experience. Social media is a fairly new technology—what else qualifies them to help you with your marketing efforts?

- Are they affordable? A social media consultant can charge anywhere from $50 to $500 per hour, and some charge by the project.

- Have they had experience working with indie authors? If so, ask them to describe their successes.

You need to decide what's best for you: Do you have the time to devote to figuring out how to do it all on your own, or would it make sense just to hire someone who could do it all (or at least most of it) for you?

I hope this helps you make your decision!

Rachel Thompson
BadRedhead Media (www.badredheadmedia.com)

Rachel Thompson is the author of four award-winning books published by Booktrope, where she directs the Gravity imprint, helping authors share their stories of trauma and recovery. She founded BadRedhead Media, a company designed to create effective social media and book marketing campaigns for authors. Her articles appear regularly in The Huffington Post, the *San Francisco Book Review*, and BookPromotion. com. Rachel hates walks in the rain, running out of coffee, and coconut. She lives in California with her family.

Authority Publishing – Gold River, CA 877-800-1097
service@authoritypublishing.com, http://authoritypublishing.com
"custom nonfiction self-publisher (selective titles) offering social
media marketing services to their authors"

BadRedhead Media – San Francisco, CA
badredheadmedia@gmail.com, http://badredheadmedia.com
"best-selling writer/former marketer Rachel Thompson helps
authors develop their social media platform, including branding
& marketing strategies"

Bakerview Consulting – BC, Canada
bakerviewconsulting@gmail.com, http://bakerviewconsulting.com
"author social media platforms, WordPress websites as well as
consulting & training services"

Caroline O'Connell Communications – N. Hollywood,
CA 818-506-1775 oconnellpr@sbcglobal.net,
http://oconnellcommunications.com "assists authors in setting
up + maintaining social media: also offers traditional media/
publicity such as book tours & interviews"

Creative Content Coaching – Bodega Bay, CA 707-875-3225
http://creativecontentcoaching.com "Anne Hill helps authors
set up + build their platform/online presence; also shares advice
& info on her website/blog"

Elance – Mountain View, CA 877-435-2623/650-316-7500
support@elance.com, https://www.elance.com "web-based
freelance marketplace for social media consultants & other
creatives"

Kate Tilton's Author Services, LLC – Berlin, NH
assistantk8@gmail.com, http://katetilton.com "Kate Tilton
connects authors and readers through social media & outreach
to book bloggers"

Kincade, Jason – Brooklyn, NY jason_kincade@yahoo.com,
http://jasonkincade.tumblr.com "social media marketing +
consulting, including book & author website production"

Miller Mosaic, LLC – Beverly Hills, CA
marketing@millermosaicllc.com, http://www.millermosaicllc.com
"social media consultants to help authors harness the power of
the Internet to market their books + promote their brand"

Queen Bee Consulting – Edwardsville, IL 618-530-7166
http://queenbeeconsulting.com "coordinated book marketing
through social media, website, Amazon author page; also offers
book/publishing coaching & consulting"

Ratzlaff, Cindy – Allentown, PA 610-393-5192
cindy.ratzlaff@gmail.com, http://cindyratzlaff.com "social
content marketing strategies, brand visibility & publishing
consulting for authors"

Social Media Just for Writers – San Francisco, CA 707-292-2505
http://socialmediajustforwriters.com "writer Frances Caballo
offers consulting services + creates, optimizes & maintains social
media marketing platforms for fellow authors"

Book Review Services

Book review services: where to find them and how to use them

Books don't just sell themselves. Getting reviews is an essential part of book marketing, and every author's marketing plan needs to include reviews. Review outreach is probably where you'll spend a good chunk of your time, so make sure you have a strategy that works for you. Does your plan include giving away your book for free? Blog tours? A KDP promotion? Do you have your book available in all formats so the reviewer can easily read and review your book?

Reviews can make or break your book. Readers usually check a book's reviews before they decide to buy it. They want to see what others are saying about a particular book. So if you have 600 reviews on Amazon that are mostly four or five stars, that will likely compel potential readers to hit the buy button.

If you have a few hundred one-star reviews, on the other hand, that will most likely dissuade users from buying your book. That's why it is so important to get your book in front of the people who are known to be interested in your genre or subject matter.

A book review is a power-marketing tool because it means that someone loved or hated your book enough to take the time to write a short note about it. A positive review is basically an endorsement of your book. Someone has vouched for your work and said, "YES—this is a book worth reading."

Places to get reviews include:

- **Colleagues and people you know.** Just be careful with this, as Amazon is cracking down on reviews from family and friends. But if you work with other authors or in a professional environment and your book is relevant to what they do, colleagues could be a great choice to review your book.

- **Beta readers.** A beta reader is typically someone you don't know who can give you critical feedback on your book once it's been edited. It's a good idea to have at least five to ten beta readers giving you feedback. These beta readers are also great people to give you reviews. It's important to remember to thank them in your acknowledgments.

- **Bloggers.** There are lots of great sites where you can reach out and find bloggers. You typically want to get reviews from bloggers who review books in your genre or, for nonfiction, on the specific subject you are writing about.

- **Professional review sites.** These are sites like Publishers Weekly, or sites such as Kirkus, IndieReader, and BlueInk that charge for reviews. Receiving a positive review from one of these sites is a great stamp of approval for your book, and you can paste this on your website, feature it on your Amazon page, or include it in the front matter of your book.

- **Amazon top reviewers.** The super readers of Amazon are highly influential. A review from one of these people looks really good on your Amazon page.

- **Companies that organize reviews**. You can also hire companies that specialize in helping you gather reviews by reaching out to bloggers and reviewers for you.

Here's a suggested template for requesting a review from a blogger:

Dear Jane Doe:

I got your name from [where you found them] and thoroughly enjoyed your review of [name of book]. I recently wrote a book that appeals to a similar audience, "[Name of your book]."

If you think you might be interested in reading it and perhaps reviewing it, I'll gladly send you a complimentary copy.

Thank you so much for your time.
Best Regards,

[Author Name]
[Your website]
[Your social media links]

To start getting reviews, you can reach out to some of the companies mentioned in the following pages, but don't forget to check out beta readers and bloggers as well.

Also, there are a few easy things you can do to get reviews. Below are a couple of ways you can engage with your readers right away. They're so simple you can implement them today.

- Have a short author's note at the end of your book asking readers for a review.

- Set up a link to your author mailing list at the end of the book asking readers to sign up.

Here's a sample note for the end of your book:

Author's Note

Thank you for joining me in telling the story of [x and y]. I hope they touched your soul the way they touched mine.

If you enjoyed the book and have a minute to spare, I would really appreciate it if you could take the time to write a short review on the page or site where you bought the book. Your help in spreading the word is greatly appreciated. Reviews from readers like you make a huge difference in helping new readers find stories like [x].

Thank you!

Name
URL
[Links to your Amazon, Barnes & Noble, iBooks, Kobo, and Goodreads pages]

Right now Amazon is cracking down on book reviews from fake sources and family and friends, as I've mentioned, so it's more important than ever that your review outreach strategy is solid and that you have at least ten to twenty reviews before you start marketing and promoting your book.

Miral Sattar
Bibliocrunch (www.learnselfpublishingfast.com)

Miral Sattar is the CEO of LearnSelfpublishingFast.com, a fast track to learning how to self-publish your book in less than twenty-four hours in a full video course series. She also runs Bibliocrunch, a marketplace that connects authors with vetted editors, designers, and book marketers. She has been featured in *Businessweek*, BBC, *Time, Forbes, Money Magazine, Consumer Reports, and PBS.*

BlueInk Review – info@blueinkreviews.com,
http://www.blueinkreviews.com "objective reviews by
professional critics whose bylines have appeared in major
publications, as well as editors from major publishing houses"

BookIdeas.com – doug@bookideas.com,
http://www.bookideas.com "free + paid reviews from screened
volunteer, recreational & professional reviewers/bloggers"

BookLife – New York, NY 212-377-5500 service@booklife.com,
http://booklife.com "Publishers Weekly website for self-
published authors, free registration lets you submit your book
for possible review in Publishers Weekly and gives you access to
other BookLife benefits

Bookowl – Toronto, ON Canada contact@bookowl.com,
https://www.bookowl.com "online community of authors,
readers, illustrators + publishers where authors can showcase
excerpts of prepress works & receive a report, based on
feedback, to help define audience & market strategies"

BookReview.com – Madison, WI 888-272-7873/608-442-4475
zanne@bookreview.com,
http://www.bookreview.com/$spindb.query.bottom.booknew
"paid express reviews include listing in searchable database by
title, author & genre"

Book Reviewer Yellow Pages –
http://www.bookrevieweryellowpages.com "book reviewer
directory available in print, eBook & PDF, updated annually;
includes genre preferences, submission guidelines & book
reviewer contact info"

Clarion Reviews – Traverse City, MI 231-933-3699 M-F 8a-5p EST
allyce@forewardreviews.com,
https://publishers.forewordreviews.com/reviews "division of
Foreword Reviews offers paid 400-500–word reviews/critiques
from qualified reviewers in approximately 4-6 weeks"

Feathered Quill Book Reviews – Goshen, MA
info@featheredquill.com, http://featheredquill.com "paid

review packages by qualified reviewers including varying degrees of promotion/publicity on website & blog; voted one of the best sites for authors by Independent Authors Association"

Hollywood Book Reviews – Sparks, NV 775-461-6281 http://www.hollywoodbookreviews.com "paid reviews from qualified professional reviewers in all genres + distribution to major websites & search engines"

IndieReader – http://indiereader.com/authorservices/#hp-services "paid reviews from IndieReader's team of professional reviewers"

Inkspand – Toronto, ON Canada 416-305-2746 admin@inkspand.com, https://www.inkspand.com "crowd-sourced book reviews, proofreading & editing"

Kirkus Reviews – New York, NY 888-285-9394 indie@kirkus.com, http://www.kirkusreviews.com "paid, impartial, reputable reviews by professional reviewers + editorial services"

The Midwest Book Review – Oregon, WI 608-835-7937 mbr@execpc.com OR mwbookrevw@aol.com, http://www.midwestbookreview.com "free reviews for print books (nominal fee for eBooks, proofs, galleys & PDF) prioritizing small publishers, academic presses & self-published authors"

NetGalley – Newburyport, MA 888-708-1936/978-465-7748 concierge@netgalley.com, https://www.netgalley.com "provides e-galleys to reviewers, journalists, librarians, bloggers, educators + other professional readers in exchange for reviews & feedback"

Reader Views – Austin, TX admin@readerviews.com, http://readerviews.com "free reader reviews plus fee-based publicity, editing & eBook conversion"

Rebecca's Reads – Austin, TX admin@rebeccasreads.com, http://rebeccasreads.com "possibility of free review + fee-based reviews & press release writing/distribution"

SPR: Self-Publishing Review – Los Angeles, CA editor@selfpublishingreview.com,

http://www.selfpublishingreview.com "paid professional book
reviews, promo services + proofreading & editing services"

Your First Review – Chicago, IL 800-662-0701 x240
http://yourfirstreview.com "paid unbiased review + 7-point
'report card' critique"

Author Assistants

What is an author assistant?

To understand how an author assistant can help you, first we need to define exactly what an author assistant is.

An author assistant is a person who provides services for an author or authors exclusively. Author assistants come with a variety of skills, much like the authors they work for. For example, an author assistant may be:

- a virtual assistant (working remotely only),
- a personal assistant (working directly with the author in a physical location), or
- a mix of the two.

Unlike a normal virtual or personal assistant, author assistants specialize in working with and for authors.

Author assistants all have different skills. I work with my authors on tasks that usually fall under one of two categories: administration and marketing. On the administration side, I handle tasks like sending information about the authors or their books to those who request it, updating websites, organizing spreadsheets, mailing out prizes to readers, and pulling sales reports. On the marketing side, I reach out to reviewers, create book jacket copy, run street teams, and create newsletters.

One of the most important things to keep in mind when looking for an author assistant is to make sure he or she can provide the specific skills you need.

Author assistants can help you by:

- **Saving your valuable time.** This is the top reason to hire an author assistant. Just because you can do a task does not mean it is cost effective. Most authors simply do not have enough time in the day to complete their writing and the other marketing and administrative tasks they need to do. By hiring an author assistant, the author has more time to focus on what only they can do—write!

- **Supporting and encouraging you.** Assistants are on your team! The publishing process, no matter what route an author takes, can be tough. Having a passionate assistant on your team can be invaluable. An author assistant can be just what you need to help you organize your material, meet deadlines, and cheer you up on gloomy days.

- **Motivation and goal setting.** Sometimes you just need someone to talk to, keep track of things, and keep you moving forward toward your dreams. Author assistants rock at that.

Hiring an author assistant

Are you feeling overwhelmed by the work piling up around you? Are there things you know you should be doing, but you can't get them done without sacrificing sleep or writing time? Are you willing to delegate your work? Do you have funds in your budget you can use to pay for help? If your answer to these questions is yes, it may be time to consider hiring an assistant.

When you're considering hiring an author assistant, first decide what your main goal is. Then make sure the person you hire has the skills and experience to help you meet that goal. Author assistants are focused on organizing everything so authors can have more time to write, and although in many cases this can lead to better sales, that is not the main focus of working with an assistant.

- If your goal is to increase sales, you need a **marketer**.
- If your goal is to increase visibility, you need a **publicist**.
- If your goal is to find more time to write, you need an **author assistant**.

When looking for an author assistant, there are a few factors to consider:

- **Price**. Like most service-based occupations, the more experience an assistant has, the more you are likely to pay, but you can find talented assistants at any experience level. A student may work for as little as $5 an hour (with college credit), while an experienced author assistant may charge $25 to $60 per hour. Compared to a marketing consultant, who may charge $150 to $300 an hour, an author assistant can offer cost-effective help at any budget level.

- **Personality**. Working with an author assistant is a partnership. Your assistant will be there to help with anything and everything, so make sure you enjoy their company and can communicate well with them.

- **Professionalism**. Check their website and social media. Are there lots of errors or poor formatting? Look for assistants who pay attention to details and have clean, professional websites.

- **Skills.** Most assistants can guide you in the services you may need, but no one knows your needs better than you, the author. Take a few minutes to research the skills of each assistant and look for those that match your needs.

- **Experience.** As if you were hiring an employee for your company, look for recommendations, current and past work experience, and book acknowledgments. It's also a good idea to check the author assistant's references, just to be on the safe side.

Once you have decided to hire an author assistant, you need to find the right assistant for you. Use the suggestions in this section of *The Self-Publisher's Ultimate Resource Guide* to start your search. And don't forget to ask your author friends for recommendations. Have they worked with an assistant before? Follow the above advice to vet your choices, taking care to make sure your potential assistant offers the services you need and feels like the right person to have on your team. Hiring the right author assistant can take you to the next level, so try to include this valuable team member in your publishing plan. She or he can make such a difference.

Kate Tilton
Kate Tilton's Author Service, LLC (www.katetilton.com)

Kate Tilton has been serving authors since 2010. Founder of Kate Tilton's Author Services, LLC, Kate works as an author assistant, social media manager, and speaker with the mission of connecting authors and readers. Kate is the creator and host of #K8chat (Thursdays at 9:00 p.m. Eastern on Twitter) and has appeared in popular media such as *Publishers Weekly and Library Journal.*

AdminiSmith – Austin, TX 512-250-
8546 Info@PublishingSmith.com,
http://www.janicasmith.com/adminismith/ "Janica Smith +
team offers bookkeeping, social media support, newsletter
management, & more"

Author Sidekick – jan@authorsidekick.com,
http://authorsidekick.com "Jan Lewis offers email management,
newsletter creation, blog + social media management, press
release + media kit creation, reviewer outreach, promotional
material design, ebook formatting, & website development"

AuthorRX – Taylorsville, North Carolina 828-308-2925
melissa@authorrx.com, http://authorrx.com/ "Melissa Jolly
offers editing, craft support, design services, ghost writing,
newsletter + email management, social media support, email
management, & more"

E-vantage Business Services – Brantford, ON, Canada
shelley@e-vbs.com, http://shelleysturgeon.com "Shelley
Sturgeon provides social media marketing, blog and website
assistance to authors"

JL Author Services – info@jlauthorservices.com, http://www.
jlauthorservices.com/ "Joanne Levy offers email management,
scheduling + calendar maintenance, research support, mailing
assistant, & more"

Kate Tilton's Author Services, LLC – Berlin, NH
assistantk8@gmail.com, http://katetilton.com "Kate Tilton offers
admin support, craft support, email management, marketing
services, promotional management, social media training for
authors & more"

My Author Concierge – (858) 431-6777 mariaconnor@msn.com,
http://www.myauthorconcierge.com "Maria Connor offers
personal liaison/point of contact services, correspondence/
mailings services, database management, schedule/travel
coordination & file maintenance/organization"

The YP Publishing – Ontario, Canada
myauthorassistant@theyppublishing.com,
http://theyppublishing.com/ "Yvonne Wu, provides services
tailored to professional writers & authors. She helps authors
with publishing & promoting their book"

Press Release Services & Sources

The power of paid press release distribution services

Two decades ago, smart authors used press releases primarily to "get press," otherwise known as publicity.

But today, thanks to the Internet and paid press release distribution services, the press release is all grown up.

Services like PR Newswire and PRWeb can attract attention for your book, your event, or your expertise far beyond traditional media. You can now reach consumers directly without having to genuflect before the media gatekeepers.

Most authors can't afford to use paid press release distribution services for all their press releases, and that's OK. Save this service for major news like a book launch. Here are some of the advantages:

- Bigger services will push your press releases directly into the Google and Yahoo! news feeds and LexisNexis, the world's largest collection of public records. This is critical to getting the widest exposure possible. Once your press release is in the news feeds, people who are searching for information using the keywords in your press release can find it.

- Press release distribution services offer RSS feeds. That means they deliver information on specific topics directly to the desktops of journalists and anyone else who requests it—bypassing email and spam filters.

- The large distribution services have long lists of reporters and editors who cover certain topics at newspapers, magazines, and other media. The services then push the releases to the media outlets whose target audiences are a good match for your book.

- Some of the bigger services offer reports on how many people have accessed your press release and which media have downloaded or used it.

- Several services have a secure site where you can upload releases, images, and other files.

- Many of the services have excellent help desks, and for an additional fee, they'll even write your press release for you.

Press releases rank well on Google

Press releases published through one of the paid services usually rank well on Google. Take A. Michael Bloom, an elder care expert from Boston, for instance. He hired a PR expert to write his release and spent another several hundred dollars to have it distributed through PR Newswire. It was worth it. The release tied into the holidays and led readers to his website at Caregiving Without Regret (caregivingwithoutregret.com), where they could find practical support during a hectic time of year. It also included a link to his Caregiving Thrival Kit and Caregiver Recharge Bootcamp.

Search for "Boston elder care expert" on Google, and chances are good his press release will show up on the first page—maybe even twice. That's because the headline starts with the phrase "Boston elder care expert," which the search spiders spot immediately.

The best press release services

Here are the services I recommend. Compare prices and be clear about exactly what you're getting for your money before you sign up.

- PR Leads Guaranteed Press Releases (www.pressreleasesender.com): Dan Janal guarantees that at least a hundred media websites will print your press release within twenty-four hours, or he'll refund your money. His program has three levels of membership. Call 952-380-9844.

- PR Newswire (www.PRNewswire.com): This is the world's largest distribution service. It sends releases to more than 200,000 print and broadcast outlets, journalists, bloggers, financial portals, social media networks, websites, and content syndication channels. For pricing, call 888-776-0942.

- ExpertClick (www.expertclick.com): This membership site lets you join their searchable database as an expert, have your own press room page, and send press releases without per-release charges. For pricing, go to www.expertclick.com/Expert/JoinAsAnExpert.aspx or call 202-333-5000.

- eReleases (www.ereleases.com): This service has four levels of pricing and distribution, including a web-only service for customers who want to reach consumers directly and are not interested in media pickup. For pricing, go to www.ereleases.com/submit.html or call 800-710-5535.

- PRWeb (www.prweb.com): The company offers press release packages for companies of all sizes. For pricing, go to service.prweb.com/pricing/?nav_location=main_menu or call 866-640-6397.

- prREACH (www.prreach.com): This digital press release service lets you publish your release to their website, accompanied by a video of on-air talent who looks like a TV reporter reading your release. Every release is nationally syndicated and optimized for social sharing, search engines, and the media. For pricing, go to www.prreach.com/pricing or call 888-296-8372.

Beware of free press release services

Do a Google search for "free press release services," and you'll find dozens from which to choose. But the truth is, you get what you pay for. These free sites have three major problems:

- Many of these services don't distribute anything. They simply park your press release at their website.

- The page on which your press release is parked might have a pay-per-click ad that your competitor bought, so your release is competing with their ad.

- Most of these sites don't offer a help desk. If your release has a mistake, like a wrong phone number or URL, there's no way to correct it. The error lives online forever.

Seven tips for working with the paid services

The larger services I've mentioned will take a press release you've written and distribute it for you. Or, if you prefer, they'll do both the writing and the distribution. Here are some tips for getting the most out of your experience:

1. **Before you hire them, know exactly what you want your release to accomplish.** Do you want to pull visitors to your website where they can give you a name

and email address in exchange for a digital freebie? If so, make sure your call to action says that. Do you want to position yourself as a subject matter expert by sharing news about trends you're seeing in your industry? If so, what do you want people to do after they read the release? Contact you to check on your speaking availability? If so, include your phone number or email address in the release.

2. **Know which keywords and keyword phrases are most important to you**. Remember that most people won't be searching for your name or company name because they don't know you. They'll be searching for the type of books they want to read, like "Civil War romance novels," or solutions to problems like "how to fix a leaking toilet" or "safest car seats for babies." If you do business locally, be sure your keywords include your town, region, or state.

3. **Use multimedia**. Research shows that images expand your audience up to 92 percent and help your release stand out among text-only releases. A mix of photos, videos, and multimedia content can pull five times as many people to your release. Multimedia can also include audio, PDFs, infographics, and slide decks.

4. **Return periodically and update your content to keep it fresh**. Remember, this is news. News is timely. Pay special attention to links.

5. **Know exactly what you're paying for**. If they're writing your press release, how many links will they include? How many revisions will they do? Will they proofread it for you? What kinds of statistics will they provide on the number of people who have viewed the release? Most

of the major services offer multiple levels of service and pricing.

6. **Give yourself enough time to get your account set up before sending your first press release**. New accounts can take a day or two before they're live. You might need additional time to correct bad-quality photos, convert content to the correct file format, write a caption for a photo, or submit a high-resolution image.

7. **Be prepared to include a phone number and email address as contact information**. If you don't want to use your home or office phone number, make arrangements for a service like Google Voice. Create a secondary email address if you don't want to use your primary email address. To keep your email address from being harvested, most services require readers to fill out a form if they want to email you. The service then forwards the message to you.

PR Newswire has a free Press Release Boot Camp, a four-page PDF document that goes into more detail on what you need to know about writing releases and working with their service. You can access it here: www.prnewswire.com/knowledge-center/Press-Release-Boot-Camp-What-You-Need-to-Know.html.

How to measure the success of your press release

Knowing whether your press release is effective depends on what you expect to happen as a result of writing it. Here are some ways you can determine whether it's working for you:

- Go back to the goals you set before you wrote the release. If you wanted the release to sell more books, how many did you sell? If you wanted more speaking engagements, how many meeting planners have called you? When they do, ask how they heard about you. I try to remember to ask everyone who contacts me how they heard about me.

- How many people are sharing your releases on social media?

- How many calls from traditional media are you receiving? And how many of those have turned into free publicity, also known as "earned media"?

- If you're offering a free digital giveaway in exchange for someone's email address, create a special list in your email management program just for this promotion so you know how many people are signing up through your press release.

- Check your Google analytics to see which sources or websites are sending visitors your way and in what numbers.

- Do a Google search for keyword phrases used within the release and see where you rank in the organic (unpaid) listings.

Remember that you'll seldom see overnight success. It takes time for your press release to build buzz and get results. Online press releases live on the web forever and will keep pulling traffic. That's why it's important to keep them up to date.

Much of your success also depends on how hard you work at sharing the release after you've published it through one of the online services or at your own website. Are you willing to send customized pitches to bloggers and journalists and link to the press release? Are you willing to connect with them first on the social media sites? Have you taken the time to research your media contacts and learn as much as you can about them before sending them anything?

Press release distribution services are only one of many PR tools you can use to promote your expertise and sell books. Incorporate them into your book launches, event promotion, and author platform.

Joan Stewart
The Publicity Hound (www.publicityhound.com/tips/sample)

Publicity expert Joan Stewart, a.k.a. The Publicity Hound, works with authors, publishers, speakers, experts, and entrepreneurs who want to self-promote to build their platform and sell more books. Subscribe to her free snack-size email tips, delivered twice a week, at the address above.

24-7 Press Release – Vancouver, BC Canada 888-880-9539/
646-417-8294 M-F 8:30a-5p PST
contact1950@24-7pressrelease.com,
http://www.24-7pressrelease.com "press release distribution
services"

Bill Stoller's Publicity Insider (Stoller & Bard Communications)
– Fort Lee, NJ 201-224-3737 info@publicityinsider.com,
http://www.publicityinsider.com/release.asp "free samples +
tips about public relations, press releases & establishing media
contacts"

Constant Content – Federal Way, WA support@constant-content.com,
https://www.constant-content.com "70,000 freelance writers
who can provide press releases, copyediting, copywriting, SEO
content & blog articles"

ContentProz – 800-879-3182 care@contentproz.com,
http://www.contentproz.net "press release writing + distribution
& comprehensive Internet marketing including website/blog/
social media"

Elance – Mountain View, CA 877-435-2623/650-316-7500
support@elance.com, https://www.elance.com "web-based
freelance marketplace for press release writers & other creatives"

eReleases – Baltimore, MD 800-710-5535 M-F 7a-7p EST
http://www.ereleases.com/write.html "press release writing &
distribution service"

Eworldwire – Succasunna, NJ 888-546-6397/973-252-6800
salesteam@eworldwire.com, http://www.eworldwire.com
"press release writing, editing & distribution"

Expertclick – Washington, D.C. 202-333-5000
Mitchell@YearbookofExperts.com, http://www.expertclick.com
"Membership site & searchable database of experts, distribution
of press releases without per-release charges"

fiverr – New York, NY social@fiverr.com, http://www.fiverr.com/
categories/writing-translation/writing-press-releases "web-

based freelance marketplace to find press release writers & other creatives"

Freelancer.com – Sydney, NSW Australia support@freelancer.com, http://www.freelancer.com/jobs/Press-Releases "web-based crowd-sourced freelance marketplace for press release writers + other creatives"

Guru – Pittsburgh, PA 888-678-0136 http://www.guru.com "global network of more than 900,000 freelancers' profiles listing their skills & experience, including press release writers"

iFreelance – contact@ifreelance.com, http://www.ifreelance.com/freelance-jobs/press-release-writing-freelance-jobs "find freelancers including press release writers by posting project & requesting bids or searching profiles/portfolios"

myPressManager – Bell, FL 888-544-2100/850-222-4636 M-F 8a-5p EST info@mypressmanager.com, http://www.mypressmanager.com/press_release_tips.aspx "press release distribution including editing & writing services"

oDesk – Mountain View, CA 855-946-3375 M-F 6a-6p PST https://www.odesk.com/o/profiles/browse/title/press-release "freelancers respond to your job post or you can review their profiles/portfolios listing skills, experience & client ratings"

PeoplePerHour – London, UK http://www.peopleperhour.com/freelance/press+release "post your job for bids from relevant freelancers or search their profiles/credentials & request a proposal directly"

Press Release Writers – 888-289-2459 x49 support@pressreleasewriters.org, http://www.pressreleasewriters.org "press release writing + distribution including SEO & reporting"

Press Release Writing Service – 888-289-2459 x50 support@pressreleasewritingservice.biz, http://www.pressreleasewritingservice.biz "press release writing, editing & distribution"

PR Leads Guaranteed Press Releases – 952-380-9844
sales@prleads.com, http://www.pressreleasesender.com
"Principle Dan Janal guarantees that at least 100 media websites
will print your press release within 24 hours, or he'll refund your
money. His program has three levels of membership"

PR Log – http://www.prlog.org "free press release submission
+ distribution plus optional paid premium (ad-free) online
newswire distribution service"

PR Newswire – (offices worldwide) 800-776-8090 8a-5p EST
http://www.prnewswire.com/news-releases "press release
distribution, enhancement (via images, video, audio & landing
pages) + tracking ROI"

PRnine Press Release Services – Los Angeles, CA
http://www.prnine.com/press-release-writing-services
"affordable SEO, press release writing + online distribution by
graduate students"

ProfCopy.com – 347-497-7557 support@profcopy.com,
http://www.profcopy.com/press-release-writing-service "press
release writing/distribution + website, blog, landing page & SEO
content writing"

ProPRCopy – Milwaukee, WI 800-746-3121 info@proprcopy.com,
http://www.proprcopy.com/about-copywriting-services/press-
release-writers "press release writing + local (free) & national
distribution"

prREACH – San Diego, CA 888-296-8372 http://www.prreach.com
"digital press release service accompanied by a video of on-air
talent. Every release is nationally syndicated & optimized for
social sharing, search engines & the media"

PRWeb – Beltsville, MD 866-640-6397 http://service.prweb.com
"offers press release packages for companies of all sizes"

Send2Press Newswire – Los Angeles, CA 866-473-5924/
310-373-4856 M-F 9a-5p PST support2@send2press.com,
http://www.send2press.com/services/release_writing.shtml

"press release writing or revision/rewriting + targeted local to national distribution services"

Textbroker – Las Vegas, NV 702-534-3832 clients@textbroker.com, http://www.textbroker.com "marketplace for freelance marketing content writers"

wikiHow – http://www.wikihow.com/Write-a-Press-Release "learn how to write your own press release"

WriterAccess – Boston, MA 855-597-4837/617-227-8800 9a-6p EST http://www.writeraccess.com/blog/tag/freelance-press-release-writers "content writers for press releases, websites, blogs, etc., including editing & project management support"

Best Blogs on Self-Publishing

Just a few years ago, you could have read all the blogs on self-publishing in a short afternoon. Now there are literally hundreds of authors, editors, agents, designers, and more creating content for authors who plan to publish their own books.

Blogs play an important part in the world of indie publishing. Authors use blogs for many purposes, among them:

- **Content marketing,** where the author publishes content intended for a specific group of readers, in the hope of building an audience that will sustain her publishing efforts

- **Reader engagement,** where the author gets a chance to interact with her readers

- **Market intelligence,** because the conversation an author has with her readers and other authors in her field gives her some of the best and most current market information available

- **Building an e-mail list** that will allow the author to communicate directly with a large number of readers

- **Publishing news** about the author's own books, awards, and recognition from industry groups

- **Creating a hub** for the author's social media outreach, because a blog creates a more personal site for her readers

- **Reinforcing your brand,** since the author totally controls her own blog, unlike her social media accounts

In the list that follows, you won't find every blogger who focuses on self-publishers. What you will find is a carefully curated list of sites that will help keep you up to date on the latest changes in the indie publishing scene. You'll also find education, opinion, news, marketing tips, and much more that will help you on your own publishing journey.

Whether you write fiction, nonfiction, memoir, how-to books, or just about any other kind of literature, you'll be able to find blogs where topics of interest to you are being discussed in real time. There's no better way to get a feel for the indie publishing scene, to learn the ins and outs of e-book production, or to get tips on the latest innovations in software than by reading the posts from these accomplished bloggers.

Of course, you can't read every one of these blogs because then you wouldn't have time to write and publish your own books. Our advice is to glance over the ones that intrigue you and then subscribe to the bloggers who most closely address the issues that concern you.

Joel Friedlander
The Book Designer (www.thebookdesigner.com)

Allen, Moira – Writing-World http://writing-world.com "articles & tips on writing for various genres, plus information on publishing options"

Amir, Nina – How to Blog a Book http://howtoblogabook.com "marketer, writer, speaker & self-publishing coach"

Baker, Bob – Bob Baker's Fulltimeauthor.com http://fulltimeauthor.com "tips on marketing, pricing & crowdfunding"

Barrett, Mark – Ditchwalk: A Road Less Traveled http://ditchwalk.com "writer seeking to understand and pursue the craft, art & business of storytelling in the digital age"

Baum, Henry – Self-Publishing Review http://www.selfpublishingreview.com "writer & blogger"

Benesh, Patricia – AuthorAssist … Helping Writers Succeed http://authorassist.com "tips & coaching on publishing success"

Bolme, Sarah – Marketing Christian Books http://marketingchristianbooks.com "marketing advice & tips on reaching the Christian marketplace"

The Book Marketing Network – http://TheBookMarketingNetwork.com "the inside scoop on all things Kindle"

BookWorks: The Self-Publishers Association – http://www.bookworks.com/blog "our own BookWorks blog written by indie author experts Robin Cutler, Penny Sansevieri, Carla King, Betty Sargent, Ron Callari & Randy Stapilus"

Bricker, Dave – WGB http://theworldsgreatestbook.com "author, editor, graphic designer & coach"

Briles, Judith – The Book Shepherd http://thebookshepherd.com "coach, blogger & strategizer"

Buroker, Lindsay – http://www.lindsayburoker.com "fantasy writer & blogger"

Clark, Brian – Copyblogger http://copyblogger.com "blogger, adviser & serial entrepreneur"

Coker, Mark – Smashwords Blog http://blog.smashwords.com "founder of eBook publisher & distributor Smashwords"

Donovan, Melissa – Writing Forward http://www.writingforward.com "tips + ideas to inform & inspire the writing process"

Eckstein, Kristen – The Book Ninja http://www.ultimatebookcoach.com "writing coach offering tips & industry news"

Fields, Jonathan – Tribal Author http://tribalauthor.com/tribal-author-blog "author, blogger & serial entrepreneur"

Friedlander, Joel – The Book Designer http://www.thebookdesigner.com "author, speaker, book designer & popular blogger"

Friedman, Jane – http://janefriedman.com/blog "blogger, professor, & speaker, offering insights on the future of publishing"

Fry, Patricia – Matilija Press http://matilijapress.com "articles & advice on writing nonfiction"

Gaughran, David – Let's Get Digital http://davidgaughran.wordpress.com "writer & blogger"

Godin, Seth – http://www.sethgodin.typepad.com "author, entrepreneur, speaker & blogger"

Grant, Alexis – http://www.thewritelife.com "contributors specialize in ebook promotion, blogging, finding an agent, & more"

Hamilton, April L. – http://www.aprillhamilton.com "author & indie publishing agitator"

Hise, Stephen – Indies Unlimited http://www.indiesunlimited.com "author & consultant"

Hitz, Shelley – Training Authors http://www.trainingauthors.com "book marketing resources, tips & tutorials"

Howard, Catherine – Catherine, Caffeinated
   http://catherineryanhoward.com "writer & blogger"

Howey, Hugh – http://www.hughhowey.com "best-selling author,
   speaker & blogger"

Kawasaki, Guy – How to Change the World
   http://blog.guykawasaki.com "author, marketing guru, speaker
   & educator"

King, Carla – http://carlaking.com/blog "travel writer, adventurer &
   self-publishing expert"

Konrath, J.A. – http://www.jakonrath.blogspot.com "mystery/
   thriller/horror writer & blogger"

Kremer, John – BookMarket.com http://www.bookmarket.com
   "resources to help authors with publishing, marketing &
   publicity"

Lindsey, Julia – Our Little Books http://ourlittlebooks.com "tips on
   setting goals, finding your audience & producing your book"

Lyons, C.J. – No Rules, Just Write http://www.norulesjustwrite.com
   "best-selling author & pediatric ER doctor"

Marcus, Michael N. – Bookmaking
   http://www.bookmakingblog.com "writer & blogger"

Matthews, Jason – How to Make, Market and Sell Ebooks
   http://ebooksuccess4free.wordpress.com "self-publishing
   expert & teacher specializing in marketing/metadata"

Penn, Joanna – The Creative Penn http://www.thecreativepenn.com
   "writer, blogger, speaker & adviser"

POD People – http://podpeep.blogspot.com "news, views &
   reviews for self-published books"

Poynter, Dan – Para Publishing http://parapublishing.com, "tools
   to make self-publishing faster, easier & more suc-cessful"

Publetariat – http://publetariat.com "an online community for
   people who publish"

Quale, Amy & Beevas, Dara – Wise Ink Creative Publishing
http://www.wiseinkblog.com "an editor/marketer partnership
creates this information-packed blog"

Ratzlaff, Cindy – http://cindyratzlaff.com/tag/blog "marketer,
speaker, coach & social media expert"

Rinzler, Alan – http://www.alanrinzler.com "editor & blogger"

Sansevieri, Penny – Author Marketing Experts, Inc. http://www.
amarketingexpert.com/about-ame/penny-sansevieri OR
http://www.marketingtipsforauthors.com "marketer, blogger,
consultant & public speaker"

Self-Publishing Resources –
http://www.self-publishingresources.com "news, articles +
advice for self-published authors"

Shiel, Walt – Making It Easy http://fiverainbows.com/5rainbows
"self-publishing information + guidance from author & writing
coach"

Scott, D.D. – http://www.ddscott.com "romance writer offers tips
on self-publishing"

Shepard, Aaron – Aaron Shepard's Publishing Blog
http://www.newselfpublishing.com/blog/index.html "writer &
blogger"

Serafinn, Lynn – Spirit Authors http://spiritauthors.com "teacher,
coach, author + marketer offers tips & advice"

Simonds, Jacqueline Church – Small Press World
http://www.smallpressworld.com "insights into small press
publishing"

Sivils, Kevin – The Self-Publisher's Notebook
http://theselfpublishersnotebook.blogspot.com "marketer +
blogger, for new & experienced self-publishers"

Smith, Dana Lynn – The Savvy Book Marketer
http://www.bookmarketingmaven.typepad.com "marketing
tips & resources"

Strauss, Victoria – Writer Beware: The Blog
http://accrispin.blogspot.com OR http://victoriastrauss.com
"exposes scams + unscrupulous book service providers & offers
advice for writers"

Stucker, Cathy – http://www.idealady.com "mystery writer,
marketer, speaker & consultant"

Umstattd, Thomas, Jr. – Author Media http://authormedia.com
"social media experts, web designers & platform builders"

Vandagriff, David – The Passive Voice
http://www.thepassivevoice.com "Passive Guy (pen name), an
attorney, entrepreneur, former tech executive & writer whose
site aggregates articles on self-publishing"

Weber, Steve – Kindle Buffet http://www.weberbooks.com/kindle
"author & blogger with insights on self-publishing, sales &
distribution"

Virtual Book Tours

Sell more books with virtual book tours

In the old days, authors traveled all over the country to visit bookstores and other venues to promote books and meet their fans. It's still wonderful to meet your readers in person if you have the opportunity, but with a virtual book tour, you can reach a much larger audience at little or no cost, from the comfort of your own home.

Of course it takes time and effort to organize a virtual book tour, but the return on that investment can be huge. Here are some of the benefits of virtual tours:

- **Sell books.** You will sell books both during the tour and afterward.

- **Spend less.** Virtual tours are less expensive and time consuming than traveling. Generally the only cost of a do-it-yourself tour is simply the cost of mailing your book to tour hosts.

- **Reach far more people** and a more targeted audience with a virtual tour. In contrast, live appearances by authors who aren't well known tend to have low attendance.

- **Get great links.** The virtual tour provides quality, lasting links to your website. These links have search engine optimization value and may continue to bring you new visitors for months or years to come.

- **Get out there!** Making a commitment to a tour gives you an incentive to promote your book and get content onto other websites.

- **Get book reviews.** If any of your tour hosts review your book, you'll get an added benefit.

- **Build buzz.** Tours get people talking about you and your book and sharing information about it with others.

- **Earn implied endorsements.** When others host you on their blog or show, there is an implied endorsement of you, which enhances your author platform.

- **Interact with your readers.** You have the chance to interact with readers and potential customers.

- **Earn a higher Amazon rank.** Getting a lot of book sales in a short period of time pushes up the Amazon rank of your book, leading to greater visibility on the site.

- **Develop relationships.** You get a chance to develop relationships with bloggers and other key influencers in your field or genre.

- **Let readers sample your work.** The content of a virtual book tour gives potential book buyers an opportunity to see your work.

- **Grow your reputation as an expert.** Nonfiction authors can enhance their expert status by posting content on other venues.

- **Expose your book to new audiences.** You get exposure to new audiences that you might not reach any other way.

- **Build your mailing list**. Additional traffic to your website during the tour gives you the opportunity to build your mailing list and blog subscribers.

How to organize a successful tour

Organizing a virtual book tour isn't difficult, but it does require good planning and logistical skills, along with an investment of time. Here is a list of the steps involved in planning a successful tour:

- Before you start, have basic promotional tools in place, including a website and social networking accounts.

- Begin planning at least two months in advance.

- Determine your goals for the tour and whether you will hire someone to help you.

- Set the length of the tour and tour dates.

- Create a recordkeeping system to keep track of the tour details. Spreadsheets are ideal for this.

- Decide what kind of content, giveaways, and/or contests to offer on the tour. Content can include articles, interviews, and book reviews posted to other blogs; radio and podcast interviews; online audios and videos; and social media chats.

- Make a list of prospective hosts and research them to determine which are the best fit.

- Write a compelling invitation and send it to the top pro-spective hosts.

- Correspond with hosts, sending confirmations and details.

- Set up a schedule of tour stops, assigning hosts to specific dates.

- Send books to the hosts who will write book reviews.

- Develop a promotional plan and materials for the tour and begin pretour promotions.

- Write articles and interview questions and send to hosts.

- Monitor and promote your book daily during the tour. Respond to comments made at your tour stops.

- Coordinate giveaways and contests, sending out prizes as necessary.

- Evaluate the success of the tour and take care of follow-up tasks.

Create killer content

The three most important aspects of a successful book tour are finding great hosts who reach your target audience, creating compelling content for those audiences, and promoting the tour effectively.

Here are some tips for creating killer content that will showcase you and your book:

- Don't underestimate the amount of time it will take to create the content for your tour, and start as early as possible. You may find it easier to block out several days and get a lot of articles done at once, or at least get the rough drafts done for polishing later.

- First, make a list of potential article topics and feature stories. For nonfiction books, use your table of contents for ideas.

- It's a good idea to vary the type of content, including how-to articles, interviews, book excerpts, feature articles, book reviews by tour hosts, audio, and video.

- Find out if your hosts prefer a particular word count. They may have article guidelines posted on their websites. Look at the length of other articles on their sites, or just ask.

- Read your hosts' blogs to get a feel for their style.

- Write your best stuff and proofread carefully.

- Add a short introduction to the beginning of each article, explaining that it's part of your virtual book tour and linking to the tour page. Your tour host may expand on this introduction.

- To increase the odds of getting traffic to tour posts from search engines, use important keywords in the title and the article.

- Include a call to action at the end of your articles, with a link to where readers can buy the book.

- For audio interviews, find out if your host prefers to send you a list of questions or if you should write them. Provide the interviewer an introduction and a conclusion that contain information about your book and where to buy it.

- Plan to send articles or interview questions to your hosts at least 10 days in advance and schedule this on your calendar. Be sure to include your book cover image and author photo.

Do it yourself vs. hiring help

Some authors plan their own tours, while others turn to outside help. Here are three ways to organize your virtual book tour:

Do it yourself

When you organize your own tour, you will save money, and you'll have complete control over the entire process. As the author, you're in the best position to understand your audience and find ideal tour hosts. You'll also have more opportunity to develop relationships with your tour hosts, who may become valuable contacts in the future.

Hire assistance

Another option is to use an assistant to help you. You'll need to consider all the tasks involved in planning and executing the virtual book tour and decide which ones you can delegate.

Hiring help will save you time, but you'll still need to do some of the planning yourself, and you'll probably need to write all or most of the content for the tour. If the person you're working with isn't familiar with researching venues and organizing virtual book tours, you'll need to educate them.

Hire a tour manager

If you don't have time to organize everything yourself or would just prefer to have someone else handle the details, consider hiring a virtual book tour manager. But keep in mind that you will still need to devote time to creating content and promoting the tour.

One advantage of hiring a tour manager to promote your book is that someone who specializes in doing tours in your genre they may already have valuable contacts with bloggers who would be good tour hosts. The disadvantage is the cost and the lack of control over details.

Some book publicity and promotion firms offer virtual tour management, and there are also individuals and companies that specialize in organizing virtual book tours.

Tour services and prices vary widely, so be sure to compare services and be clear about exactly what you're getting. Also find out if the company specializes in any particular genre and how much experience they have.

Regardless of which method you choose, you'll still benefit from a good understanding of virtual book tours and how to produce compelling content to showcase you and your book. And, of course, you will reap the many rewards of a virtual book tour!

Dana Lynn Smith
Savvy Book Marketer (www.thesavvybookmarketer.com)

Dana Lynn Smith is the author of *Virtual Book Tour Magic*, a comprehensive guide to planning and implementing a successful virtual tour. Dana has seventeen years of publishing experience and a degree in marketing. She teaches authors how to sell more books through her blog, guidebooks, and author training programs.

Air Book Tours (UK) – across genres – http://airbooktours.wix.com/air-tours "book reviews, guest posts, tour page, cover reveal, social media promotion"

ATOMR Tours – YA (Young Adult), NA (New Adult), adult titles, romance – atomrbookblogtours@gmail.com, http://atomrtours.com "cover reveal, book reviews, social media promotion"

Bewitching Book Tours – paranormal, urban fantasy, paranormal erotica – RoxanneRhoads@bewitchingbooktours.com, http://bewitchingbooktours.blogspot.com "book reviews, blog posts, social media promotion, tour button, tour banner"

Book Lovers Tours – across genres – jenschaper@yahoo.com, http://bookloverstours.wordpress.com "A new book promotion company offering inexpensive packages for blog tours & other online promotions"

Coffee and Characters – across genres – coffeeandcharacters@gmail.com, http://www.coffeeandcharacters.com/blog "cover reveal, release blitz, social media promotion, author interviews, book reviews, spotlight posts, tour banner, media kits"

Dark Scream Book Tours (UK) – across genres – http://darkscream.com/virtual-book-tours "website, blog spots, social media promotion, videos, marketing images"

Enchanted Book Promotions – across genres/specializes in sci-fi, romance & fantasy – http://www.enchantedbookpromotions.com "cover reveals, social media promotion, book reviews, book excerpts, guest posts, giveaways, media kits, press releases"

Enticing Journey Book Promotions – across genres – enticingjourney@gmail.com, http://www.enticingjourneybookpromotions.com "cover reveal, blog tours, promo tours, sales blitz, review tours & more"

Fire and Ice Book Tours – across genres – fireandicebooktours@hotmail.com, http://fireandicebooktours.wordpress.com "spotlight blog posts, book cover, author photo, giveaways, social media promotion, media kit, guest posts, author interviews, book reviews, tour banner"

Girls Heart Books Tours – across genres – girlsheartbookstours@gmail.com, http://www.girlsheartbookstours.com "giveaways, social media promotion, cover reveal, blog spots, author photo"

Goddess Fish Promotions – romance, genre fiction, YA, middle grades – goddessfish@gmail.com, http://www.goddessfish.com/tours.htm "cover reveal, blog spots, book reviews, author interviews, giveaways, cover graphic, social media promotion, book banner"

iRead Book Tours – across genres – http://www.ireadbooktours.com "giveaways, social media promotion, reviews, hosted home page, tour coordinator"

InkSlinger – YA, NA – inkslingersocial@gmail.com, http://www.inkslingerpr.com/author-services/blog-tours "cover reveal, press releases, features on blogs, blog reviews, tour buttons, social media promotion, media kits, tour page, giveaways"

Innovative Online Book Tours – across genres – innovativeonlinebooktours@gmail.com, http://www.iobooktours.com "book reviews, author interviews, guest blogs, book excerpts, social media promotion, cover reveal, giveaways"

Jean Book Nerd Tours – across genres – jeanbooknerd@gmail.com, http://www.booknerdtours.com "book reviews, spotlight posts, author interviews, book banner, giveaways, social media promotion"

Jitterbug PR – across genres – alicia@jitterbug-pr.com, http://jitterbugpr.blogspot.com/p/blog-tours.html "media kits, tour banner, blogger reviews, tour page, author interviews, guests blogs, giveaways, live interview on blog radio, press releases, social media"

Kismet Book Touring – across fiction genres – kismetbt@kismetbt.com, http://www.kismetbt.com "full tours, review tours, social media, & more"

Lady Amber's Tours – romance – agarcia6510w@gmail.com, http://ambersupernaturalandya.blogspot.com/p/lady-ambers-tours.html "cover reveal, book blitz, blogger posting"

Litfuse Publicity Group – across genres – info@litfusegroup.com, http://litfusegroup.com/services/blog-tours "giveaways, social media promotion, author photos, blogger interviews, author posts, press releases"

Lola's Blog Tours – middle grade, YA, NA adult fiction – lola@lolasblogtours.com, http://www.lolasblogtours.net "cover reveal, book blitz, tour banner, blog reviews, guest posts, author interviews, book reviews, giveaways"

Novel Publicity & Co. – across genres – http://www.novelpublicity.com/blog-tour " book reviews, author interviews, social media promotion, giveaways, blog spots, tour page"

Partners in Crime – crime, mystery, thriller – http://www.partnersincrimetours.net/p/tour-pricing.html "book reviews, guest posts, author interviews, giveaways, social media promotion, tour page"

Premier Virtual Author Book Tours – across genres – teddyrose@virtualauthorbooktours.com, http://www.virtualauthorbooktours.com/ "virtual book tours with a minimum set number of reviews, also includes guest posts & interviews"

Pump Up Your Book! – across genres – thewriterslife@gmail.com, http://www.pumpupyourbook.com "media packets, tour banner, tour page, social media promotion, press releases, author interviews, guest posts, book reviews"

RBTL World of Books Blog Tours – contemporary, dark erotica/ erotica, fantasy, dystopian, historical romance, paranormal romance, sci-fi, steampunk, YA – sadase98@gmail.com, http://www.rbtlreviews.com "author interviews, guest posts, author spotlight, giveaways, book reviews, book excerpts, book reveals"

Rockstar Book Tours – YA – rockstarbooktours@gmail.com, http://www.rockstarbooktours.com "book tours, cover reveal, giveaways, guest posts, author interviews, blog spots, tour banner"

Sage's Blog Tours – across genres – sweetcandydistro@gmail.com, http://www.sagesblogtours.com/book-your-blog-tour.html "tour page, tour banner, book reviews, author interviews, book excerpts, giveaways, guest posts"

Sizzling PR – romance, erotica, paranormal, urban fantasy, YA, NA romance – marissa@sizzlingpr.com, http://sizzlingpr.com/services "guest blogs, author interviews, character interviews, excerpt posts, giveaways, book reviews, social media promotion, tour website, book banner"

Virtual Book Tour Café – across genres – bkwalkerbooks@comcast.net, http://www.virtualbooktourcafe.com "blog spots, media kit, tour banner, author interviews, guest posts, book excerpts, giveaways"

Worldwind Virtual Book Tours – across genres – worldwindtours@ymail.com, http://worldwindvirtualbooktours.weebly.com "book reviews, book excerpts, guest posts, author interviews, book spotlights, tour banner, tour page, social media, media kit, giveaways"

WNL Virtual Book Tours – Christian, children's books – http://wnlbooktours.com "book blasts, giveaways, media kit, social media promotion, book banner, author interviews, guest blogs, book excerpts, book reviews, interviews on blog talk radio, tour page"

Xpresso Book Tours – YA, NA – xpressobooktours@gmail.com, http://xpressobooktours.com "book reviews, tour banner, tour page, blog spots, media kit, social media promotion, book excerpts, guest posts, author interviews"

YA Bound Book Tours – YA, NA, adult – yaboundgirls@gmail.com, http://yaboundbooktours.blogspot.com "tour banner, social media promotion, giveaways, cover reveals, author photo, book excerpt, book reviews"

Marketing & Publicity

Book marketing basics

When I first entered the book marketing business, only five hundred books were published each day; now forty-five hundred books are published each day, and that number continues to grow. What does this mean for indie authors? Now, more than ever, it is essential that you become more creative and consistent in marketing your book. For any marketing to be successful, regardless of the genre, there are several "must-dos" that need to happen. Let's take a look at these.

When to start marketing

Industry experts will often tell you that you should start marketing your book before it comes out, but in a world where a consumer has many (many) choices when it comes to books, it's often *not* smart to push your book too hard before it is actually available for sale. So instead of considering this time as marketing time, let's look at it as planning time. Why? Because every good marketing plan starts off with a solid foundation.

Before you put pen to paper, it's a good idea to know the market you're writing for; more than that, it's a good idea to know what other folks in your industry are writing about. I offer our authors a checklist of things they should know about other authors in their market. For example:

- How many books have they published and how often do they publish?

- Is there a consistency to the covers in this market; i.e., is there a "look" for books in your genre? (This will help you later when we talk about branding.) I know some authors who go through pages and pages of covers on Amazon to see what they like and what stands out for books in their category. It's a great idea, not only to get to know your market but also to get a feel for what you like and don't like when it comes to designing your cover.

- What's the focus of the books that are similar to yours? What do they address? If the books are fiction, are they specific to your genre? If so, is there a subniche they are writing to?

- How many reviews do these books have, and what is their Amazon sales rank? Why should you care about that? Frighteningly, sometimes I find authors have done none of this research and discover they are writing a book that has no market. So doing research in advance will help you decide if this is the book you should be writing, or if a small redirect on your topic or focus could help you reach a wider audience.

The importance of infrastructure

During my career as a marketing and publicity specialist, I've often encountered authors who don't even think about setting up their website or social media until their book is out. This is a mistake that I liken to handing out fliers for your new store, but not deciding on its location until opening day. I think a lot of authors feel that they only need to list their book on Amazon and it will sell. Unfortunately, that's not the case. You need to have an infrastructure in place to not only draw readers in, but engage with them as well. So here's a checklist of the things you need to have in place:

- **Website**. Your website doesn't have to be big or complicated or expensive. It just needs to show off your book(s) in the best possible light.

- **Newsletter**. You're going to want one at some point, so it's better to start early. You can get a free account at sites like MailChimp (free up to a thousand subscribers) and add the signup to your website. You don't have to send a newsletter on day one, but at least you're building a list.

- **Social networks**. When it comes to social media you don't have to be everywhere, just everywhere that matters; find the networks that make the most sense to your market, and make sure to add their icons to your website.

- **Is everything linked? Make sure that everything is linked and ready to go**. This is important, because there's nothing more frustrating than social links on a website that go to the wrong pages—or worse, that lead nowhere. Make sure your "Contact us" link works too in case some big blogger, reviewer, or media person is looking for you!

- **Branding**. Branding is often misunderstood. When we hear the term *branding* we think of big marketing firms; long, complicated meetings; and a hefty price tag at the end. Well, you can certainly go that route, but if it's your first book I don't recommend it. By branding I mean a uniform "look" that's consistent across all your platforms. The idea is that this "look" becomes recognizable to your reader. And keep in mind not to personalize it too much, or it'll look more like your personal Facebook page, rather than your overall brand. For example, if your book is about a dog, then by all means include a dog in your branding, but if it's not, then leave Fido out of it.

Fans, readers, super fans

I talk a lot about the odds of getting the attention of bloggers for your first book. While you aren't getting intentionally ignored, it may often feel that way when you send out a boatload of pitches, only to get just one response. We love our bloggers and reviewers, but in an age where there are forty-five hundred books published each day, you can bet they're pretty busy. This is why you want to build fans early. Yes, you'll still want to pitch bloggers, but you need readers. I had an author tell me once that she didn't care what the average reader said about her book. This is a mistake, because the average reader can really help drive sales. Going one step further, the average super fan can not only drive sales but also help spread the word about your book.

So how do you engage readers and turn fans into super fans? Well, it takes a bit of work, but it's worth it! First, if you don't have a book published yet, start blogging. You don't want to start too early, as I've said, but allow enough of a window that you can start some momentum going in your blog. I would suggest that you start blogging three months prior to your book release. This will also help you get a feel for what you'd like to talk about and what your readers are interested in. Don't worry if you don't have any blog comments. Remember you've just put on your training wheels.

Then when the book launches, you start to get in touch with fans. Encourage them to write you by putting a thank you letter in the back of your book. Be engaging with it: tell them you sincerely appreciate the time they are investing in your book, and now you'd like to hear from them. Getting a fan to contact you is golden. Once you have some fans writing to you, you can start engaging more with them and increasing their dedication. Make them feel exclusive—give them something to make them feel special. Maybe it's an early release of your next book or a special "behind the scenes" extra from your first one. We had an author who created a "director's cut" of her book with deleted scenes and a behind-the-scenes diary; she gave it to fans and they loved it! If fans are engaging with you already, the next step is to keep them talking and keep them active. This doesn't have to be a daily thing, but a few times a month you definitely want to reach out to them and keep building your relationship.

Work it, or not

There's a fallacy in publishing, and it's this: "instant best seller." Anyone who has spent any time in the industry knows there is no such thing as "instant," and certainly the words "overnight success" do not apply to books. And yet there is this odd belief that a "miracle" will just happen when you publish. Personally I love miracles, but they tend not to happen with books, sadly. Book promotion should be viewed as a long runway—meaning that you should plan for the long term. Don't spend all your marketing dollars in the first few months of a campaign, but make sure you have enough money or personal momentum to keep it going. Whether or not you hire a firm, you must work it—work your marketing plan, work your goals, work everything you can to make your book succeed. Publishing is a business. You'd never open up a store and then just sit around hoping people show up to buy your stuff. You advertise, you run specials, you pitch yourself and your store to local media. You work it.

But what does "working it" really mean? Well, it means that if you have a full-time job, you find time each week to push the book in some way. You find time, or you make time. You should be engaged in your own success, even if you hire someone to do the marketing. Sometimes it doesn't take much, but it does take a consistent effort. I call it the compound effect: everything you do adds up.

Living by metrics

Metrics is a funny thing—sometimes it works and sometimes it doesn't. Often I find in the book world it just doesn't. I speak with authors who want metrics on everything and that, frankly, isn't realistic. For this reason, authors often forgo getting reader reviews because "there's no metric in it." That's true, technically, but you never know if a new buyer will see a particular review and be prompted to buy your book. Metrics when it comes to things you can actually measure is great, but for everything else, it's a waste of time. Again, most of what we do is the compound effect. Yes, you could pitch a hundred bloggers and get only one response and think: *The metrics of pitching bloggers is terrible; I won't do that again*. But maybe your pitch was weak or your e-mail subject line was misleading, or maybe the book wasn't right for them. I know that sometimes it's easier to blame metrics, but in most cases, metrics aren't the real issue. Use metrics as a guide, but know that they should not be the basis of your entire marketing plan.

Not understanding timing

Timing in publishing has essentially become obsolete. Things like advanced reviews, advanced pitching, and early sales into bookstores aren't the be-all and end-all they once were. Still, timing is important. While it's true that sometimes older books can see a surge of success, this is not the rule. As I said above, you'll want to be prepared with your marketing early.

You should have a plan in place months before the book is out. That doesn't mean sending two hundred review copies out; it just means having your ducks in a row, so to speak. Also, timing can affect things like book events (especially if you're trying to get into bookstores). Understand when you should pitch your book for review and start to get to know your market and the bloggers you plan to pitch. Create a list and keep close track of who to contact and when you need to get your review pitch out there. Though many things have changed in regard to timing, it doesn't mean you shouldn't plan. A missed date is a missed opportunity.

Don't drink dirty water

There's a lot of negativity out there, and let's face it, there's a lot to complain about. I get it. And while I'm not trying to go all Tony Robbins on you here, your mental attitude has a lot to do with your success and your ability to keep going and keep marketing.

Sure, there are a lot of books out there, and a lot of other authors competing for the same virtual shelf space you are. When you go to a conference to learn how to sell more than a hundred books, you may run into someone who just hit their ten-thousandth book sale, and it can be discouraging. The thing is, the more you can stay positive, the more wind you will have in your sails. Believe me, this is true. I'm not asking you to stick your head in the sand and ignore the realities of publishing, but rather encouraging you to try to stay above it all.

I once worked with an author who was one of the most talented writers I've ever seen. Honestly. Every book this author wrote had mega-best seller plastered all over it. But he was always, always negative about everything. He didn't get enough reviews. He wasn't making enough sales, though

I knew his books were selling really well. Then, one day, despite his "everyone hates me" attitude, he got a traditional publishing deal. They published one of his books and then dropped him. I had a friend at this publishing house and asked her what the scoop was, and she said that he was so negative, so hard to please, and so hard to work with that no one could stand him. Don't drink dirty water—it will help you keep up your marketing efforts.

In a world where forty-five hundred books are being published every day, you need a positive attitude, a strong foundation, and the momentum to keep on marketing. Eventually, you will see the reward. Remember, overnight success rarely occurs overnight.

Penny Sansevieri
Author Marketing Experts (www.amarketingexpert.com)

Penny C. Sansevieri, founder and CEO of Author Marketing Experts, Inc., is the author of fifteen books, and a book marketing and media relations expert. She is an adjunct professor teaching self-publishing for NYU.

All About Publicity for Indie Authors and Their Books

Welcome to the 2016 edition of *The Self-Publisher's Ultimate Resource Guide*. I am Amy Edelman, founder of IndieReader and IndieReader Author Services, and I am here to explain what public relations is all about—specifically as it relates to you, the indie author—and what you need to know to do your own PR well.

What is book publicity anyway?

Book publicity—any publicity, really—is a means by which you can bring your product to the attention of people who are potentially interested in buying what you are selling. For authors, this means readers.

The secret ingredient to creating great publicity, especially today, when there are so many people and companies shouting to be heard, is to focus on how your product is different from everything else out there in the marketplace.

I hear you thinking: *Well, a book's a book … how different can mine be?* But there are many ways in which your book or you as an author can stand out. It all comes down to figuring out what makes your story different, and how skilled you are at communicating what those differences are.

What's your platform?

A platform is based on who you are. It is your personal story, and it's your platform that will enable you to stand apart from the crowd.

While you don't have to be a Kardashian (although clearly that doesn't hurt), having a unique story to tell—colorful, even tragic—can immediately make your platform more interesting to readers. Remember, authors are competing for attention on a daily basis with reality stars, celebrity chefs, and Oscar winners. You need to figure out what makes you different and then roll this information into your platform in a way that catches your readers' attention.

Indie author Hugh Howey, for example, worked as a yacht captain, roofer, audio technician, and salesperson in an indie bookstore before he self-published his first sci-fi series, *Wool*. He frequently cites his experience both as a bookseller and yacht captain to explain both the themes of his books and the choices he has made as an author.

Lisa Genova, the author of the originally self-published *Still Alice*, has a PhD in neuroscience from Harvard University. Lisa also had a grandmother who suffered from Alzheimer's. She used both her personal and professional experience to write and promote her book about a fifty-year-old Harvard professor who suffers from early-onset Alzheimer's disease. Lisa became somewhat of a poster girl for successful, self-published authors and was subsequently featured in stories in *The New York Times* and *Time* magazine. (Fun fact: those stories are what prompted me to launch IndieReader.)

What's your pitch?

Your platform is about your personal life and your connections. Your pitch should be about your book and should include its title, genre, and a short "sexy" synopsis. (NOTE: The term "sexy" is not so much about sex, but more about the electricity that should resonate from your pitch, even if your book is a nonfiction title dealing with climate change.)

An author who has spent a lot of time writing her book is probably an expert on her subject, but the trick is not to try to communicate *everything* about her book in her pitch, just the *most interesting* things. Keep it short, sweet, and riveting. Think of it this way: If Oprah still had her book club on TV, and she invited you to sit on her couch and talk about your book, what's the first thing you would say?

Break your pitch down to its essential components in words that the listener will remember. One method is to describe your book in comparison with other, preferably successful titles, so there's an immediate sense of recognition from your audience. For example, the following descriptions were taken from a recent issue of *Publishers Lunch*:

- Science and math writer Julie Rehmeyer's *Through the Shadowlands*—pitched as *Brain on Fire* meets *My Stroke of Insight* with a dash of *Wild*

- Guggenheim Fellow Donald Ray Pollock's *The Heavenly Table*—pitched as a Sam Peckinpah-meets-Erskine Caldwell epic

- Sarah Cooper's *100 Tricks to Appear Smart In Meetings: How to Get By Without Even Trying*, an illustrated business-humor book—pitched as *The Worst-Case Scenario Survival Handbook* meets *Dilbert* and *Office Space*

You get the idea.

As a longtime PR person, I am a big proponent of having, and being able to deliver, a great pitch. The ability to sell yourself and your book in as much time as it takes an elevator to descend ten floors is a skill that everyone—particularly indie authors—should master. And the best part is that it won't cost you a dime.

You have your platform and your pitch—now what?

You should include your book's platform and pitch in all your correspondence with the media, on your Amazon and Goodreads pages, and on your website. It should be well-thought-out, well-written (no typos!), and no longer than one page of twelve-point text. No one has the time to spend reading pages and pages of information. Be succinct. In this case, less is more, and shorter is better.

Do you need a press release?

A press release should ideally take a less personal tone than your pitch and is used primarily to announce something—a book signing, the winning of an award—to the media. It should be double-spaced and written in twelve-point Times Roman font and include your book's title and your contact information. It's always best to save a press release for more special announcements.

The importance of manners and outreach

I would suggest *not* including your book as an attachment until the editor/reviewer agrees to read it. Aside from seeming pushy, many people have spam blockers, and a submission with an attachment might not get through.

As for your outreach, be polite and concise. Cut and paste your pitch. Spell-check ... twice. Make sure you provide your contact information so they can get back to you. Follow up ("I just want to confirm that you received my pitch ...") exactly one time (no more!) if you haven't heard back in a week.

How do you find the right contacts?

As both an author and a lifelong PR person, I feel you should know what's going on in the book publishing industry, even if you'll never have the occasion to pitch there.

The three main trade publications, which address mostly traditional publishing, are *Publishers Weekly* (PW), *Publishers Lunch* (PL), and *Shelf Awareness* (SA). SA focuses more on news relating to brick-and-mortar bookstores. Each offers a daily e-mail highlighting the latest book publishing news. I suggest you sign up for them right away.

As far as more traditional media (e.g., newspapers, magazines, wire services, and broadcast media), you'll have to dedicate some time to research and learn who is open to receiving self-published books. It's always smart to start with your local newspaper. Look beyond the book editor. This is where your platform comes into play. If your book is about baseball, reach out to the sports editor. If it's chick lit, heavy on descriptions of clothes, reach out to the style editor. Think big. You might be turned down, but, as the saying goes, if at first you don't succeed, you can always try again.

The new world of social media

In the "olden" days (pre-Facebook), people were limited to traditional media to promote their wares. Today, thanks to social media, authors wanting to generate publicity can leave out the middleman (i.e., traditional media outlets) and go directly to their audience: their readers.

The new landscape can be both good and bad: "good" because there are so many more places to go and "bad" because, well, there are so many more places to go. It can become overwhelming. My advice would be to start slowly. Make sure you have kick-ass Amazon and Goodreads pages that include your pitch and a short biography. Build your

Twitter and Facebook presence (and friends and followers) not just by imploring people to buy your book but also by supporting other authors. Share the posts that resonate with you and pass along helpful info that you've read or learned along the way. There's a kind of karma at work here: the positive things you do for other authors are usually repaid in kind. What goes around comes around, as they say.

Don't be afraid to be imaginative and color outside the lines

Author of the self-published mystery novel *Blood Orchids*, Toby Neal offered some tips on the innovative way she promotes her books in a recent interview with IndieReader: "To build interest in an upcoming book, I post fun photos and videos of locations …" Toby's most recent book, *Rip Tides, is a mystery* that takes place in the world of surfing, so she traveled to Oahu; researched the professional surfing scene; and posted photos, quotes, and snippets of video from her research, along with personal reflections on why surfing is important to her. Another good idea? Pitching to sports writers at newspapers, magazines, and blogs who cover professional surfing.

But my book is self-published!

Yes, *you* know that and *I* know that, but that doesn't mean everyone else has to. Create an imprint and publish under that name. Believe me, no one has the time these days to double-check to see if you're the only author who is published under that imprint!

And, hey, it's 2015. Although many of the old assumptions and perceptions of self-published books remain—they're badly written and only authors who couldn't get published anywhere else do it—for some people in the media, self-publishing has gotten kind of cool. These are the people you want especially to target and cultivate and pitch!

The most important thing (aside from the pitch) for an indie author is reviews

Because you don't have the luxury of saying that a bona fide, big-name publisher thought your book was great enough to buy and publish (even if you never wanted them to), you still need some type of stamp of approval. That means, while the praise from your mother and father and partner is all well and good, you still need people who don't share your bloodline to give their honest feedback of your work.

Both Amazon and Goodreads have a list of top reviewers that you can find by Googling. Before sending your book to them, make sure that the reviewer is open to your book's genre and is currently accepting submissions.

In addition to free reviews, having at least one paid, professional review is worth it, if only because—if it's good—you can use it everywhere from your Amazon and Goodreads pages to your pitch to the media.

Outlets that provide paid reviews include the following:

- IndieReader (indiereader.com/authorservices/services/professional-review-service-alt-1)
- BlueInk Review (www.blueinkreview.com)
- Kirkus Indie (www.kirkusreviews.com/indie)

Can your book become a best seller?

Like most everything in life, there are no guarantees. My first (traditionally published) novel got a three-quarter-page, favorable review in Kirkus and People magazine and I was interviewed on the *Today* show (and those are just the highlights). While my novel sold fairly well for an unknown author, it didn't, as I had hoped, make *The New York Times* best-seller list or even earn out the advance I was paid. There are many,

many examples of great books that never receive the acclaim they deserve, and it's usually not for lack of trying.

My advice is to not give up. Write the best book you can, keep pitching and improving, and keep widening the circle of people you reach out to. At least you won't be able to beat yourself up for not trying.

What if you just want to hand things over to an experienced publicist?

One thing you need to do before you make the decision whether to hire someone is to *check their references*. There are as many publicists out there as there are indie authors, and some of them are quite good. But you'll never know—until you ask—what they've done before, if they have experience with your genre, who's on their media lists, who they'll be pitching your book to, and where the books they've promoted in the past have appeared. Unlike advertising, there are no guarantees with PR. If someone promises you that they will get you on the Today show or your book reviewed in *The New York Times*, you should run the other way.

In the end the onus is on you, the author, to be sure the person you're hiring will do her best for you and your book.

Amy Edelman
IndieReader (www.indiereader.com)

Amy Holman Edelman has spent her professional life as a publicist for consumer products like M&M's, Dunkin Donuts, and Hanes. She launched IndieReader , the essential consumer guide for self-published books and the people who write them, in 2009, with the goal of making self-publishing not only respectable, but also downright cool. She's still working on that.

Annie Jennings PR – Belle Mead, NJ 908-281-6201
annie@anniejenningspr.com, http://anniejenningspr.com
"full-service PR firm specializing in book promotion/publicity,
author/expert public relations, media presence & author
platform"

Ascot Media Group – The Woodlands, TX 281-333-3507
tstevens@ascotmediagroup.com, http://www.ascotmedia.com
"full service marketing, promotion, public relations &
advertising firm"

Authority Publishing – Gold River, CA 877-800-1097
service@authoritypublishing.com, http://authoritypublishing.com
"custom nonfiction self-publisher (selective titles) offering social
media marketing services to their authors"

Author Marketing Club – http://www.authormarketingclub.com
"free + paid premium membership access to marketing info,
tools & resources"

Author Marketing Experts – San Diego, CA 866-713-2318/
858-560-0121 http://www.amarketingexpert.com "full service
firm founded by Penny Sansevieri, recognized expert in book
marketing + media relations, specializing in social media
promotion for books & authors"

Blue Cottage Agency – http://www.bluecottageagency.com
"Offers author branding, author websites, website support,
social media, book tours, press releases, book launches & event
planning"

Brody Public Relations – Stockton, NJ 609-397-3737
beth@brodypr.com, http://www.brodypr.com "publicity
through media placement, speaking engagements &
promotional/marketing materials"

Bryan Farrish Marketing – Santa Monica, CA 310-998-8305
interviews@radio-media.com, http://www.radio-media.com
"specializes in publicity through radio interview promotion"

Burgett, Gordon – Novato, CA 800-563-1454 glburgett@aol.com,
http://www.gordonburgett.com "specializes in niche

publishing & empire-building from writing, speaking, & product development"

Caroline O'Connell Communications – N. Hollywood, CA 818-506-1775 oconnellpr@sbcglobal.net, http://www.oconnellcommunications.com "firm specializing in author tours + book publicity for nonfiction, especially business, travel, beauty, environmental via traditional & social media"

DeChant-Hughes Public Relations – Chicago, IL 312-280-8126 dha@dechanthughes.com, http://www.dechanthughes.com "PR firm dedicated to national media coverage for authors, specializing in books on religious thought, spirituality & culture"

EMSI Public Relations – Wesley Chapel, FL 800-881-7342/727-443-7115 info@emsincorporated.com, http://emsincorporated.com "pay-for-performance firm offering national/local media exposure + online & offline branding/marketing campaigns"

Gail Leondar Public Relations – Arlington, MA 781-648-1658 gail@glprbooks.com, http://www.glprbooks.com "specializing in promotion of progressive authors/books with a focus on radio"

Gulotta Communications – Newton, MA 617-630-9286 victor@booktours.com, http://www.booktours.com "full service book promotion + publicity for authors of fiction & nonfiction"

Jane Wesman Public Relations – New York, NY 212-620-4080 jane@wesmanpr.com, http://www.wesmanpr.com "book publicity + marketing including radio/TV/ interviews, Internet/ social media & branding"

Jennifer Prost Public Relations – Montclair, NJ 973-746-8723 jprostpr@comcast.net, http://www.jenniferprost.com "traditional publicity for authors/books including media exposure, author tours, press release/kits & promotional copywriting"

Julia Drake Public Relations – Los Angeles, CA 310-359-6487 M-F 9a-6p PST info@juliadrakepr.com, http://juliadrakepr.com "boutique literary publicist specializing in author platform/

branding via social media, website, book events/videos, press campaigns & author reels"

Kathryn Hall, Publicist – Ukiah, CA 707-468-8201 khpbooks@aol.com, http://www.kathrynhallpublicist.com "specializes in 'national print media tours' for limited genre nonfiction titles"

KT Public Relations & Literary Services – Fogelsville, PA 610-395-6298 kae@ktpublicrelations.com, http://www.ktpublicrelations.com "all phases of author marketing + publicity including press/promo materials, radio/TV/print interviews, book tours/signings, online/blog outreach & media relations"

Max Communications – Atlanta, GA 404-447-6242 mimi@maxbookpr.com, http://www.maxbookpr.com "book publicity, including press releases, book publicity plans, media lists, trade + review mailings, & more"

Media Masters Publicity – Tryon, NC 828-859-9456 tracey@mmpublicity.com, http://www.mmpublicity.com "maximize book exposure via local/national print/TV/radio media, author + virtual tours & websites/blogs/social networking sites"

Meryl Zegarek Public Relations – New York, NY 917-493-3601 mz@mzpr.com, http://www.mzpr.com "full service marketing + public relations firm specializing in comprehensive publicity campaigns for books & authors"

Milton Kahn Associates – Santa Barbara, CA 800-969-8555/805-969-8555 milton@miltonkahnpr.com, http://www.miltonkahnpr.com "book publicist, publishing consultant + marketing specialist offers public relations campaigns/promotion for authors & entertainment industry"

Monteiro & Company – New York, NY 212-832-8183 bam@monteiroandco.com, http://www.monteiroandco.com "specializing in book publicity via tailored campaigns in traditional + social media, ongoing public relations & sales/marketing consulting"

My Author Concierge – (858) 431-6777 mariaconnor@msn.com, http://www.myauthorconcierge.com "Maria Connor offers promotional plan development, author branding assistance, newsletter management, virtual party planning, blog management & more"

Nissen Public Relations – Summit, NJ 908-376-6470 info@nissenpr.com, http://nissenpr.com "specializing in publicity for business, current affairs + all nonfiction books through print, TV, radio & online/blog outlets"

Page-Turner Publicity – Miami, FL 949-254-3214 jperez@pageturnerpublicity.com, http://www.pageturnerpublicity.com/ "literary publicity firm offering strategic media placement, author tours, promotional events & press materials"

PR by the Book – Round Rock, TX 512-501-4399 x706 info@prbythebook.com, http://www.prbythebook.com "author publicity + branding via traditional/online media outreach, social media strategy, book/speaking tours; also training & consulting to build a long-term platform"

Public Eye – Minneapolis, MN 612-436-3957 http://www.publiceye.com "Hillcrest Media division for book marketing/publicity including traditional, online & social media marketing"

The Publicity Hound – Port Washington, WI 262-284-7451 JStewart@PublicityHound.com, http://publicityhound.com "Joan Stewart will brainstorm story ideas, review media kits + help with book publicity campaigns & pitching your book"

PW Select – New York, NY 212-377-5500 service@booklife.com, http://booklife.com/pwselect "Publishers Weekly service that promotes your book across PW's properties, reaching booksellers, librarians, publishers, agents, media and more for $149"

Sam Petersen Associates – Menlo Park, CA 660-854-5575
sampetersenpr@aol.com, http://www.sampetersen.com "20
years' experience arranging publicity, promotion + author tours
for books on photography, travel, art, architecture, design,
current/environmental issues, home, gardening & cooking"

Sandra Goroff & Associates – Canton, MA 617-750-0555
sgma@aol.com, http://www.sandragoroff.com "full service
PR firm offering high-level media (print/TV/radio/online)
placement, promotional book tours/events, branding, project
analysis & consulting"

The Sayles Organization – Woodland Hills, CA 818-999-9571
nancy@saylesorganization.com,
http://www.saylesorganization.com "targeted book publicity
tailored to specific audience, objective & budgetary needs of
author"

Sherri Rosen Publicity – New York, NY 212-222-1183
http://www.sherrirosen.com "comprehensive, tailored
book publicity campaigns as well as prepress manuscript
development, eBook design & consulting"

S.J. Miller Communications – Randolph, MA 781-986-0732
staceyjmiller@bookpr.com OR bookpromotion@gmail.com,
http://www.bookpr.com "full service book/eBook publicity
including traditional promotion/media outreach + online
marketing, (social media/blog/virtual tours), platform building
& branding"

Skye Wentworth Public Relations – Newbury, MA 978-462-4453
skyewentworth@gmail.com, http://www.skyewentworth.org
"author media relations + publicity services including press kits,
book tours, print/TV/radio & Internet"

Smith Publicity – Cherry Hill, NJ 856-489-8654 x306
info@smithpublicity.com, http://www.smithpublicity.com
"publicity for indie authors of most genres, including eBooks,
via media/press exposure, Amazon optimization, social media
launch, book tours & events"

Spence Media – Leesburg, VA 214-939-1700
http://www.spencemedia.com "comprehensive author/book
publicity with emphasis on radio, TV & print appearances"

Stephanie Barko Literary Publicist – Austin, TX
stephanie@stephaniebarko.com,
http://www.stephaniebarko.com "literary publicist for
nonfiction + historical fiction authors offering comprehensive
media campaigns/promotion & pre/post-pub marketing
consulting"

Storyrally – jason@storyrally.com, http://storyrally.com/coaching/
"Jason Kong offers personalized marketing consulting for
authors & free online marketing strategies for fiction writers"

Susan Schwartzman Public Relations – Bronxville, NY
877-833-4276/914-776-1380 sjschwa@aol.com,
http://www.susanschwartzmanpublicity.com "book + author
publicist with reputation for tenacity, specializing in media
placement & brand-building"

Susannah Greenberg Public Relations – Dix Hills, NY 646-801-7477
publicity@bookbuzz.com, http://www.bookbuzz.com "full-
service PR firm offering outbound (radio/TV/print publicity) +
inbound (online/social media) book marketing"

VidLit – liz@vidlit.com, http://www.vidlit.com "book marketing
& content-creating company offering artist management &
guidance, public relations campaigns, media relations, social
media strategy, strategic marketing & more"

Sites to List E-books

Whether you are looking for free publicity or planning on purchasing paid ads for your book, it is important to know what sites are indie-book friendly and good at book promotion. Aside from the countless book bloggers we know and love, there are entire sites dedicated to selling books at all prices.

Why might an author take advantage of these sites?

Book listing sites offer great visibility for books at a variety of price points. These sites are marketing tools you can use—in many cases for free or at little cost. When trying to get your book in front of as many readers as possible, adding it to some of the sites in this section is a must. There are three ways you can use the sites below to market your book.

Free promotions

One of the most controversial marketing techniques is offering your e-book for free. While we could get into a book-long discussion on the benefits and downsides of free promotions and what this means for the future of literature, I suspect you are likely to try at least one free promotion in your career as an author.

As an author assistant I have helped many authors with their free promotions, and my advice remains the same—submit your book to sites that list free books. The bottom line is even a free book will need to be shared with readers, and the platform from which you can sell your book is only so big. Tapping into the platforms of major listing sites, the ones that exist with the sole purpose of telling readers about free books, is a no-brainer.

Now, whether you decide to pay to be listed on these sites or opt for the free listings (which offer no guarantee of your book being listed) is up to you. I suggest authors submit their books to sites that offer a free listing. In the worst-case scenario, you've spent an hour submitting your book to these sites, it doesn't get picked up, and it does as well as it can without the extra boost. In the best-case scenario, your book is picked up by numerous sites and sees a jump in downloads you wouldn't have gotten any other way. For most authors, you'll find if you give these sites enough advance notice (try a month to three weeks in advance of your sale date), a few sites will pick up your book and you'll reach a wider audience at the cost of only a little of your time.

Discount promotions

Like running a free promotion of your book, discounting the price of a book is another common marketing tool for indie authors. The difference between a discount promotion and a free promotion lies in the finances, obviously. A discount promotion gives you the chance to make some money, but the opportunities for free listings on sites go down, as more sites charge for listing discounted e-books versus listing free e-books. Still, there are many benefits to running sales on your books, and listing sites are here to help you make the most of your promotion.

When an author wants to do a discounted promotion, I always suggest we look at listing the book on the appropriate listing sites in addition to their other marketing efforts, such as their newsletter, blog, and social media. While there are fewer sites that offer free listings for discounted books, there are still a few that do. Start with the free sites and consider adding a paid ad or two. BookBub is a well-regarded listing site for free and discounted books, but it is also one of the most expensive and difficult sites to get your book listed on. Yet many authors have found a paid BookBub ad can lead them to make sales that cover the expense of the initial ad— and it has provided other benefits, such as new newsletter subscribers.

So when it comes to paying for ads for your discounted e-book, remember to look not only at the cost of the ad but also at the potential benefits it may bring you. Talk to other authors and see what sites they have tried and where they had the most success. Run experiments of your own, and try a new site each time you run a discount. As an indie author, you have one of the best gifts in publishing—control. You get to see what works for you and what doesn't, so it is always a good idea to try new things.

General visibility

Remember, in order for a reader to buy your book, she must first find out about it. Many authors use social media and book bloggers to help get their books in front of new readers, but why not try a well-placed listing or even an ad or two? You may be surprised what leads a reader to your book.

Use the sites below to create a section in your marketing plan for book listing sites. You won't be sorry you took the extra step, I promise.

Kate Tilton
Kate Tilton's Author Services, LLC (www.katetilton.com)

Kate Tilton has been serving authors since 2010. Founder of Kate Tilton's Author Services, LLC, Kate works as an author as-sistant, social media manager, and speaker with the mission of connecting authors and readers. Kate is the creator and host of #K8chat (Thursdays at 9 p.m. Eastern on Twitter) and has appeared in popular media such as *Publishers Weekly and Library Journal.*

Addicted to eBooks – http://www.addictedtoebooks.com "free listing for qualified free & low-cost eBooks + paid advertising options"

Author Marketing Club – http://www.authormarketingclub.com "links to some of the top places to list free eBooks + training tools to help authors promote & market their work"

Bargain eBook Hunter – admin@bargainebookhunter.com, http://bargainebookhunter.com "fee-based listings for free & bargain eBooks"

Book Deal Hunter – http://bookdealhunter.com "subscribed authors can submit free Kindle books for inclusion (paid/ sponsored listings will be available in future)"

Book Marketing Tools – http://bookmarketingtools.com/ submission-tool-features "paid eBook submission tool for faster reporting to 30+ websites"

eBook Booster – info@ebookbooster.com, http://www.ebookbooster.com "paid submission service for free & 99-cent eBooks"

eBook Lister – info@ebooklister.net, http://www.ebooklister.net "free listing for site-approved, author-submitted free & bargain-priced Kindle books"

The eReader Cafe – theereadercafe@gmail.com, http://www.theereadercafe.com "free & bargain Kindle books may be submitted for inclusion or you can purchase featured listing"

Ereader News Today – bookpromos@ereadernewstoday.com, http://ereadernewstoday.com "will list free + 99-cent eBooks that meet the criteria for 25% commission on earnings made via their links"

Free Booksy – info@freebooksy.com, http://freebooksy.com "fee-based featured listings for free eBooks + book giveaway promotions & advertising for non-free eBooks"

Free eBooks Daily – http://www.freeebooksdaily.com "nominal fee to submit your free eBook (must have 4-star or higher rating on Amazon) for inclusion + options for additional promotion on site/blog/social media"

Indie Book Bargains – admin@indie-book-bargains.co.uk, http://www.indie-book-bargains.co.uk "enrolled authors can submit free + bargain eBooks for inclusion & add author profile to site"

YourDailyeBooks.com – contact@yourdailyebooks.com, http://www.yourdailyebooks.com "subscribed authors can post their free eBooks"

News & Views

It's crazy out there. Every day new websites pop up for self-publishers, new service providers, new gimmicks, and new outrageous promises for secret ways to make millions of dollars from your book with only a modest investment. It's pretty hard to separate the wheat from the chaff, to tell who is legit and who isn't, to know whether someone is offering a reputable, professional service or just wants to take your money and run.

The best way to sort out all the advice and pitches vying for your attention and wallet is to stay on top of what's happening in book publishing in general. And the best way to do that is to check in with a few of the leading publishing news sites every few days or so. There are many to choose from, but those listed in the following pages tend to be the ones most people in the traditional publishing business rely on religiously.

Whether you are traditionally published, a hybrid author, or an indie author, you'll find that these sites are packed with information about how New York book publishing *really* works, what editors are looking for in a manuscript, and what genres are outselling others, and you'll often come across marketing tips and insights you'd probably never have thought of on your own.

If you get into the habit of checking in with these sites every few days or so, as I do, you will be right on top of the New York publishing scene—and if you should someday decide you'd like to try to find an agent and publish your next book with one of the Big Five publishers (Penguin/Random House, Hachette, Harper Collins, MacMillan, or Simon & Schuster), you'll be much better prepared to go about it like a pro.

I suggest you check them all out, find the ones that resonate with you and the kinds of books you are working on, and sign up. Some offer a great blog or a newsletter in addition to the general content on the site. Once you get into the habit of checking in with these websites every few days, you'll be right up to date on all the breaking news in both the traditional and the self-publishing world, as well as have access to the personal opinions of many of the major movers and shakers in the ever-changing book publishing business.

Betty Kelly Sargent
BookWorks (www.bookworks.com)

Alltop – http://www.publishing.alltop.com "an aggregation of the most popular stories from articles & publishing blogs across the web"

DBW (Digital Book World) – http://www.digitalbookworld.com "annual conference + year-round platform providing information, educational & networking resources designed to address the radically changing publishing environment"

GalleyCat – http://www.mediabistro.com/galleycat "hosted by Mediabistro.com, billing itself as *the first word on the book publishing industry*, covering publishing news, deals, booksellers, writer resources, jobs + book reviews"

The Hot Sheet – http://hotsheetpub.com..."eNewsletter from Jane Friedman & Porter Anderson on essential publishing industry news"

Huffington Post – http://www.huffingtonpost.com/news/book-publishing "news, views, blogs & book recommendations"

Mediabistro – http://www.mediabistro.com/publishing "publishing news, views and events"

Publishers Lunch – http://lunch.publishersmarketplace.com/ "the most widely read daily dossier in publishing, known as *the publishing industry's daily essential read*"

Publishers Marketplace – http://www.publishersmarketplace.com "a service of Publishers Lunch available for a monthly fee; it works in part because it's driven by more than 40,000 publishing professionals who read Lunch every day"

Publishers Weekly – http://www.publishersweekly.com "website, digital + print publication covering all facets of publishing, including industry news, book reviews, libraries, self-publishers & job opportunities"

The Shatzkin Files – http://www.idealog.com "Mike Shatzkin, longtime publishing insider, covers the latest developments + news, offering trenchant opinions & forecasting emerging trends affecting traditional as well as self-publishing"

E-book Aggregators & Book Distributors

How to use an e-book distributor to reach more readers

Next to the quality of your writing and fabulous cover design, broad distribution is probably the most important factor determining the success of your book. If a book isn't available in bookstores where readers go to discover and purchase books, then it is invisible to readers. We are going to explain here how to use an e-book distributor to maximize your ability to reach readers, and we will also give you some important tips on how to leverage tools such as e-book preorders and enhanced series metadata to make it easy for your potential readers to find and buy your book.

What's an e-book distributor?

An e-book distributor distributes e-books to retailers, libraries, and other sales channels. E-book distributors are sometimes called aggregators because they aggregate ("collect into a mass") the distribution of books from hundreds or even thousands of authors and publishers. Retailers, by contrast, are the online bookstores where readers go to discover, purchase, and download books. Apple iBooks, Barnes & Noble, Gardners, Kobo, and Amazon are examples of e-book retailers. As a distributor, Smashwords distributes e-books from authors and publishers to online retailers like the ones we just mentioned.

Why use an e-book distributor?

E-book self-publishing is very popular and full of advantages such as faster time-to-market, lots of creative control, and higher royalties, to name a few. But one of the greatest challenges of being a self-published author is figuring out how to make your book more discoverable to more readers. The easiest way to ensure your book is as discoverable as possible is to have your book available at the places where readers go to find books. Distributors help authors reach many more retailers than the authors could manage on their own, and they do it more quickly and efficiently. In fact, best-selling self-published authors cite massive time-saving, global distribution reach, discoverability tools, and ease of use as reasons why they like to work with distributors.

One of the greatest benefits of working with a distributor is you gain consolidated, centralized control over your e-book publishing through the author dashboard. From your dashboard, you can easily view and manage different aspects of your publishing such as Sales & Reporting, Metadata Updates, and Marketing and Distribution tools.

The dashboard provides centralized metadata management for pricing, book updates, sales reporting, and more. Next we'll discuss the importance of these features and how a distributor helps.

- **Simplified uploading and updates.** Perhaps the greatest value a distributor provides to authors is the ability to save time. When you work with a distributor, you simply upload your book to the distributor once, and the distributor ensures your book reaches multiple (dozens or even hundreds) of retail and library outlets. If you want or need to update your cover image, price, book description, book content, or any other metadata, you make the update once on your distributor's dashboard, and your distributor propagates the updates to all sales channels. This is a tremendous time saver for authors.

- **Channel management**. Most distributors allow you to opt in and out of particular sales channels. For example, at Smashwords, since we don't distribute all our books to Amazon, most Smashwords authors upload directly to Amazon KDP and then use Smashwords to reach all the other retailers as well as our library channel partners. To expand your global reach, we recommend opting in to as many different channels as possible. By doing so, you can get your book listed at hundreds of retailers and libraries in more than a hundred countries.

- **Price management**. Most distributors allow centralized pricing control. Centralized pricing enables you to change the price of your book once and have the pricing update reach all the retail channels your distributor reaches. Some distributors offer advanced tools (e.g., Smashwords Pricing Manager) that allow you to set different pricing for libraries than for retailers.

- **Series management**. If you publish series, take advantage of distributor tools that allow you to attach enhanced metadata to each book in your series—at Smashwords we call this the Smashwords Series Manager. Retailers use this enhanced metadata to make your series books more discoverable in their stores. With enhanced series metadata, readers can clearly identify which of your books are part of a series, the reading order of the series, and the series name.

- **Sales reporting.** Another huge benefit of working with a distributor is the aggregated sales reporting. Aggregated reports, especially same-day and next-day aggregated reporting, give you at-a-glance intelligence to help you monitor the effectiveness of your marketing campaigns.

- **Aggregated payments.** Another time-saving benefit of working with a distributor is aggregated payments. When your books are selling, the retailer pays the distributor and then the distributor pays you. Aggregated payments are especially helpful for end-of-year tax reporting. At the end of the year, instead of managing multiple forms from multiple retailers, you receive a single tax reporting form.

- **Preorders.** Most distributors allow you to set up preorders. At Smashwords, we've been doing preorders since 2013, and we've proved that books born as preorders sell more copies than books that are simply uploaded the day of release. In 2015, we enhanced our preorder capabilities to support assetless (a.k.a. "metadata only") preorders that only require a title, description, release date, price, and category. With an assetless preorder, you can get your book listed for preorder at retailers such as iBooks, Barnes & Noble, and Kobo up to 12 months in advance, even before the book is finished. This longer preorder period enables more effective advance marketing because you can capture a sale in advance of your book's release date. The magic of preorders is that all your accumulated preorders register as sales on the day your book is released, thereby increasing your chances of hitting the best-seller lists. Preorders have helped dozens of Smashwords authors hit best-seller lists including the *New York Times* and *USA Today* lists. To learn how to hit best-seller lists by leveraging e-book preorders, visit "How to Reach More Readers with Ebook Preorders" (blog.smashwords.com/2015/06/how-to-reach-more-readers-with-ebook.html)

- **Library distribution.** Each year, libraries around the world spend millions of dollars on e-book purchases. Libraries purchase these e-books through library e-book aggregators such as OverDrive, Baker & Taylor's Axis 360, and Gardners Books' Askews & Holts service. When selecting an e-book distributor for your book, ask if they work with library aggregators. A good e-book distributor such as Smashwords can distribute your books to these library aggregators so that your e-books are available for purchase by public and academic libraries.

Being a self-published author is a wonderfully liberating experience, but as you'll soon discover if you haven't already, there is a lot of work involved. E-book distributors are valuable partners to self-published authors because they help you maximize your global retail reach efficiently. Why do best-selling self-published e-book authors choose to work with a distributor? At Smashwords, they tell us it's because we help them spend more time writing and less time managing myriad retailer requirements. By partnering with a distributor, you simply upload your book and metadata once, and your distributor takes care of everything else. It's fast, it's easy, and best of all, you are in control.

Mark Coker
Smashwords (www.smashwords.com)

Since Mark Coker founded Smashwords in 2008, it has grown to become the leading e-book distributor serving indie authors, small presses, and literary agents. More than 100,000 authors from around the world publish and distribute more than 300,000 books with Smashwords. Mark's three books on e-book publishing best practices—*The Smashwords Style Guide, The Smashwords Book Marketing Guide,* and *The Secrets to E-book Publishing Success*—have been downloaded more than 700,000 times and are considered essential reference guides for indie authors.

Blurb – San Francisco, CA 888-998-1605 M-F 3a-6p PST
http://www.blurb.com "self-publishing platform for full-color
print + eBook with multiple digital book-building tools; offering
direct sales through author's website, sales through Amazon &
distribution worldwide through Ingram"

BookBaby – Portland, OR 877-961-6878 M-F 9a-8p EST
book@bookbaby.com, http://www.bookbaby.com "full service
publishing + distribution packages; offering cover design,
editing, conversion/formatting, ISBN's as well as promotional
tools for both print (POD) & eBooks"

Draft2Digital – Oklahoma City, OK 866-336-5099 M-F 8a-4p CST
sales@draft2digital.com, https://www.draft2digital.com "eBook
formatting, publishing + distribution platform to Apple, Nook,
Kobo, Scribd & Page Foundry"

Ingram Spark – La Vergne, TN
ingramsparksupport@ingramcontent.com,
https://www1.ingramspark.com "publishing platform with fully
integrated print, digital, wholesale + distribution services to
every major/emerging eBook retailer worldwide"

INscribe Digital – San Francisco, CA 415-489-7000
http://www.inscribedigital.com "global eBook distributors
to Kindle/KDP, Nook, Kobo, Apple; also offering conversion &
marketing services"

Smashwords – Los Gatos, CA https://www.smashwords.com
"eBook self-publishing + distribution platform to all major
e-retailers (except Amazon Kindle, which author must upload
directly) founded by Mark Coker; allows author/publisher
complete control, providing tools for marketing, distribution,
metadata management & sales reporting"

Vook – New York, NY weloveauthors@vook.com, https://vook.com
"publish + sell your eBook (including enhanced, video,
interactive) to Amazon, iBooks, Barnes & Noble, Kobo, Google
Play and Blio (Baker & Taylor) across 192 territories"

Major Retailers

Major retailers and what they offer indie authors

The retail landscape for self-publishing is complex, filled with a mix of traditional retailers offering self-published titles on demand and online retailers who spend a great deal of effort supporting authors and opening up avenues to promote self-published books. In an effort to capture and keep market share, many companies have their own digital ecosystems, offering branded e-book readers and apps, with their own catalog of titles for sale. Though fragmented, the market has consolidated around several major retailers, where the bulk of all consumer print and e-book buying takes place.

Getting your book into one of these retailers may seem daunting, but knowing the major players, and how to get in, will greatly increase the visibility of your book, and its potential sales audience. We will take a look at five of the largest vendors for print and e-books and explain how you can get your book listed in each one. We will also touch upon what each vendor has to offer in the areas of e-book readers, apps, and print-on-demand technology.

Amazon

Amazon is the largest online bookstore, selling print editions as well as e-books through its Kindle platform. Amazon is also the main seller of the Kindle e-book readers and apps—offering many Kindle-style tablets and readers that integrate into their ecosystem. As a seller, Amazon offers customers an easy buying experience, with typically fast shipping and competitive prices. Often touted as a one-stop shop for print and e-book buying, Amazon offers an extensive range of titles provided by their CreateSpace print-on-demand label, the KDP e-book label, and the full Ingram catalog of titles.

To further their integration and product offering, Amazon offers their Prime subscription service for an annual fee. Customers who subscribe to Prime may enroll in the Kindle Owners' Lending Library, where they can digitally borrow books to read on their Kindle devices, one per month, without an additional charge. It has become a draw for a number of customers, and offering your book in the Lending Library can be a solid strategy for gaining traction with a large audience.

Publishing with Amazon has become the top priority for the majority of authors, since Amazon is a primary retail channel that readers use to purchase books. Getting into Amazon is easy, since they include titles made available through all major POD and e-book distribution services, as well as their own CreateSpace and KDP systems. The KDP system, which is Kindle exclusive, is of particular interest to authors who only want to offer their work on Amazon, where they can take advantage of promotional opportunities granted by Amazon in exchange for exclusive distribution rights.

Barnes & Noble

The largest brick-and-mortar bookstore chain, and home of the Nook e-book readers and apps, Barnes & Noble stores are a staple of the book-buying landscape. The large and welcoming retail locations are designed to mix reading and retail and are often packed with places to sit and thumb through the books you are interested in, in the hopes you will decide to buy the book and take it home to finish it.

Barnes & Noble offers the Nook line of e-book readers. Though not as widespread as the Kindle, the Nook has been moderately successful and owners tend to enjoy their devices. The integration of the Nook into the Barnes & Noble ecosystem mirrors the Amazon model in many ways, offering readers a choice of print and e-book titles all under one roof.

Like Amazon, Barnes & Noble offers the entire Ingram catalog of print and e-book titles for sale. To have your book available for order at Barnes & Noble is as simple as finding a POD or e-book distributor that includes the title in the Ingram catalog, which is offered by all major vendors. Unlike Amazon, Barnes & Noble does not offer an in-house print-on-demand service. Barnes & Noble does have a direct option to submit your e-book for Nook distribution, which operates much like KDP.

Getting your book on the physical store shelf can pose a real challenge, since shelf space is limited and the requirements for getting in, like offering returns on titles, may pose a financial burden on an author. However, it is not impossible to have your book printed and included on the shelves of a Barnes & Noble store, and they do have a submission process for those who would like to have their book considered.

Books-A-Million

Books-A-Million is the second-largest brick-and-mortar bookstore chain. Books-A-Million stores have recently been shifting their focus from simply selling books to also moving magazines, toys, novelties, and movies. They have also begun to focus on children's titles, anime, and manga, as well as teen and young adult titles and accompanying merchandise. This broadening shift has changed the quiet vibe of many locations to a more energetic and youthful one, likely changing the audience and brand appeal as well.

Like Barnes & Noble, Books-A-Million offers the full Ingram catalog of books for order through their online store, as well as in-store at the counter. Books-A-Million does not currently offer a house-brand e-book reader or platform, but they do have apps for Android and iOS devices, as well as offering a version of the Nook for sale.

One of the more exciting directions for Books-A-Million is the BAM! Publishing platform. Using the Espresso Book Machine, a small number of Books-A-Million locations are now able to print entire paperback books in store, for rapid delivery to a waiting customer. This process allows a customer to ask for your book at the counter and leave with it in the same visit. Though there are currently only a few locations doing this, if the platform expands to more stores, authors will have a new opportunity to sell the physical version of their book without a wait.

Kobo

As a large online e-book retailer based in Canada, Kobo offers books and magazines delivered digitally. Kobo is well known for offering books in a number of languages, making it a very popular digital vendor with a global market reach. Kobo gains further traction by offering its content for the Kobo e-book reader family that it sells, as well as numerous Kobo reader apps for all major phone and tablet platforms. This makes Kobo a viable and versatile retailer that focuses on delivering digital content to a broad market. If you want your book to appeal to a wide international audience, Kobo is a great digital retail channel to use.

Like other vendors, Kobo offers the full Ingram catalog for e-books, so getting into Kobo is as simple as using an e-book distributor that lists your book in the Ingram catalog or a direct channel into the Kobo store. Kobo also has a direct path to publishing on its platform, Kobo Writing Life, where you can upload your own EPUB-formatted e-book to the system.

Apple iBooks

Apple's online e-book retailer and home of the iPad, iPhone, and iBooks app, is a more recent addition to the digital landscape. Due to the integrated nature of Apple's publishing ecosystem, iBooks, also integrated with iTunes, is readily visible and available on the millions of Apple devices in use worldwide. Having your book in iBooks opens up a host of great selling opportunities for your title due to the enormous number of users who enjoy the convenience of Apple devices, such as the iPad and iPhone, and their content delivery systems.

Getting into the iBooks store is, again, as easy as using a vendor that offers inclusion in the Ingram catalog or direct inclusion in the iBooks store. iBooks Author, available only on Mac devices, allows authors to publish their books directly to the iBooks store using an easy-to-operate application.

Tracy Atkins
Book Design Templates (www.bookdesigntemplates.com)

Tracy R. Atkins is a technical expert with over fifteen years of experience building end-user technology platforms, holds numerous industry certifications, and is a Microsoft Certified Professional. He excels in simplifying complex technological solutions into easy-to-use tools for the average Joe. Tracy is also a successful self-published author who is intimately familiar with the many issues that independent authors encounter on their road to publication. This powerful combination of technology and self-publishing experience makes Tracy the go-to guy for building great tools that help authors succeed.

Aerbook – San Francisco, CA 347-567-8670
getintouch@aerbook.com, http://aerbook.com "direct retail +
marketing of print & eBooks via the cloud on the mobile, social
web through integrated services with Ingram Content Group"

iBookstore (Apple) – 800-692-7753 https://www.apple.com/ibooks
"eBooks can be purchased through the iBookstore for use on all
Apple devices, iPad, iPhone, iPod touch or Mac"

KDP (Amazon Direct Kindle Direct Publishing) –
https://kdp.amazon.com "upload + publish your eBook directly
on the Amazon site for sale worldwide in the Kindle store."

Kobo – Toronto, ON Canada 416-977-8737
http://store.kobobooks.com "global eBook retailer (especially
the Canadian market) + eReader of same name"

Nook Press (Barnes & Noble) – https://www.nookpress.com "self-
publishing + retail platform; all eBooks in NOOK Bookstores
are available on BN.com, NOOK.co.uk, NOOK devices & on free
eReading software for Android, iPad, iPhone, Windows 8, Mac &
PC"

OverDrive Inc. – Cleveland, OH 216-573-6886
https://www.overdrive.com "digital distribution, DRM +
download fulfillment of audio + eBooks for publishers, self-
publishers (via Smashwords, Vook, INscribe), libraries, schools &
retailers"

Oyster – New York, NY partners@oysterbooks.com,
https://www.oysterbooks.com "digital member-fee
subscription service that allows readers to download eBooks to
tablets, phones & web readers"

Scribd – San Francisco, CA https://www.scribd.com "digital
member-fee subscription service that allows readers to
download eBooks + PDFs to tablets, phones & web readers"

Writing Contests, Fellowships, & Prizes

The good, the bad, and why they matter for indie authors

Writing is not usually thought of as a competitive activity, but it is. At the highest levels of literature and publishing, the Nobel Prize, the Pulitzer Prize, the National Book Award, and the PEN/Faulkner Award are prestigious and coveted honors, and England's Man Booker Prize—televised like the Oscars—has the power to utterly transform an author's career. While these awards are not available to indie authors, there are thousands of lesser-known competitions—as well as fellowships and grants—that are available, and they are definitely worth considering.

Everyone has a story to tell, and many of us will write them. The problem, if you are not a recognized writer or celebrity of some kind, is how do you get your story read, let alone published? A contest may be the answer.

Winning a contest can give you a leg up on all the other writers struggling to attract a reader's attention. For one thing, the minimum prize is usually the publication of your work in whatever journal sponsored the contest. Other possible benefits include an introduction to an agent, prize money you can put toward self-publishing, and sometimes even a traditional book contract. Imagine your book with the tag "winner" on the cover. Contests can be an effective weapon in your arsenal.

A quick online search for "writing contests" returns more than eight million results. Of course, anyone can organize a writing contest, but most of the legitimate ones are conducted by journals, magazines (both online and print), small presses, and universities. Some require an entry fee and ask for first publication rights to your book. Some have a theme or are geared to a specific subject or publication. They can be fun and inspiring and often provide cash prizes as well as prestige.

What contests and fellowships have in common are rewards and bragging rights. A fellowship may offer a cash grant or a retreat for a writer. A fellowship is often a gift of time and space to start or finish a project. It can be a welcome respite from the day-to-day needs of earning money and doing chores, providing as it does the opportunity to devote a set amount of time to just writing. Universities, foundations, and government agencies often sponsor fellowships.

In the case of both contests and fellowships, the following rules apply:

- **Read the eligibility instructions.** Don't waste your time on something you may not be qualified for. Are you too old or too young? Is this contest or fellowship limited to a specific region? Does it focus on a particular subject? Are previously published writers excluded? Important questions all.

- **What are the submission rules?** What's the desired word count? Is there a formatting requirement? Is your subject right for them? When is the deadline? Be sure to revise your piece accordingly to ensure that it is ideally suited for each individual competition or fellowship. This is never a waste of time. Revision is the heart of writing.

- **Enter as many competitions as possible.** The more you enter, the better chance you have of winning.

- **Track your submissions.** Keep a submission log. Each of your submissions should have its own chart, which includes: the name of the contest, the submission date, the date the announcement of the winner is expected, and a status column to record feedback (if there was any) and whether or not you won. Your submission is valuable even if you didn't win. You can always enter it in another contest.

Sadly, however, not all contests are legitimate. There are companies that try to take advantage of a writer's desire for recognition. Here are a few simple questions to ask before you enter, and the answers can save you time and money.

- **Has this contest been run before?** This is in no way to say that every first-year contest is a scam, but a track record with few complainants is a good sign.

- **Who is running the contest?** When you do a quick search, do you feel satisfied that the company running the competition is reputable?

- **Who are the judges?** Are they well-respected professionals?

- **What is the entry fee?** Does it seem reasonable? Can you afford it? Remember that there are contests and fellowships that don't require any fee. Is the fee worth the payoff, or are they charging too much to enter in relation to the prize? Entry fees higher than $40 might be considered excessive.

- **Are there additional fees?** Supplemental fees like the cost of editing, publishing, and membership fees are flashing neon warning signs that a contest is a scam.

- **Who are the past winners?** This is always a good area to research. Do you find the past winners compelling? Is this the company you wish to keep? This will also help with your submission. Past winners will give you an indication of the type and style of writing this contest rewards.

- **What rights to your work might you be surrendering by entering the contest?** Know what they are asking you to give up and when. You should never enter a contest at the cost of ownership of your work. In some cases it may be worth it to give up some rights in the short term, but never give up your rights in perpetuity.

- **Are there additional fees?** Supplemental fees like the cost of editing, publishing and membership fees are flashing neon warning signs that a contest is a scam.

- **Who is running the contest?** When you do a quick search do you feel satisfied that you know that the company running the competition is reputable?

- **How many categories are there?** There should be different contests for different genres. A poetry book shouldn't be competing with a nonfiction business book. Writing is not one size fits all, and the contest shouldn't be either.

Always read the fine print, which is as binding as a contract once you enter. Do not skim. Read and understand every word. Warning signs may include lines about prize substitution, using your entry for publicity, or the required use of the contest sponsor as your agent. If you have any questions or concerns, e-mail the contest organizers before entering. A legitimate competition will want your entry and e-mail back. If that little voice inside your head says the contest is a scam or you don't understand any part of the terms and conditions, walk away, no matter how tempting the prizes may be.

The good news is that most contests and awards are legitimate and can boost your career. Be thoughtful about choosing the contest that's right for you, keep track of your submissions, and above all, have fun!

Liz Dubelman
VidLit (www.vidlit.com)

Liz Dubelman is the founder and CEO of VidLit Productions, LLC, the world-renowned book marketing and content-creation company. She coedited and contributed to *What Was I Thinking? 58 Bad Boyfriend Stories* (St. Martin's Press, 2009) and is a magazine writer of both fiction and nonfiction.

Alabama State Council on the Arts – (individual artist grants for poetry, fiction & creative nonfiction) Montgomery, AL 334-242-4076 x236 anne.kimzey@arts.alabama.gov, http://www.arts.state.al.us/programs/literary_arts/literary_arts.aspx "fellowships given annually"

Arrowhead Regional Arts Council – (fellowships & grants for poetry, fiction & creative nonfiction) Duluth, MN 800-569-8134/218-722-0952 info@aracouncil.org, http://www.aracouncil.info "fellowships & grants given twice a year to Minnesota writers"

Artist Trust – (literature fellowships for poetry, fiction & creative nonfiction) Seattle, WA 866-218-7878/206-467-8734 info@artisttrust.org, http://www.artisttrust.org/index.php/for-artists/money "fellowships awarded biennially"

Association of Writers & Writing Programs – (award series for poetry, fiction & creative nonfiction) Fairfax, VA 703-993-4308 supriya@awpwriter.org, http://www.awpwriter.org/contests "two cash prizes + publication by a participating press given annually"

Bard College – (Bard Fiction Prize for fiction) Annandale-on-Hudson, NY 845-758-7087 bfp@bard.edu, http://www.bard.edu/bfp "cash prize + semester appointment as writer-in-residence at Bard College given annually"

Bridport Arts Centre – (Bridport Prize for poetry & fiction) Dorset, UK http://www.bridportprize.org.uk "two cash prizes + publication in the Bridport Prize anthology for previously unpublished work given annually"

Brown University – (International Writers Project Fellowship for poetry & fiction) Providence, RI 401-863-3260 writing@brown.edu, http://www.brown.edu/academics/literary-arts "fellowship + stipend given annually"

Blue Mountain Center – (Richard J. Margolis Award for poetry & creative nonfiction), Boston, MA award@margolis.com, http://award.margolis.com "cash prize + monthlong residency"

The Center for Fiction – (Flaherty-Dunnan First Novel Prize for fiction) New York, NY 212-755-6710 info@centerforfiction.org, http://www.centerforfiction.org/awards "cash prize given annually for a first novel"

Claremont Graduate University – (Kingsley Tufts Poetry Award) Claremont, CA 909-621-8974 tufts@cgu.edu, http://www.cgu.edu/tufts "cash prize + a week in residency"

Dayton Literary Peace Prize Foundation – (literary awards for fiction & creative nonfiction) Dayton OH 937-298-5072 sharon.rab@daytonliterarypeaceprize.org, http://www.daytonliterarypeaceprize.org "two cash prizes given annually"

Delaware Division of the Arts – (individual artist fellowships for poetry, fiction & creative nonfiction) Wilmington, DE 302-577-8283 roxanne.stanulis@state.de.us, http://www.artsdel.org/grants "cash awards given annually to Delaware writers"

Fellowship of Postgraduate Medicine – (Hippocrates Prize Open International Award for poetry) London, UK hippocrates. poetry@gmail.com, http://www.hippocrates-poetry.org "cash prize + publication in the *Hippocrates Prize Anthology* given annually to previously unpublished work"

Goethe-Institut Chicago – (Helen and Kurt Wolff Translator's Prize for poetry, fiction & creative nonfiction) Chicago, IL 312-263-0472 christiane.tacke@chicago.goethe.org, http://www.goethe.de/ins/us/lp/kul/mag/lit/rec/enindex.htm "cash prize given annually for published German-to-English translation"

Graywolf Press – (prize for creative nonfiction) Minneapolis, MN 651-641-0077 http://www.graywolfpress.org "cash prize +

publication by Graywolf Press given to writer not yet established in the genre"

Imagine – (Milton Postgraduate Fellowship for poetry, fiction & creative nonfiction) Seattle, WA 206-281-2988 miltoncenter@imagejournal.org, http://www.imagejournal.org/ page/fellowships/the-milton-center/postgraduate-fellowship "nine-month fellowship + stipend given annually to Christian writer working to complete their first book-length manuscript"

James Jones Literary Society – (James Jones First Novel Fellowship for fiction) Wilkes-Barre, PA jamesjonesfirstnovel@wilkes.edu, http://www.wilkes.edu/pages/1159.asp "cash prize given annually for a novel-in-progress (unpublished) by a US writer"

Lake Forest College – (Madeleine P. Plonsker Emerging Writer's Residency for poetry, fiction & creative nonfiction) Lake Forest, IL 847-735-5274 andnow@lakeforest.edu, http://www. lakeforest.edu/academics/programs/english/press/plonsker. php "cash prize + two-month residency at Lake Forest College given in alternating years to emerging writer (no major book publication) to complete a manuscript"

Lambda Literary Foundation – (Outstanding Midcareer Novelist Prize for fiction) Los Angeles, CA 323-643-4281 awards@lambdaliterary.org, http://www.lambdaliterary.org/ awards/mid-career-novelist-prize "two cash prizes given annually to LGBT novelists who have published at least 3 novels or 2 novels + substantial additional work"

Leeway Foundation – (Transformation Awards for poetry, fiction & creative nonfiction) Philadelphia, PA 215-545-4078 info@leeway.org, http://www.leeway.org "cash prizes given annually to women, transsexual, transgender, gender-queer, Two-Spirit poets, fiction writers & creative nonfiction writers in the Delaware Valley region"

The Loft Literary Center – (various grants and fellowships for poetry, fiction & creative nonfiction) Minneapolis, MN 612-215-2575 loft@loft.org, https://www.loft.org/programs_awards/grants_awards "cash grants given annually"

Maine Arts Commission – (individual artist fellowships for poetry, fiction & creative nonfiction) Augusta, ME 207-287-2710 julie.richard@maine.gov, http://mainearts.maine.gov/Pages/Grants/Individual-Artist-Fellowships "fellowships given annually"

Manchester Metropolitan University – (prizes for poetry, fiction & children's poetry) Manchester, UK +44 (0) 161 247 1787/1797 writingschool@mmu.ac.uk, http://www.manchesterwritingcompetition.co.uk "two cash prizes given annually for unpublished work"

Massachusetts Cultural Council – (artist fellowships for poetry, fiction & creative nonfiction) Boston, MA 617-858-2706 dan.blask@art.state.ma.us, http://www.massculturalcouncil.org/programs/artistfellows.asp "grants given biennially"

Milkweed Editions – (Lindquist & Vennum Prize for Poetry) Minneapolis, MN 612-215-2533 http://milkweed.org/about-us/editorial/lindquist-vennum-prize-for-poetry "cash prize + publication by Milkweed Editions given annually to unpublished manuscripts only by poets residing in the Upper Midwest"

Mississippi Arts Commission – (literary artist fellowships for poetry, fiction & creative nonfiction) Jackson, MI 601-359-6035 csoutolearman@arts.ms.gov, http://www.arts.state.ms.us/grants/artist-fellowship.php "grants given in alternating years"

PEN American Center – (PEN/Bellwether Prize for Socially Engaged Fiction) New York, NY awards@pen.org, http://www.pen.org/content/penbellwether-prize-socially-engaged-fiction-25000 "cash prize + publication by Algonquin Books given biennially for previously unpublished work"

PEN Northwest – (Margery Davis Boyden Wilderness Writing Residency for poetry, fiction & creative nonfiction) Elmira, OR

johndaniel48@yahoo.com,
http://www.johndaniel-author.net/mdb-res.php "seven-month
residency + cash honorarium given biennially (publication
credits not mandatory)"

Pulitzer Prizes – (Prizes in Letters for poetry, fiction & creative
nonfiction) New York, NY pulitzer@pulitzer.org, 212-854-3841
http://www.pulitzer.org "three cash prizes given annually"

Rattle – (Rattle Poetry Prize) Studio City, CA 818-505-6777
tim@rattle.com, http://www.rattle.com/poetry/prize/about
"prizes include cash + publication in *Rattle*, given annually for
previously unpublished poem"

San Jose State University – (Steinbeck Fellowship in Creative
Writing for fiction & creative nonfiction) San Jose, CA
408-808-2067 mhccfss@gmail.com,
http://as.sjsu.edu/steinbeck/steinbeck_fellows "one-year
residency + stipend given annually to 2-3 writers"

Stanford University Libraries – (William Saroyan International Prize
for Writing: fiction & creative nonfiction) Stanford, CA 650-736-
9538 sonialee@stanford.edu, http://library.stanford.edu/saroyan
"two cash prizes given biennially for newly published work"

Sustainable Arts Foundation – (writing awards for
poetry, fiction & creative nonfiction) San Francisco, CA
http://www.sustainableartsfoundation.org "up to seven cash
awards given twice annually to artists & writers with families"

Tennessee Arts Commission – (individual artist fellowships for
poetry, fiction & creative nonfiction) Nashville, TN 615-741-2093
hal.partlow@tn.gov, http://www.tn.gov/arts/grants/grants.shtml
"up to three grants given annually"

The Story Prize – (The Story Prize for fiction) Montclair, NJ 973-932-
0324 ldark@thestoryprize.org, http://www.thestoryprize.org
"several cash prizes given annually"

University of East Anglia – (David T.K. Wong Fellowship for
fiction) Norwich, UK davidtkwongfellowship@uea.ac.uk,
http://www.uea.ac.uk/lit/fellowships "one-year residential

fellowship + stipend given annually to author writing in English on the Far East"

University of East Anglia – (Charles Pick South Asia Fellowship for fiction & creative nonfiction) Norwich, UK charlespickfellowship@uea.ac.uk, http://www.uea.ac.uk/lit/fellowships "six-month fellowship + cash stipend given annually to new, unpublished writer"

University of Pittsburgh Press – (Agnes Lynch Starrett Poetry Prize) Pittsburgh, PA info@upress.pitt.edu, http://www.upress.pitt.edu/renderHtmlPage.aspx?srcHtml=htmlSourceFiles/starrett.htm "cash prize + publication by Univ. of Pittsburgh Press given annually for book of previously unpublished poems"

University of Pittsburgh Press – (The Drus Heinza Literature Prize for fiction) Pittsburgh, PA info@upress.pitt.edu, http://www.upress.pitt.edu/renderHtmlPage.aspx?srcHtml=htmlSourceFiles/drueheinz.htm "cash prizes + publication by Univ. of Pittsburgh Press given annually for unpublished manuscript"

University of Wisconsin – (Wisconsin Institute for Creative Writing Fellowships for poetry & fiction) Madison, WI institutemail@english.wisc.edu, http://www.creativewriting.wisc.edu/fellowships.html "an academic year in residence at the Wisconsin Institute for Creative Writing + grant is given annually to up to six writers with no more than one previously published book"

Washington College – (Hodson-Brown Fellowship for fiction & creative nonfiction) Chestertown, MD jwortman2@washcoll.edu, http://hodsonbrown.washcoll.edu "fellowship + stipend given annually"

Book Awards for Self-Published Authors

Why awards matter and why some matter more than others

So you've written and self-published your book, and it's available for sale online. You drum your fingers on your desk, checking your stats every twenty minutes, anxiously waiting for the sales to start going through the roof. You know you've produced an amazing book, and you're just waiting for the world to discover it and the reviews and accolades to come pouring in.

But days pass, and the sales are nowhere near what you'd expected they'd be, even though you've been working hard and steadily building your author platform (blogging, social media networks, e-mail subscription list, and all that fun stuff). But we all know that just because a book doesn't sell, that doesn't mean it's not fantastic. It may just mean that not enough people know it's out there waiting to be read, despite all your marketing and promotion efforts to date.

Estimates are that in excess of a half-million books are self-published every year in the United States alone. Add to that all the other new books from all the other countries in the world, and all the not-so-new books out there, and that's a lot of books written by a lot of authors all competing for the same consumers' attention and hard-earned cash.

Somehow, you need to shake things up a bit and figure out how to rise above the masses of books in the marketplace to get your book the attention it deserves.

One way to do it? Book award contests.

Not all book awards are created equal. Some are more prestigious and better recognized than others and will carry more weight in the eyes of your readers. If you're not sure about a particular award, research it. Identify the previous winners of the award on Amazon or another site offering book reviews to see how many reviews their books have there and what people are saying about them. The number of reviews can give you an idea of the number of books sold. Very few or no reviews might mean that winning the award has had little impact on sales—but keep in mind it could also mean that the author hasn't tried very hard to market and promote the book. It's difficult to know for sure. If there are a lot of reviews, try to determine how many there were before the book won the award and how many after the award was won. While you can never be absolutely certain of the impact of the award, a lot of reviews after the book won suggests the award increased the visibility of the book and its sales, and that's what you're aiming for.

Some book award contests are primarily money-making schemes. Just as subsidy publishers are known for making their money by charging authors inflated fees for the services they offer to publish the book and not from actual book sales, there are book award contests out there designed to line the pockets of the contest sponsors. The contests might be run frequently and the entry fees may be high compared to other contests and the prize you'll receive if you win. Winning these contests, while presumably very exciting initially, won't really do much to help your cause in the long run.

Before entering a contest, do your research. It's important to consider the following:

- **Where did you learn about the contest?** From a spam e-mail or a respected online site? Major contests should be well publicized.

- **Who's running the contest?** Do you recognize the name of the organization or publication? Search online for information about the contest and reviews from neutral third parties.

- **Is it an annual contest or is it run multiple times a year?** If the contest is run annually, this could be an indication that it's an established and respected contest, but you still need to do your research. If a contest is run every other month, for example, odds are its focus is making money, not recognizing literary accomplishment.

- **Is there an entry fee or is the contest free to enter?** Entry fees can be legitimate, as there are costs associated with running a contest (for example, they may offer an honorarium to their judges). This isn't a reliable indication of the contest's legitimacy, therefore, but exorbitant entry fees should be seen as red flags and cause for further investigation.

- **Are there hidden fees if you win?** If the contest is for unpublished works, a hidden fee, for example, could be a mandatory charge for editing if the prize is a publishing contract. The contest sponsors might also pester you to purchase other services from them such as reviews. If it's not clear in the terms and conditions of the contest, try to find out online what others are saying.

- **What is the prize?** Cash, services, publicity? Make sure you clearly understand what you stand to gain. If the prize is only a mention on an obscure website, is it worth your efforts to enter the contest? Are you required to hand over any rights to your book if you win the contest? It's important to know this before entering.

Check whether the rules and entry guidelines clearly state:

- When the entry deadline is
- When the winners will be announced
- Who is judging the contest
- Who is eligible to enter
- Whether or not the contest accepts self-published books (not all do)
- What the categories are and whether you can enter your book in multiple categories
- The entry fee
- The accepted format for entries
- The publication year range for entries to the contest— with many contests, this date range changes from year to year

It's important you learn and understand the answers to these questions. Be sure to exercise due diligence before proceeding.

What could you potentially gain by winning a reputable book award contest? Depending on the contest, it could be:

- A shiny sticker to put on your print books so everyone can see your book has been judged a winner
- Free publicity through press releases and the social media channels and website(s) of the sponsor of the award

- An opportunity to do a bit of bragging on your own. Why not send out your own press release to spread the word? Don't forget about your own blog and social media networks.
- Maybe an agent or a publishing contract
- Maybe cash, an award certificate, or a trophy
- Tickets to the award ceremony
- And, perhaps most important, recognition that could translate into increased book sales

Excited yet?

The following pages contain listings for reputable book award contests. Check them out. You know you want to, and maybe, just maybe, you'll be glad you did!

Good luck!

Shelley Sturgeon
Bound and Determined (www.shelleysturgeon.com)

Shelley Sturgeon is a virtual assistant who works with authors to help them create and maintain their author platforms. Interested in writing since childhood, Shelley hopes to one day complete her own novel. In the meantime, she enjoys working with her clients on their journeys to success.

Axiom Business Book Awards – sponsored by Jenkins Group,
Traverse City, MI 800-644-0133 x1011/231-933-0445
jimb@bookpublishing.com, http://www.axiomawards.com
"awarded annually in more than 20 business book categories;
entry fees apply per title/per category"

Beverly Hills Book Awards – sponsored by Smarketing, LLC,
Beverly Hills, CA 310-862-2573/805-403-5285
support@bhbookawards.com, www.bhbookawards.com
"annual awards in more than 80 categories, including fiction,
nonfiction & poetry; entry fees apply per submission/per
category"

CIPA EVVY Awards – sponsored by Colorado Independent
Publishers Assoc., Lakewood, CO 970-315-2472
admin@cipacatalog.com,
http://www.cipacatalog.com/pages/CIPA-EVVY-Awards "annual
awards in more than 40 categories of fiction, nonfiction, poetry,
editing + cover design, open to members & nonmembers; entry
fees apply"

Digital Book Awards – sponsored by Digital Book World, New York,
NY http://www.digitalbookworld.com/the-digital-book-awards
"annual awards in more than 15 categories representing all
forms of digital production, including eBooks, apps, transmedia,
education + learning; winners receive admission to 3-day DBW
event & awards ceremony in NYC"

eLit Book Awards – sponsored by Jenkins Group, Traverse City,
MI 800-644-0133 x1004/231-933-0445 info@elitawards.com,
http://www.elitawards.com "annual awards in more than 60
categories of fiction + nonfiction eBooks; entry fees apply"

EPIC's eBook Competition – sponsored by Electronic
Publishing Industry Coalition, Marianna, FL 850-526-5004
competitions@epicorg.com, http://epicorg.org/competitions/
epic-s-ebook-competition.html "more than 20 categories of
mainly fiction genres, poetry + nonfiction awarded annually,
open to members & nonmembers; entry fees apply"

**The Eric Hoffer Award for Short Prose & Independent
Books** – sponsored by The Eric Hoffer Project, Titusville, NJ
info@hofferaward.com, http://www.hofferaward.com "for indie
books (small presses, academic, self-published) + short prose
(fiction, creative nonfiction); cash grand prizes & merit awards
awarded annually with deadline for entries in January"

Global eBook Awards – sponsored by Dan Poynter, Santa
Barbara, CA 805-968-7277 becky@globalebookawards.com,
http://globalebookawards.com "awarded annually in over 80
categories of fiction + nonfiction eBooks; entry fees apply"

IACP Cookbook Awards – sponsored by International
Association of Culinary Professionals, New York, NY 646-
358-4957 x101/866-358-4951 x101 awards@iacp.com,
http://www.iacp.com/award/more/cookbook "awarded
annually in 18 categories for print + eBooks; entry fee applies"

IBPA Benjamin Franklin Awards – sponsored by Independent Book
Publishers Association, Manhattan Beach, CA 310-546-1818
info@ibpa-online.org, http://ibpabenjaminfranklinawards.com
"awarded annually to indie publishers including self-published
authors in more than 50 categories of fiction/nonfiction +
cover/interior book design, open to members & nonmembers;
entry fees apply

IndieFab: Foreword Reviews Book of the Year Awards –
sponsored by Foreword Reviews, Traverse City, MI 231-933-3699
victoria@forewordreviews.com OR
jennifer@forewordreviews.com,
https://publishers.forewordreviews.com/awards "more than
240 awards in 62 categories for print + eBooks given annually;
entry fees apply"

IndieReader Discovery Awards – (multiple sponsors) Montclair, NJ
973-783-3052 amy@indiereader.com, http://indiereader.com/
the-indiereader-discovery-awards-welcome "annual awards for
fiction/nonfiction print + ebooks in approx. 50 categories; entry
fee applies"

International Book Awards – sponsored by Keen Multimedia Group, Beverly Hills, CA iba@keenmultimedia.com, http://www.internationalbookawards.com/home.html "awarded annually with more than 100 categories of fiction + nonfiction print books (galleys accepted); entry fee applies"

The International Rubery Book Award & The Rubery Short Story Competition – Birmingham, UK http://www.ruberybookaward.com "annual awards for indie/self-published print + books & unpublished short stories including most genres of fiction & nonfiction; cash prizes with nominal entry fees"

IPPY Awards – sponsored by Jenkins Group, Traverse City, MI 800-706-4636/231-933-0445 jimb@bookpublishing.com, http://www.independentpublisher.com/ipland/ipawards.php "awarded annually in more than 70 fiction + nonfiction print + eBook categories; entry fee per submission/per category"

Living Now Book Awards – sponsored by Jenkins Group, Traverse City, MI 800-706-4636/231-933-0445 jimb@bookpublishing.com, http://www.livingnowawards.com "annual awards in 30 categories focusing on lifestyle in both nonfiction & fiction; entry fee per submission/per category"

Middle Shelf Magazine's Competition for Best Independently Published Children's, Middle Grade, and Teen Books – sponsored by Shelf Media Group, Richardson, TX 214-704-4182 margaret@shelfmediagroup.com, http://www.shelfmediagroup.com/pages/competition-ms.html "annual awards for self-published children's, middle grade, & teen print + eBooks in all genres; entry fee applies"

Moonbeam Children's Book Awards – sponsored by Jenkins Group, Traverse City, MI 800-706-4636/231-933-0445 info@moonbeamawards.com, http://www.moonbeamawards.com "annual awards in more than 40 categories of children's print + eBooks in English & Spanish; entry fee applies"

The National Indie Excellence Book Awards – sponsored by
Smarketing, LLC., Beverly Hills, CA 310-862-2573/805-403-5285
ellen@indieexcellence.com, http://www.indieexcellence.com
"awarded annually in more than 100 categories of fiction +
nonfiction print books only; entry fee applies"

Nautilus Book Awards – sponsored by Marilyn McGuire & Assoc.
marilyn@nautilusbookawards.com
OR marilyn@marilynmcguire.com,
http://www.nautilusbookawards.com "awarded annually to
inspiring works promoting social change, responsibility, green
values, wellness, social issues, consciousness/awareness, art +
creativity for adults & children; submissions to reopen Sept. 2015"

Next Generation Indie Book Awards – sponsored by Independent
Book Publishing Professionals Group, Lake Oswego, OR
(US)/Calgary, AB (Canada) info@indiebookawards.com,
http://www.indiebookawards.com "cash + trophy prizes awarded
annually for fiction/nonfiction print & eBooks; entry fee applies"

Readers' Favorite Book Award Contest – sponsored by Readers'
Favorite, Hawesville, KY 800-737-3843
support@readersfavorite.com,
https://readersfavorite.com/annual-book-award-contest.htm
"awarded annually in more than 100 categories, for print, audio,
eBooks, graphic novels, short stories, poetry, published or
unpublished, multiple cash prizes and benefits: entry fees apply"

Reader Views Literary Awards – sponsored by Reader
Views, Austin, TX admin@readerviews.com,
http://readerviews.com/literaryawards "annual awards in more
than 30 categories for fiction/nonfiction with a variety of cash
prizes for print books; entry fee applies"

**Shelf Unbound Writing Competition for Best Independently
Published Book** – sponsored by Shelf Media Group,
Richardson, TX 214-704-4182 margaret@shelfmediagroup.com,
http://www.shelfmediagroup.com/pages/competition.html
"annual awards for self-published print + eBooks in all genres;
entry fee applies"

Shirley You Jest! Book Awards – sponsored by Liz D Publicity & Promotions, Burbank, CA 310-433-2581 http://www.shirley-you-jest.net "eligible fiction includes farce, satire, parody, dark comedy + novels with strong comedic/ humorous elements in genres: romance, mystery, thriller/ suspense, horror, fantasy, sci-fi, paranormal, YA (no erotica, graphic novels/comic books) & nonfiction (no joke books); submissions to reopen May 2015"

Southwest Book Design and Production Awards – sponsored by New Mexico Book Association (NMBA), Santa Fe, NM http://www.nmbook.org "annual award open to books published in Arizona, Colorado, New Mexico, Oklahoma, Utah, or West Texas; entry fee applies"

USA Best Book Awards – sponsored by USA Book News/Keen MultiMedia Group, Glendale, AZ & Beverly Hills, CA usabooknews@keenmultimedia.com, http://www.usabooknews.com/2015usabestbookawards.html "annual awards in more than 100 categories for fiction + nonfiction print books (galleys accepted); entry fee applies"

The Wishing Shelf Independent Book Awards – sponsored by UK indie children's author Edward Trayer aka Billy Bob Buttons, http://www.thewsa.co.uk "annual awards open to fiction/ nonfiction print + eBooks for children through adults available in UK market, with all entries receiving feedback/review from the reading groups who help inform the judging; entry fee applies"

Writer's Digest Self-Published Book Awards – sponsored by Writer's Digest, "annual awards in 9 categories for fiction, nonfiction + poetry, print & eBooks, includes cash prizes & publicity perks; entry fees apply" http://www.writersdigest.com/competitions/selfpublished (print), http://www.writersdigest.com/competitions/ writers-digest-self-published-ebook-awards (eBooks), http://www.writersdigest.com/popularfictionawards (popular fiction), http://www.writersdigest.com/competitions/poetry-contests (poetry)

Consumer Protection

As soon as an author starts to consider self-publishing, questions begin to come up. Some are fear-based questions like: What will others think? Will I have the same status as a "properly" published writer? These we can ignore, as we must ignore all self-doubt that interferes with creative output and flow. But valid, work-centered, creative questions also arise:

- Do I have what it takes to go it alone and publish well?
- What services and support do I need?
- What kind of provider will best suit me as an author given the kind of book I want to publish?
- How much will it cost?
- How much can I make? Do I want to make a living at this?
- Who offers the best services for me on this particular project?

It's not easy. A whole industry has sprung up around self-publishing, and it's growing at an alarming speed—to the extent that trade publishers that traditionally invested in authors are now getting in on the act of charging some authors for services.

To become a self-publisher is to step from one work sector into another. Writing is self-expression; publishing is business. And while writing requires solitude, business requires connection and collaboration. It takes us away from our own imagination back into the stream of life.

"Self"-publishing is really a misnomer. Nobody who publishes a good book does it alone. We all need editors and a good marketing plan, at minimum, if we are to do this job well. Many others need assistance with design and production issues and publicity. This is why author services are now in big demand.

When demand for any service is high, scammers and schemers circle. The publication-for-payment industry has a long history of schemes and scams, and new ones are mushrooming up all over the place, taking advantage of self-publishing's growing kudos. These may be fired by technology, but they are indistinguishable from the vanity services of old.

Acid test: You can usually spot them if their business model is not selling books to readers but selling largely ineffectual services to uninformed authors.

Victoria Strauss of Writer Beware, a contributor to the Alliance of Independent Authors' (ALLi's) Watchdog Desk, has tracked the amazing growth of these scams for years. "Self-publishers face a wide array of dangers," she says. From "editing services" that do little more than run manuscripts through spelling and grammar checks to overpriced designers, artists, and formatting services, to bogus publicists who charge a premium for junk-mail "marketing," to predatory self-publishing services that advertise themselves misleadingly and engage in relentless upselling.

This is an unregulated market: on the one hand creative, innovative, and exciting; on the other, idiosyncratic, illogical, and incoherent. Some services are run by people who are knowledgeable, dedicated, helpful, and fair; others by people who are clueless, greedy, callous, and manipulative.

Authors must make their publishing choices in an unregulated environment where the same service can cost $500 or $15,000, depending on where you shop—where services gloss over the challenges of writing and publishing well and overstate the value of ineffective services, particularly around marketing and promotion. And where one large operation with many imprints dominates the information stream.

It's not surprising that so many self-publishers fall victim to literary fraud, scams, and misleading practices, duped by the pretense that their book is being "published," while in reality it is only being printed or formatted.

"Lack of competence is also a big problem," says Victoria. "There are skilled providers for every step of the self-publishing process, but there are also many people offering services—often for a lot of money—that they aren't qualified to deliver. These people may not be scammers; in fact, they may have the best of intentions. But goodwill is not a substitute for experience. For most writers, the difference between a scammer and an amateur is negligible: either way, they wind up with a smaller bank account and an inferior product."

How, then, do you make your way in this complicated, confusing new realm?

Starting out, many writers type "Self-Publishing" into Google and instantly find themselves overwhelmed by choice or bogged down in jargon, completely confused about who does what, and for how much. The answers to their questions are in there somewhere but framed in different ways, using different terms and jargon, by different people.

Instead of clarity, the writer emerges with a whole new suite of questions:

- How much should an editor cost?
- How do I protect my copyright?
- Is it worth paying for promotion?
- What is an ISBN? Do I need one? How do I get one?
- Who should I choose to help me?

The answer to that final question is no one. Not at first. Not until you understand the mechanics of publishing.

What is publishing?

The printing and formatting of e-books is production, not publishing. Production is just one of six stages in the process of publication, which literally means "to make known." Those six stages (after writing, of course, the first and last stage, the alpha and omega of it all) are:

- **Editing:** content, copy/line editing, proofreading

- **Design:** e-book and print cover design, interior design

- **Production:** manuscript conversion, e-book and print layout/formatting, audiobook production.

- **Distribution:** getting the book out to vendors

- **Promotion:** letting people know the book exists and why they should buy it

- **Rights Licensing:** trading the right to translate your book or turn it into a film or TV program or other subsidiary rights

One of the jobs we do daily at ALLi is guide our members through what Victoria has described as "shark-infested waters." Our aim is to help our members, and the wider indie-author community, self-publish with ethics and excellence. (And, an important point to note: excellent publishing means selling books.)

Much of our work is education: teaching indie authors how to think and act like publishers. To develop an indie mindset is, first and foremost, to take control. To see yourself as the creative director of your books from concept to completion— which means all the way through to reaching readers.

With the freedom afforded to us by technology comes responsibility.

"Some writers want to self-publish without thinking or acting like a publisher in any way," says ALLi's legal advisor, Helen Sedwick. "They hand off their manuscript to a company without doing their homework, failing to research the company's reputation until they realize they've made a mistake.

"They buy a template cover, then discover five other books that look just like theirs. They don't understand a contract but sign it anyway, assuming it can't be questioned. They are talked into buying videos, blog tours, and banner ads without considering whether they will increase sales enough to justify the cost. And then, disappointed and poorer, these writers give up the dream of getting their books into readers' hands.

I want to say to these writers: 'Come on!'"

Self-publishing success requires you to take charge of the process and maintain knowledge and control. To think and act like a business investor, an entrepreneur, the boss. To go comparison shopping. "If you are planning on successfully self-publishing, comparison shopping is essential," says Victoria. "There are scores of self-publishing services, offering a range of prices—from free to five figures—and features. Only by comparing one to another and getting to know what's possible can you be sure to find the best match for your needs and goals."

Be educated. A good knowledge base is your best defense against schemes and scams. Take the time to learn about self-publishing before jumping into it.

Be social. Hang out with other self-publishers—you'll learn a lot from both their successes and their mistakes. ALLi's member forum is invaluable, and the active Kindle boards are a treasure trove of information.

Be smart. For any person or service you're thinking of hiring, check references, credentials, and reputations. Don't take anything at face value. If you have questions, please ask our Watchdog Desk by submitting an e-mail through our contact form.

Admit your mistakes. If you signed on with the wrong company or freelancer, admit it and find a way out, even if it costs you money. "Everyone makes mistakes," says Helen. "I've paid for cover designs I never used, and I wish I could get back money I paid for worthless promotions. Sometimes you just need to pay the piper and move on."

DIY or assisted?

Whether you are moving on or it's your first time out, before publishing you need to stop and ask yourself how much help you need—and what you'll be getting for your money. If you can afford it, you may be thinking about paying a company for a one-stop-shopping package covering editorial, design, production, and marketing. This generally more expensive option may, depending on the contract offered by your service, limit your options. The alternative is to take a more independent route and employ your own editors, designers, and, perhaps, publicist.

The most successful indie authors tend to take this second option: picking and choosing single-service providers to maximize creative and financial freedom and control. This is hands-on book preparation and design, learning by doing. It requires you to draw together online tools and collaborators and combine them with your own competencies and self-taught skills and, the first time out, will take you on a steep learning curve.

This is why some people like to break themselves in gently by starting with a supported service and others value the support on an ongoing basis. "I'm with Adam Smith on division of labor," says historical novelist Alison Morton. "I did not want to spend my time learning a whole new skill set which may or may not be up to the highest possible industry standards when others, professionals, could do it for me. On the practical side, I send them a copy-edited MS Word file, which they turn into a beautiful paperback and e-book: formatting/typesetting and interior design, compilation of front and back matter, bespoke cover to my specification, all filing/registration fees, ISBN allocation, Nielsen Enhanced listing, preorder and look inside on Amazon, PDF ARC, proofs, POD setup, digital archive fee, e-book formatting for different retailers, legal deposit, bookseller information sheet, print ordering, quality control checks, and project management. Also a lot of advice, hand holding, and twenty-four-hour or less response; an author book-promotion toolbox, author community, and events; plus links into the publishing industry, e.g., representation/exhibiting at the London Book Fair. I gain time to write. Whether you go DIY, buy services on an 'as and when' basis, or buy a full-service package, the choice really is yours. And isn't that what independent publishing is all about?"

You are the publisher

If you hire anyone to help you self-publish, remember: they are your service provider, not your publisher. You are the publisher.

- You should not allow anyone else to decide your book's retail price, size, design, cover image, or title. When deciding your book's price, think about why you settled on that particular price.

- You should not give anyone exclusive ongoing rights to your book.

- If you are using a temporary exclusivity program (e.g., Amazon KDP's Kindle Select program), be sure you know what you are losing in exchange for any exclusive benefits.

- You should not give anyone an option on your next book unless they have already invested serious money in your career and have a plan for that book.

- You should not sign anything you don't understand.

- You should educate yourself. Read until you understand everything regarding the granting of rights, licenses, and ownership.

- You should ensure that any contract you sign may be terminated by you at any time.

Orna Ross
The Alliance of Independent Authors
(www.allianceindependentauthors.org)

Orna Ross is the founder of The Alliance of Independent Authors (ALLi), a nonprofit association for self-publishing writers. ALLi also offers a partner membership for self-publishing companies and freelancers who offer good author-centric services and decent business practices. These partners agree to abide by Alli's Code of Standards (http://allianceindependentauthors.org/code-of-standards/) and are willing to be vetted. They can be individuals or organizations, and they range from huge retailers like Amazon and Apple to family businesses and individual freelancers. ALLi also produces a range of guides for authors, including *How to Choose a Self-Publishing Service* (http://www.selfpub-lishingadvice.org/how-to-choose-a-self-publishing-service/).

Better Business Bureau –
https://www.bbb.org/consumer-complaints/file-a-complaint

Complaints Board – http://www.complaintsboard.com "public
online complaint postings"

Consumer Financial Protection Bureau –
http://www.consumerfinance.gov/complaint

Federal Trade Commission Complaint Assistant –
https://www.ftccomplaintassistant.gov

Federal Trade Commission Consumer Protection –
http://www.consumer.ftc.gov

Pissed Consumer – http://www.pissedconsumer.com "online
reviews & complaints platform"

Ripoff Report – http://www.ripoffreport.com "consumers
educating consumers; complaints, reviews, scams, fraud,
lawsuits"

The Independent Publishing Magazine –
http://www.theindependentpublishingmagazine.com "free
digital publication edited by Mick Rooney, dedicated to sharing
information, reviews of industry service providers + coverage of
independent publishing"

USA Government Consumer Protection –
http://www.usa.gov/topics/consumer.shtml

Writer Beware: the Blog – http://www.accrispin.blogspot.com
"advice + information to help writers avoid the pitfalls/scams of
self-publishing; sponsored by the Science Fiction and Fantasy
Writers of America, with additional support from Mystery
Writers of America & the Horror Writers Association"

Acknowledgments

So many people have helped us make what we hope is the most thorough, up-to-date guide and resource book for indie authors on the market today. Here they are. We love them all and couldn't have done this without them.

Rachel Rice of Rae the Indexer (www.rachelrice.com), Cathi Stevenson of Book Cover Express (www.bookcover-express.com), Judith Briles of The Book Shepherd (www.thebookshepherd.com), Kat Vancil of KatGirl Studio (www.katgirlstudio.com), Michael Larsen of San Francisco Writers Conference (www.sfwriters.org), C. Hope Clark of Fundsfor-Writers (www.fundsforwriters.com), Sharon Goldinger of PeopleSpeak (www.detailsplease.com/peoplespeak), Carla King of Self-Pub Boot Camp (www.selfpubbootcamp.com), Robin Cutler of IngramSpark (www.ingramspark.com), Victoria Strauss of Writer Beware (www.sfwa.org/other-resources/for-authors/writer-beware), Gordon Burgett of Gordon Burgett's Website (www.gordonburgett.com), David Bergsland of Radiax Press (www.bergsland.org), Tyler Doornbos of Well Design (www.welldesignstudio.com), Rachel Thompson of BadRedHead Media (www.badredheadmedia.com), Miral Sattar of Bibliocrunch (www.learnselfpublishingfast.com), Kate Tilton of Kate Tilton's Author Services, LLC (www.katetilton.com), Joan Stewart of The Publicity Hound (www.publicity-hound.com/tips/sample), Dana Lynn Smith of Savvy Book Marketer (www.thesavvybookmarketer.com), Penny Sansevieri of Author Marketing Experts (www.amarketingexpert.

com), Amy Edelman of IndieReader (www.indiereader.com), Mark Coker of Smashwords (www.smashwords.com), Tracy Atkins of Book Design Templates (www.bookdesigntemplates.com), Liz Dubelman of VidLit (www.vidlit.com), Shelley Sturgeon of Bound and Determined (www.shelleysturgeon.com), and Orna Ross of The Alliance of Independent Authors (www.allianceindependentauthors.org).

So there you have it. We hope these resources will help make your self-publishing adventure easier and more fun. If you have any suggestions for additional categories or resources please let us know at editor@spresourceguide.com.

More Resources for Indie Authors

THE BOOK DESIGNER

PRACTICAL ADVICE TO HELP BUILD BETTER BOOKS

The largest online site for nuts-and-bolts information on publishing your own books, with articles from top writers and an archive of 1,500+ easy to read articles, contests, and an active reader community.

TheBookDesigner.com

BookWorks, founded by Betty Kelly Sargent, is a community dedicated to helping its members PREPARE, PUBLISH and PROMOTE their books, share what they learn, and help one another. Best of all, it's **free**.

BookWorks Free Membership

Beautiful, industry-standard pre-designed book templates for Microsoft Word and Adobe InDesign allow you to quickly and easily create beautiful print and ebooks, along with marketing tools for authors and "done-for-you" book production services.

Book Design Templates

CPSIA information can be obtained
at www.ICGtesting.com
Printed in the USA
FSOW02n0241040516
20009FS

9 780936 385389